Brink of Reality

New Canadian Documentary Film and Video

DISCARD

between the lines

CHAMPLAIN COLLEGE

© 1993, Peter Steven

Published by:
Between The Lines
394 Euclid Avenue, #203
Toronto, Ontario
M6G 2S9, Canada

Cover: Jeff Jackson, Reactor Design, Toronto
Backcover photo: Geri Sadoway
Typeset by Adams & Hamilton, Toronto
Printed in Canada

Photo credits: Maurice B̶███████████NF; Judith Doyle by
Mark Sherman; John Greyson ███████vis; Brenda Longfellow
by Paul Till; Zach Kunuk by ████████, photo courtesy of the
Agnes Etherington Art Centre, Queen's University;
Brenda Longfellow by Paul Till; Alanis Obomsawin by the NFB;
John Walker by Rick McGinnis.

Between The Lines gratefully acknowledges financial assistance
from the Canada Council, the Department of Communications, the
Ontario Arts Council, and the Ontario Ministry of Culture, Tourism,
and Recreation, through the Ontario Publishing Centre.

Canadian Cataloguing in Publication Data

Steven, Peter, 1950-
Brink of reality: new Canadian documentary film and video

Includes bibliographical references and index.
ISBN 0-921284-69-1 (bound)   ISBN 0-921284-68-3 (pbk.)

1. Documentary films – Canada.   2. Documentary television
programs – Canada.   I. Title.

PN1995.9.D6S73 1993   070.1'8   C93-094098-9

To my parents, Art and Jessica,
and to Geri,
for their support and inspiration

Contents

Preface and Acknowledgements

Like many books before it, this one began on a modest scale and then took off in many directions as my interviews with filmmakers and videomakers led me to pursue new lines of enquiry. By pulling together a small book of interviews I wanted to convey my excitement that documentary in Canada had entered a period of renaissance, and that filmmakers and videomakers from a range of backgrounds, working outside the bounds of the large institutions, were creating innovative work on crucial subjects. Many Canadians and countless others throughout the world know the documentaries of the National Film Board. That organization is a national icon, like Mounties, snow and trees, and hockey. Yet, while the NFB regularly fosters the creation of fine films, and I interview two of its best directors, Alanis Obomsawin and Maurice Bulbulian, other important traditions and visions are also at work in this country.

This book has grown out of my work at Full Frame Film and Video, formerly DEC Films, in Toronto. As someone involved in programming and the distribution of films and tapes, I value documentary as much through the eyes of users in a specific context as through the eyes of a dispassionate critic or theorist. I think this has helped me to consider diverse strategies of style and communication, to be wary of forming too easy links between documentary forms and documentary effects.

My attempts to understand the new, exciting work and come to grips with the context in which it emerged has only been possible through the efforts of other documentary enthusiasts. The main influence for me, as for many others, has been Bill Nichols, for many years the chair of Film Studies at Queen's University in Kingston. I took his first course in documentary in 1974 and have been grappling with his ideas ever since. Nichols has worked almost alone in developing a theory of documentary based on the entire range of specific works, rather than on abstractions – and not as a theoretical afterthought to models of narrative fiction. This is especially clear in his 1991 work, *Representing Reality.* I am also indebted to the work of Alan Rosenthal, especially his interview books *New Documentary in Action* and *New Challenges for Documentary*, which set the standard for serious discussion about documentary and provided a model for this book. Tom Waugh's superb anthology *Show Us Life* is another essential guide to the subject. Waugh created a much broader historical and international scope than normally found in U.S. textbooks. Readers of this book will see a clear debt to Waugh's framework of committed cinema. Brian Winston's articles on documentary ethics provided a sobering reminder about the rights of those persons who become subjects in a documentary, and his marvellous book *Misunderstanding Media* provided a framework for thinking about the relations between technology and the television industry.

The world of video was really opened up to me through the remarkable tapes and unwavering enthusiasms of Richard Fung, Lisa Steele, and Kim Tomczak. All three have encouraged me to see the special values of video as a medium for artistic and political change and to see the specific contexts in which video producers work. Lisa and Kim generously provided suggestions and guided me through the enormous collection of work at V-Tape. Lisa wrote letters of support and Kim read and challenged my opinions in early drafts of the manuscript.

I have a passionate interest in documentary – the new worlds that it opens up, the juxtapositions of sound and image, the arguments, new knowledge, the real people and real situations. But it's the issues too. My political approach to these works stems to a great extent from my colleagues at *Jump Cut* magazine, especially Chuck Kleinhans, John Hess, and Julia Lesage, and was first given concrete form by my three earliest colleagues at DEC Films: Ferne Cristall, Barbara Emanuel, and Jonathan Forbes. I write with these voices in the back of my mind – their silent arguments popping up on every page.

Many people have helped push this book along and set me straight. I particularly thank those who took the time to read portions of the manuscript, including Ferne Cristall, Yasmin Karim, Clarke Mackey, Arlene Moscovitch, Bill Nichols, Geri Sadoway, Ellen Seiter, and Paul Wigle. Thanks also to Blaine Allan, and to Mary Sue and Al Rankin of Kingston who provided retreats from Toronto when the book was barely germinating.

The book was aided financially by grants from the Ontario Arts Council, the Toronto Arts Council, and from the Canada Council. Thanks to the programs, the juries, and the taxpayers who made these funds available. I also thank Barbara Goslawski at Canadian Filmmakers Distribution Centre and the staff at the NFB Ontario office for providing many films.

Never enough can be said about my editor at Between the Lines, Robert Clarke, alas now in Peterborough, who encouraged this work, argued its case, and had the tact and patience to push me on through many improvements. Robert's support and expertise were matched by that of Marg Anne Morrison and Pat Desjardins, also of Between the Lines.

Finally, I am most indebted, of course, to the film and videomakers whom I interviewed. They have challenged, educated, and delighted many varied audiences. I am only the latest. I hope that readers will go on to learn more about the political and social issues treated in these films and tapes. The works of art discussed in this book deal with vital Canadian and international issues that all of us should know more about. What is happening in Eritrea since Danièle Lacourse and Yvan Patry were last there? What developments have occurred on Vancouver Island since Sara Diamond last videotaped the Cowichan First Nation? Who are the other innovative producers at the Inuit Broadcasting Corporation besides Zach Kunuk? Did Toronto's AIDS Action Now go on to use John Greyson's *Pink Pimpernel* in their educational work?

I hope too that readers will be prompted to compare the approaches of the different producers and compare what they say with my contextual chapters. I hope that readers will seek out the tapes and films and also the writings of the producers. The book is intended less as a manifesto than as a stimulus to these artists and the communities they feel accountable to.

PART ONE

I

The Look, Sound, and Feel
of the New Documentary

On the screen we see Brian Mulroney giving a speech. As he talks, a crude, hand-drawn Pinocchio nose begins to grow on his face.

Cut to the Fifth International AIDS conference in Montreal, where a series of African and Asian men speak directly to the camera – all activists, all living with AIDS. The video screen divides to form a box within a box, framing the speakers in a larger sea of manipulated images, showing AIDS demonstrators in a swirling collage. Text floats across the bottom of the screen: "Stay tuned, do not adjust your set."

Cut to a male TV reporter dressed in drag, a parody of CBC coverage, but also a performer who functions as the tape's narrator.

The videotape is John Greyson's The World is Sick (Sic), *made as an educational tool for the Toronto group AIDS Action Now. In three or four quick strokes Greyson combines humour and the didactic; we learn about the political debates between activists and officials surrounding the AIDS conference, and we come face to face with a critique of the news media.*

Information, comic relief, and an unsettling challenge all push themselves onto the screen, and out into the audience.

Since the early 1980s, a distinct group of filmmakers and videomakers has set out to rejuvenate the documentary in Canada. Their films and videos break new ground in subject matter and form, take up social and political themes in a manner that challenges the status quo, and are produced in co-operation with groups that have often been pushed to the sidelines in Canadian society.

To take a few examples: John Greyson's internationally acclaimed works focusing on gay and lesbian communities irreverently mix conventions from video art and older forms of the social-issue documentary essay. Zach Kunuk reconstructs the lives of Inuit families ninety years ago using a unique style of staging and observation. Sara Diamond's videotapes not only insist on the importance of women in Canadian labour history but also challenge the use of archival footage in standard documentary. Laura Sky doesn't simply make portraits of working women, she raises much more general questions about our health-care system and the practice of medical ethics.

Mainstream journalism tends to ignore persons and groups it considers marginal to Canadian society, and as a matter of professional practice it shuns close contact with the people being documented. The group that practises this new documentary has sought out ignored "subjects" and tried to establish more co-operative and lasting relations with them. Yvan Patry and Danièle Lacourse have developed a long-term commitment to the Ethiopians and Eritreans they got to know during the production of several films over seven years; the making of Judith Doyle's film *Lac La Croix*, produced in collaboration with the Lac La Croix Ojibwa community near Thunder Bay, Ontario, stretched over five years; Brenda Longfellow's film on domestic violence, *Breaking Out*, took final shape only after years of collective work with Ottawa women's crisis centres.

These filmmakers and videomakers might not be as well known as the star journalists who appear nightly on CBC's *Prime Time News*, but they have not exactly languished in a backwater. All the producers interviewed for this book have achieved critical attention, garnered festival awards, or made it onto Canadian television. Their attempts to rethink documentary's forms and conventions – as well as its relations with its subject matter – hold great promise for salvaging the genre for new generations of media watchers.

Even before 1980 many viewers may have noticed changes in both documentary and narrative fiction, in films and tapes that combined elements of actuality and fiction. The best known of these new mixed forms heed the format of U.S. TV movies, those works termed docudrama by the broadcasting industry – *The Missiles of October* (1974), *The Terry Fox Story* (1983), and the like. British TV developed its own mixed forms of dramatized documentary in the 1970s as the logical extension of the earlier "kitchen sink" social-realist fiction. In Canada, Allan King's "actuality drama" *A Married Couple* (1969) observed in distressing detail, but with a reshuffled chronology, the breakup of a marriage. The film caused a stir but remained an isolated example until the CBC series *For The Record* (1976–84) aired a number of controversial films that critic Peter Morris has described as "journalistic dramas." The most "notorious" of them was *The Tar Sands* (1977), Peter Pearson's "true fiction" on the saga of Peter Lougheed and the Alberta oil industry.

Films produced in Europe, in Cuba, and in the United States occasionally combined fiction and documentary as well. In *Le Bonheur* (1965) and *Lion's Love* (1969) Agnès Varda mixed documentary with fiction as her contribution to the French Left Bank cinema of the 1960s. The revolutionary Cuban cinema of the 1970s was filled with such works. Sara Gómez's documentary/fiction hybrid on "marginal" social classes, *One Way or Another* (1974), was the most influential and controversial. Haskell Wexler's powerful drama-documentary *Medium Cool* (1969), set in Chicago during the tumultuous Democratic Party Convention of 1968, used fiction to expand the context for the actuality footage shot in the streets. Jim McBride's *David Holzman's Diary* (1968), Mitchell Block's *No Lies* (1973), and above all Michelle Citron's *Daughter Rite* (1979) showed the U.S. penchant for fake documentaries, using scripted action and dialogue but made to resemble conventional documentary. Even big-budget features have occasionally tried this strategy, hilariously in Woody Allen's *Zelig* (1983) and Rob Reiner's *This is Spinal Tap* (1984), and more recently with Tim Robbins's awkward but effectively creepy *Bob Roberts* (1992).

In the 1970s video artists often combined documentary conventions with various forms of acting or performance. A wonderful Canadian example is Vincent Trasov and Michael Morris's *My Five Years in a Nutshell* (1975). The promotion described it as "a document tape of Vincent Trasov as Mister Peanut. A three dimension antromorph" (whatever that is) where we see Mr. Peanut "running in the 1974 Mayoralty Race in Vancouver." [1] For some five years Trasov's work involved variations on disguising his body as a peanut.

This book does not deal with all the forms of docu-drama, drama-doc, fiction/non-fiction, drama/observation, scripted/unrehearsed action, and performance/natural behaviour – forms that accelerated rapidly in the 1980s, accompanied by considerable theoretical fascination. Art-world critics seem to have adopted the term *hybrid* to cover all the permutations of these mixed forms. I also largely avoid using the sweeping category of *postmodernism*, an umbrella adopted by some academic observers to gather all the current mixing of genres and conventions, which some call an exciting political realignment of art forms and others label simplistic pastiche. [2]

My purpose here is to focus more precisely on documentary per se – those films and tapes that most viewers recognize as being based largely on footage of actual persons and events: works preoccupied with the actually existing world.

Within the large realm of documentary I focus on those specific works that share three elements. First, they are innovative formally; they shake up the conventional documentary forms that we see and hear on screen. Second, they challenge us to look more closely at the social, cultural, and political patterns and habits we have set for ourselves in Canada: they connect with audiences in order to produce social change. And third, they attempt to create new types of working relationships with the people or groups documented. These comprise what I call the new documentary. Some of these films and tapes may venture far into the realm of the hybrid, but my concern is not with the process of going hybrid as significant in itself, but rather with how these documentaries "fuse forms, contents, and contexts in a new way." [3]

The critical and innovative work of the new documentary provides information and encourages learning that is worlds apart from the mainstream. Viewers constantly ingest vast quantities of material, from television news and talk shows through "reality-based" series like *Top Cops* to music video and advertising. Given this daily bombardment, it seems to me that the new documentary provides an antidote – another way of seeing, with different information from different points of view. This hope for an antidote differs entirely from the prescriptive plans to develop better informed citizens, as set out by John Grierson at the National Film Board. Grierson hoped the NFB documentary would help build a stronger nation state, and that increased knowledge of Canadian industry and labour, history, and social problems would help that cause. In contrast, the new documentary promotes critical challenges to entrenched power (residing in the state, in big capital, in patriarchy).

The term "new documentary" implies historical change in itself. It is a label I use to mark off a new type of work in a new period. [4] There are, as we shall see, a number of specific historical explanations for why the documentary world took the shape it held before 1980, explanations that juggle the causal factors of technology, Canadian society, and artistic renewal – as applied, for example, to the development of observational documentary or the early years of video. I use the term *crisis* (another indicator of the nature of change) to characterize the status quo in both film and video documentary at the end of the 1970s. But in offering historical explanations I have tried to avoid the worst traps of historicism, that way of thinking that sees present events merely as the logical result of what came before. While we might argue that modern medicine is the logical (and improved) result of centuries of study and experimentation, the notion of a similar progress in the arts has little validity. The picture gets clouded somewhat in discussing film and video, in which technological invention can look like progress and appear to propel the art. But there is no logical proof that silent movies were bound to die, that television would invade the home, that cinemas will eventually fade into extinction. I argue for a new type of documentary emerging in the 1980s, but the causes have been multiple and the exact kind of emergence was by no means inevitable.

I am not aware of any books that cover similar territory. As Bill Nichols points out, "Remarkably, the last wave of single-author books on documentary occurred fifteen years ago." [5] Some very good material exists on the history of the NFB, and Gary Evans's *In the National Interest* (1991) provides a thorough, though rather defensive, guide to the NFB's contemporary work. [6] But no other books have focused on Canada's independent documentary; almost all commentary here and abroad assumes that the NFB covers the entire range.

The CBC has attracted no substantial analysis of program content or forms. Video art and film documentary have remained far apart in academia, even with producers now working increasingly in both media and with the same audiences viewing both. Almost no film or video criticism or theory examines distribution. Even mainstream Hollywood distribution remains a mystery to all but the most dedicated *Variety* readers. Non-theatrical distribution is a mystery that ranks with the workings of the Canadian Senate. And audience theory has concentrated either on television as a medium or on the specific genres of classical Hollywood. Audience studies using empirical models have ignored documentary, although some provocative work has examined audiences for British current affairs programs.

The New Documentary: Some Snapshots

Richard Fung's *My Mother's Place* examines a woman's life in Trinidad and Canada. Shot on video with a minuscule budget, it sculpts an engaging portrait of a fascinating woman – she could, I suppose, be called an "ordinary woman." Much of the tape consists of Fung's mother giving an account of her personal history and of her family's background in Trinidad and China.

The tape manages to retain a critical edge by rejecting family biography in the standard sense. Fung places his mother's life into a larger context by incorporating comments from other women who talk about the general forces that seem to have contributed to her life, especially race, colonialism, and her generation's views of marriage and children. Fung also contributes small, almost throwaway, comments himself. For instance, he tells viewers that his mother's stories, even her accent, may be slightly "dressed up" for the tape. Yet, throughout, Rita Fung holds her own. The tape avoids setting up a conflict between a voice of experience ("the subject") and the voices of experts. There is a tension to be sure, but neither the charming stories nor the layers of context totally dominate. Another fruitful tension stems from the tape's style, which crosses standard conventions of documentary biography – facts, dates, interviews, old photos, and home movies – with editing and visual devices usually associated with video art. These devices include the use of on-screen text, obvious editing transitions (wipes, long fades into black), a staged rather than "natural" setting for the experts who provide contextual comments, and hand-held, very shaky camera movements for some scenes.

These devices may remind viewers of experimental film or even home movies. Yet the anchor of a documentary portrait holds firm. The viewer is asked to consider different approaches to Rita Fung's life. "I've always liked triptychs and panels in art, as in Japanese painting," Fung says. "It's a question of getting a total sense from the different parts."

Alanis Obomsawin's *Richard Cardinal, Cry from a Diary of a Métis Child* explores the reasons behind the tragic suicide of a seventeen-year-old Métis boy in Alberta. Like many traditional documentaries, *Richard Cardinal* picks up a specific social problem and strives to supply a context, aiming ultimately, perhaps, to alleviate that problem – in this case to change Alberta's foster-children legislation. Unlike most journalistic reports or muckraking documentaries, the film never loses sight of Richard himself – his feelings and emotions. Yet unlike the ubiquitous "human interest" story, which loves to show feelings, emotions, and suffering, the film keeps pushing out to the larger picture. Obomsawin illustrates passages from Richard's diaries and the memories of Charlie, his older brother, and uses a child actor to evoke Richard's youth, to dig deeply into the lives of the Métis children. The brief scenes with the child actor, by depicting emotions and the unspoken relations between the brothers, lift the film onto a much wider psychological plane and give viewers a chance to develop associations on their own.

Obomsawin provides small doses of narration but speaks more as a participant than an outside witness. She speaks of "our people" and recounts her deep feelings in visiting Richard's grave. A conventional, typically more confrontational, approach with social workers and foster parents would have pulled the story away from the children. Instead, the film was made as much for children as adults, and because of that many viewers say at the end, "That's me up there on the screen. I almost became like Richard."

Keeping the Home Fires Burning surely ranks as one of the most unusual labour videos ever made in Canada. Sara Diamond combines historical footage of the West Coast labour movement of the 1930s with staged scenes re-creating labour meetings and working-class theatre of the 1930s and 1940s. The remarkable compilation of historical material based on extensive archival research is in itself a major achievement. Most documentaries would have rested on that achievement, adding only an overlay of narration and period music. This tape complicates that history. The extensive theatrical scenes allow Diamond to interject humour and a texture of immediacy into the historical footage and provide another avenue to develop commentary and context without using the authoritative, all-knowing, but unseen narration referred to in the media world as the "voice-of-God." In addition to its structure, the tape ploughs new ground with its feminist analysis of the labour movement. Unlike most left-wing labour documentaries, which flourished in the 1970s, this tape manages to hold together a socialist yet strikingly unromantic view of working-class organizations during the period. In comparison to the U.S. film *Rosie the Riveter* (1980), for example, Diamond says she was aiming for something "less heroic, more fragmented." The work is a document of historical enquiry, sceptical as well of that strain of conventional history that asserts the "truth" about the past.

Night and Silence by Yvan Patry and Danièle Lacourse shows in graphic detail the nasty truths of modern warfare. Not, as they say, the televised "Nintendo war" of Desert Storm but the chaos, suffering, and death on the ground among the victims. As the only foreign film journalists present during the brutal bombing of Massawa in 1991, the filmmakers document the civilians of Eritrea in their last months of war with

Ethiopia. But their presence was not a lucky accident. This film was only the latest in a string of documentaries, reports, and news items that the Québécois partners produced over six years.

Night and Silence is a scream of pain and a scream for recognition. Eritrean doctors not only act as guides and a form of conscience but also emerge as complex human beings. This is the fruit of committed film-making, the result of months and years of collaboration with those who appear on camera. As Patry said to me, their work is not a "one-stop, one voice-of-God trip." The film's narration is subtly different from that of conventional documentary. It manages to remain sober and measured, yet resists the cool detachment and false objectivity that defines the norm, especially on television. It also carefully constructs a solid point of view and reveals a firm solidarity with the Eritrean people without employing the puffed-up personality journalism of the mainstream.

The richness of the new documentary spreads well beyond the films and tapes made by those interviewed for this book to a larger group of remarkably inspired, diverse, and socially committed works. These include the following, all produced since 1980.

- Sophie Bissonnette's *A Wives' Tale* (1980) and *Quel Numéro: What Number?* (*The Electronic Sweatshop*, 1985)
- Richard Boutet and Pascal Gelinas's *The Ballad of Hard Times* (1983)
- Gil Cardinal's *Foster Child* (1983) and *Tikinagan* (1991)
- Gilles Carle's *The Devil in North America* (1990)
- Martin Duckworth's *No More Hibakusha* (1984)
- Lorraine Dufour and Robert Morin's *Le mysterieux Paul* (1984)
- Carlos Ferrand's *Cimarrones* (1982)
- Mary Jane Gomes's *Downside Adjustments* (1983)
- Jackie Levitin's *Not Crazy Like You Think* (1983)
- Ron Mann's *Imagine the Sound* (1981)
- Midi Onodera's *The Displaced View* (1988)
- Harry Sutherland's *Track Two* (1981)

This list of wide-ranging films and tapes, based on refreshingly new approaches, grows longer every year; it is certainly incomplete. It should, however, suggest the scope of the new documentary – that many other producers not included in the interviews in this book are working in the same vein.

Modes and Genres

Before 1980 documentary was usually classified as one of the three basic modes of film. The other two forms were *narrative* (such as Hollywood fiction), and the *poetic* (such as the experimental films of Luis Buñuel, Maya Deren, or Norman McLaren). The term "mode" includes three properties: a highly refined rhetoric that has developed over time (the use of actors or non-actors, certain camera and editing styles); a specific type of production practice (the studio, the independent creator, the state or corporate patron or sponsor); and a particular understanding with an audience (the viewers know these features of rhetoric and production practice when they see them on the screen).[7] In the most general terms, before 1980 the documentary mode was defined as synonymous with exposition and non-narrative.

Each of the three modes was subdivided by genres: groups of films and tapes that had developed more specific sets of conventions (of theme, style, characterization, or setting) shared between the makers and the audience. The narrative mode included westerns, musicals, and European art films; similarly, the documentary included the genres of travel, biography, and social issues.

But today many other types of non-narrative have proliferated, especially on television. There are news programs, music videos, children's programs, info-tainment, talk shows (day and night), commercials, crime show re-enactments (*Crime Stoppers*, *Top Cops*, *Missing Treasures*), and television reports by journalists (often called documentaries by programs such as *The Journal* or *CBC Prime Time News*). And documentary must now be considered as only one genre within the expository mode. These non-narrative forms continue to grow luxuriantly on television (see Figure 1). This change in status for documentary in some ways merely recognizes the need to develop more precise terms in classifying media forms. Just as Hollywood movies were often talked of as the only form of cinematic narrative even when other forms clearly existed, documentary was considered the only type of exposition. Viewers must now cope with (and seem to crave) more and more forms of reality-based programming: "Reality TV" in the industry jargon. To quote from one successful show: "After *Top Cops* everything else is just fiction."

Of course, both modes and genres are notoriously difficult to pin down, despite attempts by writers from Aristotle to Northrop Frye to do so. The conventions are not fixed and static; they are constantly shifting. Nevertheless, within a given historical period audiences seem to

Figure 1
Modes and Genres

The Old Framework

Modes	Documentary	Narrative Fiction	The Poetic
Genres	social issue	Hollywood	avant-garde
	biography	Euro-Art	abstract
	nature		experimental
	ethnography		

The New Framework

Modes	Exposition	Narrative	The Poetic
Genres	documentary	Hollywood	abstract
	current affairs	Euro-Art	experimental
	music video	African	
	ethnography	Asian	
	children's	South American	
	journalism		

Documentary Sub-Genres
social-issue documentary
nature documentary

---

share assumptions with makers about the three modes and the major genres. Each genre and subgenre requires us to classify quickly what we see (if not by name) as a particular type with its own set of specific expository conventions. Conventional documentary films and tapes are organized differently from narrative fiction, and the audience knows it right off the bat.

The common denominator for all the documentary subgenres is now extremely difficult to find. Before the development in the 1960s of newer forms of rhetoric based on observation or engagement, with names such as cinéma vérité, cinéma direct, and direct cinema, the heart of documentary as a mode was centred in the rhetoric of exposition – the development of an argument by citing examples, the rejection of counter-arguments, the citing of outside authorities, the presenting of personal "authentic" testimony, the use of standard logic (if a, then not b). All the basic conventions of this rhetoric are well known to audiences, and most documentaries, including many discussed in this book, still use the rhetoric of exposition.

Nevertheless, more than a few works that get labelled documentary by both producers and audiences borrow heavily from narrative or the poetic. The best-known works of North American direct cinema, such as Robert Drew and Richard Leacock's *Primary* (1960) and Alan King's *Warrendale* (1967), developed a narrative "crisis structure" by following the course of an extraordinary event – a political campaign, a day-in-the-life, demonstrations, or concerts. Some thirty years later Simcha Jacobovici used the day-in-the-life crisis structure in *Deadly Currents* (1991) to observe Israeli soldiers and Palestinian civilians in the Intifada. Much documentary biography straddles the line, at times emphasizing the narrative devices of growth or crisis, at other times exploring a life by exposition through themes of family, marriage, and politics. Other well-known documentaries work more in terms of poetic rhetoric, by associative or primarily visual means. Nature films and dance films are often structured this way. Sequences develop through a string of associations, motions across the screen, patterns of light and colour, or camera movement. Here the sharp division between a documentary and a poetic mode seems pointless.

Older definitions that stressed documentary's affinity to reality or actuality (set in opposition to fiction) get constantly bogged down with the baggage of meanings for the specific terms. John Grierson's famous definition of documentary as the "creative treatment of actuality" only begs the question of the meaning of *creative* and *actuality*. At the other extreme, radical opponents of realism-based definitions, such as the filmmakers Jean-Luc Godard and Trinh T. Minh-ha, who insist that "everything is fiction," may shake up critical lethargy but hardly explain what happens with audiences. Every film and tape may be a narrative in the sense that all treatments of the outside world are organized by point of view and by the results of a hundred different choices. Yet everything is not always a fiction. Still, the documentariness of documentary remains elusive, especially when so many filmmakers and videomakers today consciously set out to blur the old critical categories. In fact, many videomakers avoid the terms documentary and narrative fiction altogether and opt for more literal descriptions – or they refer to

their work as "a piece," showing the influence of conceptual and performance arts.

To speak of documentary simply in the negative as "non-narrative," which many critics have done, can also prove misleading.
Documentary has always employed narrative techniques. Even the
most analytical, essay-like film sets up expectations and enigmas, the
core of narrative, to make its case. These narrative devices seldom
replace or contest the rhetoric of exposition, yet, in modern documentary, both conventional and iconoclast, narrative devices usually work
alongside the exposition. The kind of observational documentary based
on following an event, with all its attendant build-up, conflict, crisis,
and possible resolution, is only the most obvious style of documentary
narrative. The controversial, though certainly conventional, CBC/NFB
series on World War II, *The Valour and the Horror* (1991), sets up a structure in one episode that makes its points by telling *the story* of Canadian
troops captured in Hong Kong.

With some contemporary works, mainstream and otherwise, the
use of narrative devices plays a more central role. This follows a trend
that has developed across a wide spectrum since the 1970s. The trend
appears as docu-drama in Paul Cowan's (in)famous Billy Bishop film
done for the NFB, *The Kid Who Couldn't Miss* (1982), as drama-doc in
Donald Brittain's *Canada's Sweetheart* (1985), a chilling film on the
labour racketeer Hal Banks, and in a whole range of postmodern hybrids
that mix conventions from different modes and genres. [8] In these works
narrative serves explicitly to complement or comment on the actuality
sequences. The narrative sequences introduce ideas, events, or feelings
that could not be communicated by observation or archival compilation. Producers I've talked to for this book refer to narrative devices used
as reconstruction of events, used to heighten emotion or to create a critical distance between viewers and the screen, and used as chorus to the
leading themes. The pulling of narrative from a supporting into a lead
role, especially in a clearly fictional form, often marks the boundary
between documentary and hybrid. Most documentaries use narrative
devices, whereas the hybrids (such as Brenda Longfellow's docu-drama
Gerda) also use fiction, not just reconstruction.

The Current State of Documentary

"A few years ago Radio-Canada did a big money Gallup Poll and the question was, 'What do you want to see more of on TV?' Well, about 77 per cent said two things: documentary and information. The people at CBC were appalled. 'Something must be wrong with the poll somewhere,' they said."

Maurice Bulbulian

Documentary films and videotapes are all around us – on television, in schools and libraries, occasionally even in theatres. And in combination with the other rapidly multiplying forms of exposition and hybrid they now outweigh narrative-based drama and fiction in the visual media. Although some critics have been fooled into thinking that historically the main current in documentary has been left-wing, most documentaries are part of a mainstream of utterly conventional servings of information designed to fill programming slots, deliver audiences to advertisers, and uphold the dominant voices of authority. Their subjects are politics (narrowly defined), nature (the lives of animals, the wonders of geography and travel), and celebrities.

Those documentaries comfortably paddling along in the mainstream are not, however, the only works being produced alongside the new documentary. Other films and tapes often fall into three clusters.

A group of highly skilled practitioners of the documentary craft have carved out reputations within the mainstream as innovators or stylists. The NFB's Donald Brittain is the most interesting example of this group, because he possessed a low tolerance for government hypocrisy and his work often breached the confines of documentary convention. Yet even his best films on Canadian politics, such as *The Champions* (1978–86), on Trudeau and Lévesque, *On Guard for Thee* (1981), on the RCMP, and *Canada's Sweetheart*, on the government and labour, usually struck the chord of a world-weary observer and rarely raised any of the deep or disturbing issues of Canadian society. As an admiring Robert Fulford put it, "Far from being a hell-raiser, Brittain was essentially a journalist who liked to tell a good story and would take great pains to tell it well."[9] His followers, who are many, especially in current affairs TV and at the NFB, have adopted his cynicism and, to some extent, his sense of the edited details that make up a strong story, but little else. Many of their works, not surprisingly, remain anchored within the political mainstream.

A lesser-known set of works shares with new documentary an

interest in innovative form yet constitutes a specialist or alternative practice that reverses many of the conventions within mainstream documentary. These films and tapes are usually defined in terms of experimental cinema or video art: some would be recognized by audiences as documentary; others might best be described as anti-documentary hybrids. Unfortunately, these reversals remain stuck on the level of form. They include a number of traits: a tendency to pull the producer to the front and centre of the work, often pushing the interviewed or observed subjects to the sidelines; re-enactment, fiction, and performance overtaking exposition and observation; a predominance of titles and text on screen rather than a more observational window-on-the-world aesthetic; and an emphasis on editing effects rather than seamless editing.

Unlike the new documentary, which uses many of the same devices, these works seem based on the primacy of artistic self-expression and the assumption that unusual form in itself can shake viewers into a new consciousness, a greater awareness, or even political action. This second creed, that one kind of correct form exists and that it will solve other problems, is usually described as formalism. [10] Within this variant of formalist works (mainstream realism can be just as formalist) the breaks with conventions remain simple reversals – shock tactics that overwhelm thematic purpose or coherence. Michael Rubbo's personal documentaries made at the NFB, especially *Sad Song of Yellow Skin* (1970), on Vietnam, and *Waiting for Fidel* (1974), on Cuba, run this risk and demonstrate how the search for a central metaphor via an unusual secondary character and through staging or performance becomes the centre of the work, to the exclusion of a political context that would at least partially frame the exotic nature of the characters.

During the 1980s the calls to break the conventions of documentary often mixed with fashionable academic theories claiming that history can never be known and that any attempts at representing the world (through an aesthetic such as realism) are based on a lie and best left to fiction. Consequently, much video art produced in the last ten or twelve years might best be described as anti-documentary, anti-history, and anti-popular (if not anti-social) – overwhelmingly preoccupied with formal agendas set by the art and academic worlds. For example, Vera Frenkel, an inventive and influential video artist, seems unable to break from this closed circle in her work. [11] Frenkel's witty and visually clever documentary satire on state censorship, *Censored: The Business of Frightened Desires* (1987), examines the case of a flea copulation film that unnerved the Ontario Censor Board. But for me it's a case of wit and invention being used to play to the smallest possible audience. The tone of the pseudo-narrator hovers around sarcasm and in-jokes. A typical bit refers to Mary Brown, head of the Ontario Censor Board at the time – "Let us dispel the vicious rumour of Mary being a man" – displaying a kind of personal hauteur, surely the least effective kind of anti-censorship politics.

In his video essay *Canadian Diamonds* (1982) Gary Kibbins makes an attempt to debunk mainstream Canadian history's emphasis on great men and a select number of great events. But he becomes so sidetracked with making points through performers (rather than narrators) and so hobbled by the criticism that history is only known to us through the interpretation of historians that any thematic coherence sinks without a trace. In contrast, a work of new documentary such as Sara Diamond's *Keeping the Home Fires Burning*, which uses many of the same formal devices and mix of conventions as *Canadian Diamonds* (staging, re-enactment, actuality footage), manages to induce scepticism of mainstream history without lapsing into a cynicism that all history is arbitrary bunk.

Robert Morin and Lorraine Dufour's *La femme étrangère* (1988), a biographical sketch of a blind Brazilian woman caught between the white and Yanomami worlds, tries so hard to pile metaphor after metaphor onto the story that the woman herself remains an exotic enigma, buried under the formula. This contrasts sharply with *My Mother's Place*, in which Rita Fung manages to hold her own even as her video-producer son tries to work out the context of her life. The fascinating direct cinema portraits created by Norman Cohn, such as *William Perry: Woodcutter* (1980) and *Willis Reid, Harold Pottle, Harbour Pilots* (1980), operate on one level as masterpieces of quiet observation. Yet on another level they cry out for a deeper probing into context or into the relationship between filmmaker and subject; but this is seemingly impossible due to the rigours of the direct cinema observational style, which discourages any hint of a larger thematic structure and any intervention by the filmmaker. Happily, Cohn's work with Zach Kunuk, of re-creating Inuit lives seventy years ago, takes him fruitfully into larger social and historical realms.

These alternative works constitute a practice that co-exists with the mainstream. Exhibited mainly in galleries and festivals, they spring largely from the art worlds, mainstream and alternative, cut off from the historically much wider social base of documentary. They are works that overlap the new documentary in renewing stylistic forms and conventions, but they fail to establish a commitment to social change because they parallel rather than challenge the mainstream.

A third set of films and tapes can only be described as progressive but dull – the "reach people where they are at," Lawrence Welk approach, using safe, well-known conventions. [12] These works show a strong commitment to social change, and like the works of new documentary they link film and video creation with social or political concerns. Most convey a left-of-centre politics, at times closely identified with reformist NDP or trade union campaigns exploring social issues. The CBC program *Man Alive* runs many works of this sort, and most films sponsored by trade unions fit into this category. Similarly, in the very different context of Quebec since 1960, many nationalist documentaries simply glorify positive accomplishments and popular traditions. For Réal La Rochelle, these are "the macramé cinema of Québécois folklore." [13] Other works create a more deeply radical framework by exploring systemic issues within the society and not simply an isolated problem. Katherine Gilday's *The Famine Within* (1990) starts with a treatment of women's eating disorders but quickly branches out to question fundamental aspects of women's self-image in our culture. Peter Raymont's lively *Magic in the Sky* (1981), on Inuit culture and southern TV, constructs a wide-ranging argument about cultural stress.

Many other films and tapes centre narrowly on a specific problem or, as the media theorist Julia Lesage observes about similar work in the United States, they focus rather narrowly on "problems of identity in the private sphere," such that "the emphasis on the experiential can sometimes be a political limitation, especially when the film limits itself to the individual and offers little or no analysis or sense of collective process leading to social change." [14] They thus fail to investigate the broader realms of social power or class conflict.

Yet despite their progressive politics, for me these works remain less challenging politically than those of the new documentary because they share the rhetoric of mainstream documentary and remain trapped in conventional documentary forms. They are tied, for example, to the use of third-person, pseudo-objective narration and a reliance on experts legitimized by the dominant society (sociologists, doctors, and the like). This occurs to the detriment of experience and analysis from the poor, the non-white, and the generally disenfranchised people on the so-called margins – although *Magic in the Sky* is an exception to this rule. These works tend to use editing patterns of sound and picture that have become clichés, including the slice and dice interview – where, for example, a shot of someone talking is quickly broken up with cut-aways to illustrate the producer's thematic point – and editing rhythms that seem to be set by a template and a stop watch.

The Crisis of the 1970s; the Ferment of the 1980s

The heart of this book is a series of interviews with some of the best filmmakers and videomakers in Canada, committed artists who have created what I call the new documentary. But the book is also, in essence, an argument for the need to establish a new framework for studying documentary. Although the interviews form the heart of the matter, my experience in media studies steers me away from an over-emphasis on the role of the creative producer, an approach exemplified by the auteur theory and bolstered by the commercial media.[15]

The idea that the film director should be treated in the same way as an author in literature first reached polemical levels in France during the 1950s under the guise of the "auteur theory," providing tremendous stimulus to the serious study of popular cinema. The natural and necessary reaction to the auteur theory that set in during the 1970s and 1980s was carried by the new theories of structuralism, semiology, poststructuralism, deconstruction, discourse analysis, and above all Marxism and feminism. Although this book gives a prominent place to interviews with the producers it should not be taken as an uncritical paean to unvarnished authorship. I have tried to approach documentary from all angles: an alternative title for this book might have been "Getting Started in Documentary Viewing."

I think it is equally – if not even more – important, for instance, to look at the roles of distribution and audience, to examine the work of distributors and how films and tapes get used, by whom, and in what contexts. Bringing audiences into the picture casts light on concepts of meaning and reception and serves to remind us not to make sweeping generalizations about documentary. In doing this my aim is to get beyond the standard "use and gratifications" studies of mainstream sociology (which focus on individual viewers and eschew most discussion of ideology) in order to consider as well the group dynamics of audiences.[16]

Since the 1970s, theory in film (paralleling that in fine art and literature) has analysed, often in minute detail, elements of the film or video text for their effects on spectators and their ability to provoke a particular response. This was a welcome advance over earlier film criticism,

too often based on purely literary or social studies models. But much of
the close textual analysis of the 1970s and 1980s seemed oblivious to the
audience, when in fact the concept of "text" should imply both film and
viewer as dialectical points within a communication process. We must
know more about real, flesh-and-blood audiences in all their variations.
Why, for instance, do groups of people decide to program documentaries
as a means of communicating to a larger public?

A discussion of video *and* film between the covers of one book may
seem a tack into dangerous waters. Film enthusiasts regularly sneer at
the inferior quality of the video image, while video believers castigate
the cinema for its commercial nature. Canadian video art enjoys a
strong reputation, both locally and internationally, but video documentary has been neglected and barely recognized as an artistic endeavour,
let alone analysed seriously. My study shows a new convergence
between video art and social-issue documentary, two genres previously
at odds, in works that break new ground formally and register strong
concern for the social context in which Canadian art is created. The
work is engaging, innovative, and politically significant. One key to this
convergence centres on the evolution of conventions in documentary,
as producers in the estranged but related realms of film and video have
sought new ways to grapple with subject matter and new ways to engage
audiences.

The films and tapes discussed in the interviews were all produced
within the past decade or so. My focus on this period stems not from an
attempt to summarize a decade, or from a need to limit the scope of the
inquiry, and certainly not from a desire to weaken the previous historical context. Rather, I believe that during this time a new attitude
towards documentary began to take hold in Canadian film and video
circles. This new attitude hardly developed overnight, of course, and for
many of the people I interviewed changes in their work only occurred
later in the decade of the 1980s.

During the late 1970s filmmakers of social documentaries *and*
video producers of socially conscious work began to experience crises
and a kind of exhaustion in their respective worlds. Gilles Groulx, a
pioneer in Quebec's political documentary in the 1950s and 1960s, was
certainly speaking from experience when he stated, "The cinema that
questions has disappeared. It's too demanding." [17] Many producers
were becoming increasingly impatient in working with the standard
conventions of documentary. Most laboured at a kind of mélange of
conventions – mixing together interviews, unedited observation, rapid

montage, narration – but ever more frantic calls were made for trying something radically different. This impatience was articulated in theory and criticism during the 1970s in Canada's *Fuse* magazine, Quebec's *Cinéma Québec*, Britain's *Screen*, France's *CinémAction*, and the U.S. journals *Jump Cut* and *Camera Obscura*. Critics pondered the decline of the observational forms as well as the expository oral histories and pointed to the mannered way in which each was practised in both mainstream and independent milieux. Some critics also wrote in alarm about the apparent declining interest among audiences. Whether or not these conditions of exhaustion were true, nevertheless producers, critics, and viewers took them as being true.

The crisis in the video world arrived somewhat later, but seemed fully felt by the mid-1980s. Three video realms had established significant territory for themselves during the 1970s: video art, community-based documentary, and broadcast television. The interactions were complex and never static, yet each predominantly opposed itself to the others, and all of them challenged the cinema. During the 1980s video art and video documentary began to interact much more directly, and new hybrid work started to emerge. As well, the video aesthetic began to take hold on broadcast television, especially after the launch of *The Journal* (1982) and the Much Music network (1984). By the mid-1980s TV had come to occupy the video mainstream, pushing video art well off into the backwaters. For the producers I have interviewed, the TV video aesthetic is at once the foil, the source of new ideas, and the enemy. High-brow video art no longer plays the roles it once did during its infancy in the 1970s.

Finally, for those creating politically committed film and video, the 1980s marked several turning points in Canadian society. Left-wing politics began to be shaped not only by the old concerns of class and Quebec nationalism but also by the women's movement and a broadly based gender politics. Certainly, the women's movement gained great momentum in the 1970s, but within most left circles – unions, academia, community groups – the politics of gender was not extensively addressed until the 1980s. The 1980s also revealed new international pressures on Canada to broaden its immigration policies and to learn more about other cultures and societies, linked with the new realities of Canada itself as a multiracial, multi-ethnic society. It was only a matter of time before a new generation of women, immigrants, refugees, and Canada's First Nations produced work that would shake up both the left and the mainstream.

2

The Changing Face of
Documentary 1960–80

Film Documentary Before 1980

From 1960 to 1980 most documentary filmmakers were content with handling three types of rhetoric: the "classic exposition," – an older approach in use ever since John Grierson coined the term "documentary" in 1926 – and two newer forms, one based on observation, and usually called direct cinema, and another based on intervention and engagement, usually termed cinéma vérité or, in Quebec, cinéma direct.

The "classic" expository documentary had reached its pinnacle during World War II. By and large this rhetoric spawned heavy, didactic, educational films on "significant" themes using voice-of-God narration and stirring music. As implied by the term "exposition," the films were organized around themes and ideas, using sequences based on narration, description, comparison, and contrast. Usually the images laboured as illustration to the narration. Although based on actuality footage and a style of objective documentation, these films often employed staged and re-created scenes: Robert Flaherty's igloo-building scene in *Nanook of the North* (1922) is probably the most famous. They also used the voices of actors, re-recorded studio sound (as in battle-sequence sound effects added to silent footage), and highly manipulated editing that, for instance, created new spatial geography or collapsed time. Still, a range of approaches, even a personal style, was possible. The classic documentary at its best had power, rigorous analysis, and a poetic dignity. Influential examples include Harry Watt and Basil Wright's *Night Mail* (1936), Joris Ivens's *The New Earth* (1939), John Huston's *The Battle of San Pietro* (1945), and the NFB's *Canada Carries On* series (1940–59). From 1939 well into the 1960s the NFB, spurred by the legacy of Grier-

24

son, its founder, churned out thousands of these films. Older Canadians know this expository rhetoric as well as kids today know the conventions of rapid animation on *Sesame Street*.

Significant technological developments in the early 1960s promoted major changes in the mainstream of documentary. These developments included lighter-weight cameras, tape-recorder and camera designs that allowed sync-sound recording, and faster film stocks to shoot in more natural light. Great excitement took hold of documentary filmmakers in the hope that "real life" could now be more adequately captured through observation or participation. One proponent wrote that direct cinema "is not so much a technique as a state of mind, the natural breathing of an art that has been revived through contact with the real world. With it the cinema and its history may begin all over again." [1] The scope for documentary would be greatly expanded. Filmmakers would be free to explore and probe their subjects to an extent never before possible. And parallel to this technological "revolution" came not only the desire but also the ability to overthrow the old didactic forms exemplified by Grierson.

Yet well before these technological developments, as early as 1953 creative documentarists were straining towards a more personal style with a less didactic tone. This group included Georges Franju and Alain Resnais in France; the British Free Cinema group; the Argentinean Fernando Birri; and a few Canadians, notably Terence Macartney-Filgate and Wolf Koenig at the NFB's Unit B, and Michel Brault, Gilles Groulx, and Arthur Lamothe in Quebec. It also included a number of commercial U.S. photojournalists and filmmakers who saw the need to develop a less didactic style more in keeping with the "end of ideology" rhetoric best exemplified in *Life* magazine – an ideology of the individual rather than social systems, more in keeping with the liberal anti-communism of the 1950s.

The achievements of both the English Canadians and Québécois during the 1950s and 1960s were especially notable. One of the most creative advocates of the new rhetoric was Michel Brault, a young cinematographer at the NFB French Section. His 1958 film with Gilles Groulx, *Les Raquetteurs* (*Snowshoers*, 1958), a masterpiece of social observation on the Sherbrooke winter carnival, pushed towards the new rhetoric six years before the lighter sync-sound Eclair cameras were introduced. The story in *Les Raquetteurs* was told with a light, completely un-didactic tone. Brault outlined his philosophy in photographic terms.

I understood that it was a dead-end to observe people as a voyeur. We quickly opted for the wide-angle, which brought us closer to people, and forced us to change our attitude. We had to learn how to introduce ourselves into a situation, a conversation. And, as a result, be involved with those we were filming. Filming the world from up close is not like filming for television. It was the only possible road in our quest for truth. [2]

Others took up the new equipment with relish in the atmosphere of change sweeping through Quebec in the 1960s. By 1962 the Québécois style had been christened cinéma direct and had produced two major films: Arthur Lamothe's *Les bûcherons de la Manouane* (1963) on loggers in northern Quebec and Pierre Perrault's *Pour la Suite du Monde* (1962), which re-enacted the old traditions of beluga fishing on L'Île-aux-Coudres in the St. Lawrence. In English Canada at the NFB's Unit B, since the mid-1950s several inventive directors and cinematographers had been developing a style known as Candid Eye. Those films employed a more personal form of observational journalism as compared to the older, coldly didactic expository style of their predecessors at the Film Board. Examples include Terence Macartney-Filgate's *Blood And Fire* (1958), a loosely structured day-in-the-life portrait of the Salvation Army, and *The Back-Breaking Leaf* (1959), which followed the fortunes of young tobacco pickers searching for work in southwestern Ontario. The work of Unit B has been compared to the later U.S. films, but even with Candid Eye, which was less distinctive than the Quebec style of cinéma direct, differences with the U.S. films were apparent. For example, the U.S. directors usually placed greater emphasis on dramatic incident and, as film theorist Bruce Elder has pointed out, less emphasis on formal photographic qualities than did the Canadians. [3]

In France Jean Rouch had since the 1940s established a reputation as an anthropological filmmaker in Africa, but he was becoming disturbed by the assumptions of conventional ethnography. He now turned his eye towards "that strange tribe of Parisians" and with his writer and co-director Edgar Morin adopted the term cinéma vérité in homage to Dziga Vertov's philosophy of Kino Pravda or Cinema Truth articulated in the 1920s. Rouch concluded that the presence of the camera and the crew during filming considerably influenced how people behaved in front of the camera and how events unfolded. But Rouch was not averse to this camera effect – he embraced it – and in his most famous work, *Chronicle of a Summer* (1961), shot in the streets of Paris, he elevated the "camera as catalyst" to a key principle of his documentary approach. Michel Brault was his cinematographer. [4]

In a very different milieu, the U.S. filmmakers Robert Drew, Richard Leacock, and D.A. Pennebaker developed a more extreme version of the new rhetoric in which they also reluctantly adopted the term cinéma vérité. Drew's three commandments for his work show how different the U.S. approach was to that of the French and Québécois: "I'm determined to be there when the news happens. I'm determined to be as unobtrusive as possible. And I'm determined not to distort the situation." [5] Although Drew and the others later renamed their work direct cinema, the term cinéma vérité stuck as the shorthand term for all manner of vérité and direct styles. The U.S. films rested on the belief that narration, interviews, and literary sound tracks must all be eliminated to capture a reality untainted by bias and ideology. Although such ideas of untainted reality were certainly shallow and confused, the rhetoric of observation practised by Drew and the others in works such as *Primary* (1960) and *On the Pole: Eddie Sachs* (1961) captured an immediacy long missing in U.S. documentaries.

Today all this work usually gets called cinéma vérité, but I would stress again the different philosophies that stood behind these new approaches of the early 1960s, particularly concerning the ideas of non-intervention and the engagement of the filmmaker. Where filmmakers in the United States believed they had eliminated the intervention of the camera into the events unfolding before them, thereby allowing objective observation, Rouch and the Québécois *valued* new kinds of engagement and hoped they could bring out different sorts of truths during the filming. A competitive history of who came first matters little (though it doesn't hurt for Canadians and Québécois to set the record straight once in a while); what matters is a recognition that different approaches were adopted based on new technology and the new anti-didactic rhetoric.

In all cases the practitioners made much of the technological changes affecting their practice, and although the most sophisticated among them had groped towards this rhetoric throughout the 1950s, the equipment changes opened new avenues for everyone. Some critics have drawn up a simplistic technological history, on the one hand arguing that *technology created* the new rhetoric or, on the other, that new *ideologies demanded* the new technologies. The reality was more complex. For those most creative (Brault), or most experienced (Rouch), and for those in positions of ideological power (Drew), the need for a new rhetoric anticipated the technical changes by nearly a decade. Yet for most documentary producers in both the mainstream and in opposition – those who had been content to work in the old didactic, expository style – the new equipment, and the rhetoric that accompanied it, quickly took hold. The bandwagon set out with all the fervour of a religious pageant. In 1965 the U.S. filmmaker James Blue rhapsodized, "At no time in the history of film art have mystical and moral considerations been so important in the formation of a film aesthetic." [6]

Other kinds of simple generalizations crop up regularly concerning this new chapter in documentary. Some critics lump everything under the category of "observation," which in fact best describes the U.S. styles but diminishes many French, Québécois, and South American attempts to create documentary based on innovative engagement with those in front of the camera. Fernando Birri, an Argentinean, made *Tire Dié (Toss Me a Dime,* 1958), mixing observation with narration and direct-address testimony from street children in Santa Fe, Argentina; Mario Handler of Uruguay directed *Carlos: Cine-Portrait of a Vagabond* (1965), mixing observation, the vagabond's commentary, and his own intervention through the editing of visual themes; and in *The Brickmakers* (Colombia, 1968) Jorge Silva and Marta Rodriquez created one of the most powerful documentaries ever produced, a film that mixes six years of observation, broad-ranging social research, and narration on the lives of a family of brickmakers, especially their twelve children. [7] None of these works conform to a rhetoric of unvarnished observation.

Anti-realist critics tend to see all the new rhetorical styles as part of the post-World War II craving to introduce the "real" into art. But this also downplays the desire by Québécois and South American filmmakers to speak as advocates and not simply as observers of the new societies taking shape.

By the 1970s most independent producers as well as contract producers working for the television networks had backed off from the purer forms of cinéma vérité, direct cinema, and cinéma direct. They usually worked a kind of mélange of conventions. The typical documentary now included interviews, location shooting, sync sound, *and* some narration. [8] Low-key music and modest restaging made their surreptitious return. Yet even with the presence of a narrator, most filmmakers strained to prove they had captured a slice of reality untainted by artifice, ideology, or personal bias. They did this, for example, by employing

key scenes using a hand-held camera or long sequences of uncut observation.

Radical left-wing filmmakers of the 1960s and 1970s openly
scorned the end-of-ideology, pseudo-objective stance of the mainstream. Although they didn't agree on stylistic or rhetorical strategies,
the radicals all wanted audiences informed and swayed by the arguments in their films and tapes. Observation was never enough. In the
United States, Emile de Antonio produced a new cinematic form of partisan compilation fuelled by hostility to direct cinema (*Point of Order*
[1963] and *Millhouse: A White Comedy* [1971] were the best known),
while the Newsreel group films, such as *Black Panthers* (1969) and *The
Women's Film* (1970), often succeeded precisely through their potent
mix of observation with didacticism: the observation of people and
events ignored by the mainstream, and a didacticism matched only by
World War II films. In Quebec the renaissance of culture on all fronts
beginning in the 1960s kindled strong, iconoclastic works of cinéma
direct that bravely confronted Quebec's romanticized history, the mainstream media, and the society that stood behind it. Some of the most
powerful and innovative documentaries of the postwar period grappled
with this "impure" blend of observation and exposition, in works such
as *Ballad of Hard Times* (1983), *A Wives' Tale* (1980), *Harlan County
U.S.A.* (1975), *The Wobblies* (1979), *The Battle of Chile* (1975–79), and
El Salvador: The People Will Win (1981).[9]

Nevertheless, it seemed that by 1980 a sense of exhaustion had set-
tled over the documentary in most of its forms, including both the mainstream and those most radically in opposition. Genuine documentaries
had become rare commodities on North American, and especially Canadian, television.[10] They were replaced by "pocket docs" (an industry
term for the type of short report seen on TV news programs), sensational
journalistic reportage using vérité and pseudo-objective narration, and
the most bland stew of conventions that clearly induced passivity if not
boredom among audiences. This same grey style has dominated TV and
educational documentary since the early 1970s. There is little evidence
that the practitioners see any political or artistic need to change the
recipe.

The growing importance of film schools and film theorists also contributed to the exhaustion by mounting substantial attacks on documentary realism as a special kind of cinematic fraud. A preoccupation
among academic theorists with narrative and the deconstruction of

mainstream cinema pushed documentary even further onto the sidelines. Well-reasoned doubts also surfaced from people who really cared
about documentary. The sharp-tongued Brian Winston, in articles such
as "Documentary: I Think We Are in Trouble," questioned the ethics
and effectiveness of most documentary practice: "The majority of documentaries deal with social issues and normally concentrate on people in
society who are unable to fend for themselves. This inability clearly
extends to their dealing with the broadcasters." [11] Bill Nichols challenged the political maturity of many U.S. producers who had, he
charged, lost their voice and abdicated their responsibility to critically
probe the statements made by those they interviewed for their films. [12]
Despite the wide use of documentaries by community activists and
teachers, documentary usually fared worse than fiction and the experimental when considered by theorists as a force for making change in the
world. This was a belief shared by Europeans as much as North Americans. The English writer Peter Wollen certainly favoured Eisenstein and
Brecht over Vertov and Rouch in his *Signs and Meaning in the Cinema*,
perhaps the most widely read book of film theory circulating in the
1970s. [13]

Another attack came from the ethnography corner. Radical ethnographic filmmakers such as David and Judith MacDougall began to
question the whole underpinning of neutral observation fundamental to
most ethnography. [14] Western film ethnography was criticized not simply as shaky social science but as a practice complicit in imperial and
racial domination. Third World intellectuals questioned the one-way
flow of images from South to North and asked by whose authority filmmakers documented Third World cultures at all – a critique that reached
a political high during the attempt in the 1970s to establish, through the
Non-Aligned Movement and UNESCO, a New World Information and
Communications Order. [15]

These doubts and critiques seem to have made little impression on
most film documentarians, even in the 1990s. But for the more creative
and politically conscious filmmakers, the doubts and rethinking began
to show a way forward from the impasse and exhaustion of documentary
as practised in the late 1970s.

The Rise of Video
Videomaking evolved in a context very different from film. Even when
styles converged in film and video, the reason often lay in videomakers'
attempts to question or subvert the dominant forms of cinema.

Figure 2
Video Technology Inventions

- **1956**: the U.S. Ampex Corporation unveils its videotape recorders – purchase price, $45,000.
- **1967**: Sony introduces the Portapak VTR (black and white ½-inch reel to reel).
- **1969**: machines for electronic editing of tape become available.
- **1972**: Sony introduces the UMATIC 3/4-inch cassette to North America (two years after its Japanese launch).
- **1972**: Canada launches its Anik A Communications Satellite.
- **1973**: first Time Based Corrector introduced among broadcast networks for writing on-screen titles, performing dissolves.
- **1975**: Sony introduces Betamax (½-inch colour VCR designed for home use).
- **1976**: JVC introduces the VHS cassette recorders and players.
- **1978**: various Japanese companies introduce the first portable camera and VCR combinations, now referred to as camcorders.
- **1988**: 8mm video reaches the home market, promoted first under the name Video 8, then upgraded to HI-8. [18]

As technical media, film and video exhibit crucial differences, some of them stemming from the basic inventions of video technology, but many others from how those inventions have been structured by the industry – what the film historians Robert Allen and Douglas Gomery refer to as its innovations and diffusions. [16] A great deal depends on how the technology is first put into practical use (the innovations) and then becomes widely diffused; but some of the characteristics in the first set of inventions do pose restraints on practice, or they push artists to work in specific ways.

Video technology is a spin-off from the development of television, a set of inventions worked out by the 1930s. In his book *Misunderstanding Media* Brian Winston demonstrates just how slowly these ideas and machines were brought into the marketplace. [17] His aim is to debunk the notion that we live in an age of the "information revolution." He makes a strong case against any technological determinism and argues that machines only become diffused once there exists a strong economic or political/economic need for them. Thus the radical potential of video is contained by the dominance of commercial television. Still, for the

independent artist video technology has been changing rapidly since its
first set of practical applications in the 1950s.

To a great extent the characteristics of the first set of video inventions and innovations imply a technical boundary. They shape the
working methods of the producer and even help define what is possible
(or at least probable) aesthetically. Yet artists who have consciously
tried *have* been able to breach those boundaries. Less creative or more
inexperienced videomakers have merely accepted the technical specif-
ics as a status quo.

Innovations and Diffusion

Robert Allen and Douglas Gomery define innovations as the adoption of
inventions for practical use. Following that, "The process of diffusion
begins once the technology begins to receive wide-spread use within an
industry."[20]

A. Broadcast television first adopted video recording because of its
instant playback feature. This allowed immediate broadcasts on both
U.S. coasts, a necessity for the push to develop national networks.
Videotape recording also improved on the old kinescope recording of
programs by allowing daytime production, a necessity for cutting evening labour costs. After 1960 the networks began using video as a substi-
tute for film on news programs, primarily for its playback speed in news
gathering and editing. In most cases the aesthetic differences between
film and video were not valued; it was the technical ability to relay
instant pictures and edit quickly that drew the industry's attention.[21]
The first evidence of a new video aesthetic only appeared much later on
sports and music programs, especially the U.S. MTV (launched 1981)
and Canadian Much Music (launched 1984) networks, which used video
effects for replays, slow motion, graphics, text, or transitions (although,
significantly, the high-budget music videos themselves are still shot on
35mm film). After the mid-1980s this distinct video visual style spread
rapidly throughout commercial television. In Canada this became most
evident in commercials, music shows, and news programs, especially
the high-budget, high-tech *The Journal* (launched 1982).
B. Video art made its non-commercial debut in 1963 through the star-
tling work of Nam June Paik, a Korean-born artist working in Germany
and later in the United States. Other avant-garde artists from sculptors
to dancers picked up the medium as a way of expanding their field or
moving into the rapidly developing practice of conceptual art. One critic

Figure 3
Video Technology's Status Quo

1. Video is cheaper to shoot than film: videotape is to water as 16mm film stock is to gold (actually silver). (This refers to the tape cost only.)
2. Video can be played back instantly on the camera's internal monitor or an outside monitor.
3. Portable video cameras have always incorporated sync sound.
4. Before the late 1980s, video recording required more ambient light than film to produce an acceptable image.
5. The video image looks flatter than film, usually because of the high levels of light necessary to record an acceptable image. This has changed in the 1990s, with recording now possible at lower light levels.
6. Video resolution (the ability to record and play back detail) using the North American TV standard of 525 screen lines roughly equals that of 16mm film. [19] The much touted High Definition TV (HDTV), though evolving in two or three standards, will approximately equal the resolution of 35mm film.
7. Video editing has been electronic since 1969 and digital (computerized) since 1975, which allows immediate (random) access to any image. Film requires the editor to handle the stock physically. However, until the late 1980s, as filmmaker Clarke Mackey points out, "Video editing was linear" – that is, a change in the middle of the assembly of the tape meant going back to the start to reassemble all the shots – "while film editors could make changes throughout."
8. Video-editing effects such as dissolves, wipes, and superimpositions are achieved electronically and can be viewed immediately in the editing room.
9. Prior to the introduction of computerized editing equipment in the mid-1980s, the editing of very short segments was more difficult in video.
10. Although video is technically much more capable of producing good sound than 16mm film, which has a very restricted capacity for wide-frequency recording, video *exhibition* has usually involved small monitors or television screens, hampered by poor sound quality (encouraging producers to use close-ups and pay less attention to sound).

referred to this period (roughly 1963–75) as the "Utopian Moment." Another saw it as the "pioneering phase." [22] The first exhibition of video art in Canada was probably Gilles Chartier's 1966 video feedback installation at the Musée d'art contemporain, in Montreal. By the early 1970s a range of exuberant activity had developed in four regional centres: in Halifax at the Nova Scotia College of Art and Design, in Montreal at Le Vidéographe and L'Institut Parallel, in Toronto at A Space Gallery, and in Vancouver with the numerous events of the Intermedia Collective. Exhibition was centred in small art galleries, and this in turn partially determined the nature of subsequent work.

The tapes explored a broad terrain, from recordings of conceptual art events to personal political statements to investigations of the medium's electronic properties. As with most new movements in art, large doses of the self-indulgent mixed freely with effective social statement. Although derived primarily from the fine arts, video "genres" prided themselves as distinct from cinema, the older arts, and especially television. But as video producer Kim Tomczak points out, "Just getting the equipment to work was success," so during the 1970s video genres were largely undeveloped.

If video as a technology is a spin-off from television, video art has rejected its parent every step of the way. This distinct lineage remains a key factor for proponents of video art, even today. In 1973 an organizer for the Art Gallery of Ontario's first video exhibition stated enthusiastically: "In the gigantic shadow of broadcast television and the world of established art forms, [video art] is creating the light from which it will grow. . . . This new Life is demonstrating at least a potential for brilliance as man's first electronic art form." [23]

During the early 1970s, viewers occasionally labelled video art as narcissistic. Peggy Gale, Canada's first serious video critic, countered the charge in a 1977 issue of *Parachute* magazine: "Certainly video is an ideal means of self-study." She observed that as a medium it "seems to collect secrets," and described it as "impartial," "laconic," and "specific." [24] Summing up in 1981, Clive Robertson, a founder and editor of *Fuse* magazine, remarked, "So far, the language structure that video (in all its creative forms) has developed rarely states its references and inspirations in any common recognizable form. (Recognizable, that is, for a TV audience.)" [25]

C. Community-based video first developed in Canada largely through the opportunities presented by cable TV. This work followed quickly on the heels of video art, but was created by community-based artists and organizers who saw the potential for low-cost, quickly produced work of value for social change. In its early days the cable industry accepted the role required of it by the CRTC (Canadian Radio-television and Telecommunications Commission) of providing community access, primarily in the provision of equipment and training. [26] In smaller cities this rarely occurred. Cable acted simply as a transmission device for delivering a broader range of U.S. programs to the Canadian hinterland. But in the large cities, particularly Vancouver, local activists pushed the cable companies to provide real community access. As video producers Richard Fung and Sara Diamond both point out, important political video was created in that milieu, and the principles developed there fostered good video documentary over the next twenty years. But with the advent of pay-TV in 1983 and the new political and economic clout of an industry that had grown rich, cable TV dropped its mandate to provide community access. Because the community video work produced in the 1970s touched mainly local audiences and could be adequately supported by local cable companies, the work made little national impact and drew even less critical attention.

The Canadian women's movement played a key role in video documentary during the 1970s. As video producer Lisa Steele and her colleagues put it, "This is a new medium with women working towards evolving a new style and aesthetics without having to surmount the traditions and style of a male-dominated medium such as film." [27] The first Canadian Women and Film Festival, an ambitious 1973 national tour organized by an ad hoc group of teachers, critics, and producers, kept video in the background. But soon after, tapes on women's health and labour struggles began to find wider distribution, through Vidéo Femmes, Women in Focus, and DEC Films. The works in these collections were the only video documentaries that circulated nationally at that time. In the 1970s many more women took up video production than film – through community centres and schools – largely because, as Steele suggests, the technology seemed less forbidding and less dominated by male technical ideologies. Although the 1977 Satellite Video Exchange Society Catalogue, issued in Vancouver, listed women's-issue tapes under "life-styles," the catalogue featured the work of many women producers in nearly all the catalogue categories.

D. Within the NFB, video production dovetailed with the aims of the Challenge For Change and Société nouvelle programs (launched respectively in 1967 and 1969) – federal government initiatives using the NFB "to help citizens acclimatize themselves to change as a permanent feature of their lives." [28] The most famous video work from these programs was documented on the film *VTR: St. Jacques* (1969), a widely seen intervention into Montreal community politics directed by Bonnie Sherr Klein and Dorothy Todd Henaut. Maurice Bulbulian and Yvan Patry worked in Société nouvelle, and Laura Sky worked in the Ontario office of Challenge For Change. Société nouvelle "was something special because of the collegiality," Bulbulian says. "It worked so that all kinds of people had input – directors, producers, and . . . people in distribution" who had "relationships with all kinds of audience groups – testing, etc. . . . As opposed to the act of creation by a single individual who is called the director, we were trying to help ordinary people communicate directly to the government."

In 1971, through the efforts of Robert Forget and funds from the Canada Council, Société nouvelle spawned Montreal's Vidéographe, which became fully independent in 1973. The Ontario Challenge For Change department continued to produce video documentary on a modest scale, but by the late 1970s nearly all production had shifted back to film. NFB historian Gary Evans speculates, "Some feared that the aura of being a filmmaker was being lost." [29] Laura Sky echoes that perception based on her experience in Toronto, and Maurice Bulbulian states that video quality was simply not good enough at the time.

E. **Artist-run centres** gradually began to be organized by community activists and politically minded independent artists who hoped they could stimulate video production more concerned with social change than high art. Vidéographe and Vancouver's Satellite Video Exchange Society (founded 1972) led the way, followed by Trinity Square Video in Toronto and Women in Focus in Vancouver. Although most of this work was substantially funded by the Canada Council, much of the initiative stemmed from local political activity initiated by women's groups and the left.

Unfortunately, most work produced through the artist-run centres during the 1970s veered sharply into either one of two camps: video art and the formally conventional social-issue documentary. [30] At video conferences the most creative producers discussed ways of bridging the two camps, but little came of this during the 1970s. Clive Robertson talked about the situation in 1979: "Thankfully, the historical gap between video art and video as social documentary is closing. The latter has become more sophisticated. The former is often less precious or precocious." [31] This seemed more wishful thinking than reality. Docu-

Figure 4
Video Art's Utopian Moment
Forms, Conventions, Styles: 1970–85

- a marked preference for staged or obviously constructed scenes (often literally on a stage)
- narrators as performers
- long takes
- aversion to montage sequences
- a predominance of medium close-ups and close-ups
- extreme forms of camera movement (either static camera or hand-held camera); an aversion to smooth camera movement
- art world distribution models
- distribution organized by artist rather than by themes or content
- academic training and criticism centred on the arts (film schools in Canada still largely ignore video)

---

mentary, especially outside Quebec, played second fiddle during the entire period, and video in Canada became synonymous with video art, especially as defined by the Canada Council and the large galleries. [32]

The milieu for video production, funding, distribution, and exhibition differs tremendously from that of the cinema institutions. In the 1970s, although documentary was practised in both media, other rhetorical and stylistic genres varied enormously. Whereas in cinema the fictional narrative dominated the mainstream, as it still does, in video the mainstream in the period 1970–85 was occupied by "high art" (high-concept avant-garde formalism). After 1985 the video mainstream shifted to broadcast television, because the TV style had become so strong, in everything from Much Music to *The Journal*. Whereas film-makers learn their craft in film school or work their way up by crewing on the job, video producers, even in the days of community-access cable, tended to come up through the art schools. Thus in the video world the rhetorics, forms, conventions, styles, and controversies have most often stemmed from the art world and the preoccupations of the older arts. From painting, sculpture, and dance have come "performance video," which led to a penchant for staged and re-created scenes in video documentaries in the 1980s.

Video developed its own distinctive vocabulary and rhetoric. Some of the differences stem fairly directly from the various inventions, some developed as innovations and diffusions in the period 1970–85, and some only emerged after 1985.

Commonplace video practices and conventions have not followed lockstep from video's basic technology. In some cases the technology *has* influenced the development of conventions, in other cases the conventions stem from documentary film, experimental film, and the performance arts. The long take, for example, a dominant feature in most video work of the 1970s, stems from the technical limitations of editing short segments, yet also parallels the predominance of the long take in observational documentary, *and* it seemed best suited to the performance art of the 1970s.

Although the vocabulary for this non-commercial video developed during the structural/minimalist/modernist period for experimental film, wherein as a principle the basic elements of the medium (the shot, even the single film frame) were pushed to the foreground, the larger art world had during the 1970s leapt towards the new paradigm of postmodernism. Where modernism strived to pare away all but the essentials in the particular art, postmodernism revelled in the mixed and cross-bred, drawing from a range of historical styles to comment on or parody typical conventions. In some ways video clung to experimental film modernism, but in other ways it reached closer to high-art postmodernism. Lisa Steele's *A Very Personal Story* (1974) illustrates that dual tension and shows why video art seemed so fresh and exciting during the early 1970s. Here was a new art that could shake up the prevailing rhetorics in both film and fine art.[33] Steele's intense, carefully staged, but unrehearsed account of her mother's death invokes both documentary testimony and performance art. She stated later that the account was based partly on Proust's concept of involuntary memory. The single take, head and bare shoulders close-ups, absence of background context, and minimal lighting suggest a modernist paring down of the elements to arrive at the basic tools of video. Whether we interpret these tools as *essential* or as the *historically defined* building blocks of the technology available to all producers remains a question that requires more research and analysis.

The attempt to strip away all artifice preoccupied the dominant currents of experimental cinema during the late 1960s and 1970s. It reached its pinnacle with such early works as Paul Sharits's flicker film *T.O.U.C.H.I.N.G.* (U.S., 1968), David Rimmer's *Surfacing on the Thames* (Canada, 1970), and Michael Snow's <———> (a.k.a. *Back And*

Forth, Canada, 1969). Video of the 1970s often shared this approach in the apparently opposite but equally spare aesthetics of spontaneity and documented performance, which were felt to be among the elements that made video a unique art. But by the close of the decade many video producers had reached the end of the line with the minimal aesthetic of modernism. For Steele this change accompanied a shift towards a more complex mix of conventions and genres. Her video work remained among the most provocative in Canada as she moved fully into the constructed multivalent world of the postmodern, using the melodrama to full advantage in reshaping a woman's narrative in *The Gloria Tapes* (1980).

By 1980 the video world, like the documentary film world, had reached a crisis of vision. The exciting work of the first generation, in video's utopian phase, had ended. Curator and critic Renee Baert put it this way: "The ethos has gradually shifted from that of a 'counter' culture – with its politic of engagement and challenge – to one of a 'parallel' culture – with its accommodation to self-containment and marginality."[34] Although high-art video and uninspired social-issue documentaries still churn out in galleries and church basements today, both the mainstream and those most radically in opposition began to produce something different in the 1980s. The crisis was heightened by the new video aesthetic emerging on broadcast television. By 1985 the TV aesthetic had pushed art video to the sidelines of the video mainstream. Television now provided the video mainstream.

Before we examine the contours of that new activity in documentary, we should look more closely at the long international history of film and video produced by those committed to radical political change. That tradition has created the best documentaries yet made and continues to foster debates central to the people interviewed in this book.

The Committed Documentary

The Montreal writer and teacher Tom Waugh has defined committed documentary as work that believes in the need for radical socio-political transformation, centres on activism or intervention in the process of change, and, finally, makes a commitment not simply to create works about people but *with* them and *by* them.[35]

Such work began in the 1920s on the highest political and aesthetic level with the astonishing films of Dziga Vertov and Esther Shub in the Soviet Union. After his first view of Vertov's *The Man with a Movie Camera* in Paris in 1929, the English filmmaker Oswell Blakeston said,

"Forget the other documents, for Vertov has the idea of making you conscious of the camera. The lens racks out and in, the scene comes into focus; the lens racks out and in and the eye of the cameraman is in the lens. The eye of the camera, the eye of the cameraman, and the eye of the camera recording it all. . . . The work of Vertov is no longer legendary. We have seen it. . . . Everybody must fight till they do see it!"[36] Seeing the Vertov and Shub films today leaves one with mixed feelings, of awe at their overwhelming power and yet with sadness that perhaps nothing since has matched their creative brilliance.[37] Everything seems to have been thought of right at the beginning. Nevertheless, the great tradition of documentary lies in its direct relation to specific audiences and the specific contexts of viewing. A major work in one historical context can be of limited value and interest in another (except, of course, as a model for other producers).

The committed documentary has developed four significant genres, two of them unique and two others that share conventions and a rhetoric with more mainstream practice.

1. Solidarity. One unique and particularly strong genre of the committed documentary stems from movements of international solidarity, whereby filmmakers of one country attempt to document and agitate for people of another country in need of international help. The emergence of this genre represents and reflects new social, indeed new international, relations in the twentieth century. Luis Buñuel's *Land Without Bread* (1932), Joris Ivens's *The Spanish Earth* (1937), Chris Marker's *Cuba Si* (1961), and Helena Solberg-Ladd's *Nicaragua: From the Ashes* (1982) exemplify the best in a powerful tradition. A history of these films is a history of the twentieth century's crucial events.

2. Participant. Another unique genre has developed from filmmakers and videomakers active as inside participants within a community. This genre differs from ethnography, where the producer remains an outsider, and from autobiography, where the producer occupies the centre of the work. Since the maker is active, this genre often uses the forms of cinéma vérité – principally the camera as catalyst (although most cinéma vérité practitioners work as outsiders). In Canada some of the strongest films and tapes of the 1960s and 1970s were made by Québécois about their society and by women actively engaged in the women's movement. Brault and Groulx's *Les Raquetteurs* exemplified this dynamic, as did the tapes distributed by Vidéo Femmes and Women in Focus. Claire Prieto and Roger McTair's *Some Black Women* (1976)

provided the first inside analysis of Black women's history in Canada.

Two other genres of committed documentary stem from, and share, traits with older documentary genres, although in many crucial ways they change key conventions within the genre. Since the changes can be profound, the artistic and social effects in these works often become as radical as in the genres unique to a committed stance.

3. **Committed journalism.** The prevailing type of committed documentary is radical journalism, where a sympathetic outsider documents, analyses, and interprets events, people, and relationships. Unlike journalism in its dominant form, wielding an ideology of professional objectivity and detachment, the radical journalist, while remaining an outsider, develops a partisan point of view. A good example is *A Wives' Tale* (Bissonnette, Duckworth, Rock, 1979), a portrait of the Sudbury Ontario "Wives Support Committee" at the Inco nickel mines. The film emerged directly from the women's and union rank-and-file movements of the 1970s. Arthur Lamothe's scathing investigation of life among Montreal's construction workers, *Le mépris n'aura qu'un temps (Hell No Longer,* 1970), and Denys Arcand's muckraking investigation of the Quebec textile industry, *On est au coton* (1970), rocked the foundations at the NFB and tested the liberal tolerance of all the institutions involved.

4. **Political autobiography.** A more recent genre stems from the older tradition of autobiography. Taking up feminism's 1970s' slogan, "the personal is political," many women turned the autobiography to new ends of validation and testimony. In the United States especially, the documentary expanded significantly to encompass sexuality and gender, topics previously considered acceptable only within the private sphere or in experimental films. Due to rapidly changing social relations between women and men, even the shortest, most idiosyncratic of these works carried a social force that pushed beyond the older autobiographical themes of character revelation and individual psychology. JoAnn Elam's rough but powerful *Rape* (U.S., 1978) and Lisa Steele's *A Very Personal Story* certainly work in that way.

Thus, the committed documentary seems best described as a type of political practice within the larger genre of documentary. The key issues centre on the relations between makers and subjects and between makers and the social world they hope to change. All four genres have nurtured important films and tapes, and both the mixed and the unique genres will continue to play important roles in the future.

Since the committed documentary encompasses different genres and styles it resists definitions solely in terms of form. For example, in the 1920s the committed documentary closely allied itself to the modernist avant-garde. That link seemed to vanish during World War II, only to re-emerge during the 1980s. Yet throughout the century the links between radical documentary and various avant-gardes remained stronger than the canons of criticism have allowed. Iconoclasts such as Chris Marker in France, Santiago Alvarez in Cuba, Fernando Birri in Argentina, and Bruce Baillie, Shirley Clarke, and Emile de Antonio in the United States never abandoned either the political or the avant-garde side of the equation. The techniques of modernist fragmentation, collage, disjunction of image and sound, disruption of pleasure, and contradiction have continually surfaced in the work of political filmmakers.

Nevertheless, for many left and feminist producers, the adoption of mainstream documentary conventions has seemed the only way to reach audiences less schooled in the art world. Progressives within the NFB and labour union educators hold this principle sacred. Despite the pivotal role that the Québécois filmmakers played in the early cinéma vérité/cinéma direct period, only a few radical Canadian producers tried to link the documentary with avant-garde strategies before 1980.

Little evidence exists of any Canadian committed cinema, conventional or avant-garde, before Quebec's cinéma direct of the late 1950s. Film clubs showed radical documentaries from Europe and the United States during the 1930s, 1940s, and 1950s, but these activities have slipped from our collective film memory (at least in written form). Where were the films shown? To whom? Who were the distributors? Until more research has been done on this chapter of Canadian history, an informed discussion of radical committed media can only begin with the period after 1960.

Figure 5
Key Moments for Committed Documentary in Canada

1958   *Les Raquetteurs*: Michel Brault/Gilles Groulx
1962   *Les bûcherons de la Manouane*: Arthur Lamothe
1963   *Pour la suite du monde*: Pierre Perrault
1967   *Hybrid:* Jack Chambers
1968   *Ballad of Crowfoot*: Willie Dunn
1969   *Le mépris n'aura qu'un temps*: Arthur Lamothe
1970   *On est au coton*: Denys Arcand
1971   Le Vidéographe founded
1971   Women's community-based tapes begin to circulate
1972   Satellite Video Exchange Society founded
1972   *Down On the Farm*: National Farmers Union
1973   National tour of the first Women and Film Festival
1973   *On a raison de se révolter*: Comité d'information politique/
          Champ Libre collective
1973   DEC Films founded in Toronto
1973   Vidéo Femmes founded in Montreal
1973   *Bleeker Street*: Emil Kolompar
1973   *The Tenants Act*: Red Truck Workshop
1974   *A Very Personal Story*: Lisa Steele
1974   *Sarah's War*: Recha Jungmann and Lothar Spree
1976   *Some Black Women*: Claire Prieto and Roger McTair
1972
 –76   *24 heures ou plus*: Gilles Groulx
1977   *Pea Soup* series: Pierre Falardeau/Julien Poulin
1977   *A Right to Live*: Clarke Mackey (for the Union of Unemployed
          Workers)
1978   *Fleck Women*: Kem Murch
1978   Inukshuk Project founded by Inuit Tapirisat of Canada
1978   *Truxx*: Harry Sutherland
1979   *A Wives' Tale*: Bissonnette/Duckworth/Rock

3

Producing in the Canadian Context

Mirabel Airport, Montreal: five relatively well-dressed African men walk towards the camera that is filming over the shoulder of a Canada Immigration official. Everyone is polite and honest; the official asks his questions: "What's your country of origin? Where are your documents? What's your purpose in coming to Canada?"

The men, it turns out, are from Ghana, and they tell the official that they carry false Zaire passports and they are claiming refugee status in Canada. The immigration man says, "Okay, just sit over there."

Meanwhile, on the sound track, the dry, professional-sounding voice of Ann Medina informs us on how to read the sequence:

It used to be a safe bet. You'd invest your life savings in a ticket, and maybe a false passport if you needed one to board the plane. You'd tell the first immigration official that you saw that you were a political refugee. Under Canadian law, after he heard the word refugee, he had to let you in. Chances were you were here to stay. By the late 1980s up to a thousand people a week were getting into Canada this way, which upset a lot of Canadians.

The next sequence shows a group of apparently successful applicants being photographed for Canadian documents, and the narration describes the tough new Canadian immigration laws enacted in January 1989. We learn that the new rules established a pre-screening interview and gave officials the power to deport "phoney" refugees within seventy-two hours of their arrival.

The two opening sequences of the NFB production *Who Gets In* set the historical and political context for the film: before it was easy, now they've clamped down.

44

The Ontario office of the NFB released *Who Gets In*, directed by Barry Greenwald and written by Steve Lucas, in 1989. In many ways the film is typical of the NFB's recent work, and provides an excellent example of why the Film Board provides the foil for so many engaged in the new documentary.

The Ideal Neighbour and the Ideal Viewer

According to its promotion, *Who Gets In* provides "an unprecedented front-line view of the Canadian immigration process in action." It also "reveals the many stresses related to selection, and at the same time dispels many of the social and economic myths about Canadian immigration policies." A healthy budget covered travel to Africa and Asia and allowed all the creative and technical people decent salaries. The film received the standard kinds of NFB promotion, with the release of many prints across the country, theatrical premières at small theatres, and subsequent special promotion for the home video market. Many community-based refugee-aid groups and churches have used the film in their work. *Who Gets In* exhibits the NFB's usual high-quality techniques: sharp, well-lighted photography, professional editing, and a careful sound mix. In addition the CBC co-produced the film and supplied the professional narration of Ann Medina, a well-known field reporter whom viewers might recall from *The Journal*.

The film sets out to document how the immigration and refugee system works. It introduces four groups of people: those being sponsored by family members living in Canada; African refugees; Hong Kong business people; and Asian refugees living in Hong Kong camps. Our inside guide for this investigation is one Mike Malloy, a senior immigration official stationed in Nairobi, Kenya (what the film calls a developing world "outpost"). Malloy has helped draft Canadian policy for over twenty years. Even in the Asian sequences the film returns to Malloy for comments.

As promised in the promotion, viewers are privileged with an inside look into the system. Malloy and the other immigration officers talk in remarkably candid fashion about specific cases and how they practise policy. The filmmakers have obviously spent considerable time setting the atmosphere for relaxed and frank conversation. The officers seem to fear nothing; they are completely secure in their knowledge and their opinions. They speak not only about official policy but also about their feelings and their interpretations of the policy. Malloy admits, "We often say, if this person moves in next door to my mother, what's she going to think about him?"

At the half-hour mark the film jets from Africa to Asia and moves as well onto a higher level of generalization about its subject. Beyond the details of immigration officers deciding specific cases, the film now sets up a contrast between applicants with money (who are classified and judged as members of the "business" category) and those without. The African and Vietnamese refugees have little chance of getting in, while the Hong Kong advertising executives and entrepreneurs receive royal treatment. Ann Medina's narration reinforces this point near the end of the film: "The irony is that most Canadians wouldn't get in using the present criteria." Those who see the film as an indictment of the immigration system most likely think of this comparison between rich and poor, perhaps recalling the populist media-driven outrage over those who can "buy themselves in." In this way the film reveals a thesis, albeit one that is rather subdued and vague, and a level of thematic organization capable of harnessing the rich load of popular discussion on these issues.

Who Gets In appeared in a social and political climate soaked in the media discourses of immigration and race. Throughout 1988 and 1989 *The Globe and Mail*'s resident immigration expert, Victor Malarek, regularly turned out stories on phoney refugees, on how we are losing control of our borders, and on immigrant crime in Montreal and Toronto. In 1989 Barbara Frum hosted a special live edition of *The Journal* to discuss refugees and immigrants. While many of her audience members expressed sympathy for the plight of refugees and pointed to the economic contribution they make, Frum tended to brush them off and kept returning to the theme that most worried her: how many immigrants could we possibly handle before the country fundamentally changes culturally and politically? In Vancouver the press raised the spectre of Asian real-estate moguls buying up the city. At the same time, many African Canadians were beginning to speak out about their representation and the images of Africa normally appearing in the media. While we cannot expect that mainstream journalists had paid any attention to these concerns, the debates over racial representation would have probably reached NFB consciousness by the time of *Who Gets In*.

The NFB turns out an enormous number of current-affairs and social-issue films, exuding the sense that as an institution it can cover all the important Canadian subjects – in emulation perhaps, of the CBC. This drive towards topicality and exhaustiveness has accelerated since

1980 in the face of outside criticism, and perhaps because of the dominant role played by television journalism as the latest model for visual
media. To justify its budget and existence as a social commentator, the
NFB needs to prove it can play in the big leagues of broadcasting. But
going out and rounding up all the likely subjects has its hazards. The
main problem stems from encouraging the development of media professionals quickly adaptable to almost any subject, happy to work
within the supposedly strict confines of the objective reporter, where
deep commitment to a subject can only slow down your shift to the next
topical issue. While showing signs of more research and planning than a
typical "documentary report" on *The Journal* or *Prime Time News, Who
Gets In* reveals in distressing fashion the traits of mainstream journalism – traits nicely insulated, for example, from the debates on representation raised by African Canadians.

Who Gets In provides us with an inside view of a controversial institution, but it is hardly muckraking. The film recalls the classic look at
the British Post Office, *Night Mail*, produced by John Grierson and
directed by Basil Wright and Harry Watt. After we see the institution in
action and the work done by the staff we will appreciate the complexities below the surface and rest confident that everyone does their best
for us, the general public. From the romance of the mail trains to the
vigilance of Immigration Canada, the major chord of Griersonian
documentary sounds clearly in scores of co-sponsored NFB/Canadian
government projects. One doubts whether *Who Gets In* would encounter any immigration department displeasure even though it was not
co-sponsored. And a co-sponsored film would have tarnished journalism's independent image, so this works better all around.

The way the film exaggerates the difference between the pre-1989
and post-1989 "refugee determination process" certainly betrays a prevailing theme of mainstream journalism. Phrases in the narration such
as "It used to be a safe bet" and "Chances were you were here to stay"
hardly describe the misery of waiting in limbo and the separation from
family for the thousands of refugees who arrived *before 1989*, or those
who in the early 1990s are still caught in the "backlog." Surely the refugee system presents enough of a crisis that the filmmakers need not mis-
represent conditions before 1989. It seems that the pull towards topicality encouraged setting the new 1989 regulations in a dramatic light,
completely different from the situation preceding it. Further, without
telling viewers that the total of refugee claimants for 1988 was 22,835,
far below the 1,000 a week that the narration claims, the film plays into

the worst of the newspaper reports with their biblical disaster terminology of "floods," "deluges," "being swamped" and "losing control at the gates."[1]

We might compare *Who Gets In* to other traditions at the NFB. One very different approach that veered sharply from the institutions of the Canadian state emerged from the Unit B's Candid Eye series of the 1950s and 1960s. The freshness of Unit B stemmed partly from its focus on unofficial life in the country through films in which the disorder and social problems of Canadian society had no official or pastoral remedy. Peter Harcourt portrayed their work as an "innocent eye." According to Harcourt, "There is something very Canadian in all this, something which my own Canadianness prompts me to attempt to define. There is in all these films a quality of suspended judgment, of something left open at the end, of something undecided."[2] D.B. Jones wrote that the Unit B films "contain an organic wholeness, a certain aesthetic integrity that avoids the imposition of forced connections to some large issue, some greater relevance."[3] But another tone crept into many of these films, starkly characterized by Bruce Elder: "*Blood And Fire* is fundamentally a film of irony, and the irony is (as is typical of *Candid-Eye* films), a misanthropic one."[4] Although most Unit B films view human frailties in somewhat gentler terms, a dry, ironic, and world-weary tone colours the narration in many others (*The Back-Breaking Leaf*, on tobacco workers, for example). This tone reverberates in directors outside Unit B as well and reaches its most sophisticated practice in the work of Donald Brittain (see, for example, *The Champions*, *On Guard For Thee*, or *Canada's Sweetheart*). Brittain's ironic, weather-beaten narration represents the ideal for most directors working at the Board. Thus the ironic narration heard wall-to-wall throughout *Who Gets In* continues an NFB tradition. Unfortunately, where Brittain's irony works to unearth official contradictions and often points explicitly to state duplicity and scandal, the producers of *Who Gets In* rely only on one official source. The world-weariness functions as the status-quo's wet blanket, implying that as flawed as things may be, still, no other system is possible.

Who Gets In displays none of the sensitive producer/subject relations developed by women in the NFB's Studio D, such as Bonnie Klein's *Patricia's Moving Picture* (1978) and Susie Mah's *Thin Dreams* (1986). Mah, for instance, tells how she went about her work: "I contacted four high schools in Montreal. . . . Eventually, after interviewing a lot of girls, I chose eight drama students from two different schools. We met once a week for six weeks. I videotaped the improvisations and then wrote the scenes using a lot of their dialogue. I wouldn't have been able to capture the way they spoke and what they spoke about if I had done it by myself, without their participation." [5] It seems no one involved in Who Gets In believed the subject – or the subjects – merited this kind of consideration, or practice. Most likely the journalistic dictates – of time, of supposed "objectivity" – would rule against it. As well, because Who Gets In is structured as an inside look out at people trying to get into Canada, sensitivity to personal privacy – a right to reject being filmed – finds no place. Here certainly is the terrain that Brian Winston referred to when he asked of observational cinema: at what point does an ordinary citizen's right to privacy stand above the public's right to know? [6] The problem, I suppose, is that these people are not citizens. Did the immigration or refugee applicants who appear in Who Gets In know about the arms-length relationship between the Canadian government and the NFB?

Two conceptual problems dog this film. First, the producers can only go so far after choosing to focus uncritically on insider Mike Malloy as their sole guide to the issues. Even when the narrator lists the positive characteristics of Hong Kong business people as immigration candidates, she immediately skips back to quote our man in Africa, Mike Malloy, who worries about the challenge to "Canadian culture" posed by so many Asian newcomers. The interviews with Malloy are extensive and relaxed. In the immigration interviews the camera always rests on his side of the desk or in a neutral two-shot showing him facing the interviewee. The narrator often refers simply to Mike, and in a sequence where Malloy arrives in Kampala by car the editing sets up a classic point-of-view sequence, looking out at the Africans on a crowded street. Nothing in the narration or the mise-en-scène questions his practice. How can we not assume that the film endorses Malloy? Another immigration officer who approaches her work in what seems to be a cold and somewhat snide manner is shot from a low angle at the front of her desk, emphasizing her apparently enormous case load. Her rejection of applications with only fleeting perusal seems justified given those stacks of files, which visually wedge her into a small portion of the frame. This too is evidently one of the "stresses related to selection" referred to in the film's promotion.

Perhaps most disturbing is the underplayed sense of Malloy as metaphor for Canada – a typical Canadian on the lookout for "the scoundrels out here," as he puts it. Malloy has no difficulty playing this part, as the comment about the possibility of someone moving in next door to his mother shows. He represents the immigration department's relaxed and assured view of the world: an uncomplicated, insular, white view holding firm in the "outposts" in the service of those typically like themselves back home. This too seems a function of mainstream journalism, a practice that takes its audience for granted. Unlike British and European television, the CBC has not yet embraced the possibility of "specialized" audiences – non-white, for instance, with varied cultural values and tastes. *Who Gets In* shares this uncomplicated view of the audience, and so Mike Malloy's mother gets constructed not only as the typical neighbour but also as the typical viewer.

But, some might say, shouldn't we trust viewers and let the immigration people hang themselves? Why assume that others are not as disturbed by this film's treatment of its subject as I am? This is valid, but only makes sense if the producers had really challenged Malloy. Certainly some viewers will share my disgust for how this film works; others may be shocked at hearing the attitudes of the immigration officials for the first time. Yet providing another platform for Immigration Canada to hang itself seems an awfully modest undertaking; so much for investigative journalism. Since Malloy is not challenged, what about the film's thesis that reveals wealth as a criteria for immigration? Unfortunately, that idea poses no challenge to official immigration policy either. Immigration Canada happily embraces it. The officials in Hong Kong wax ecstatic over the billions of dollars pouring into Canada with the entrepreneurs; they're only dismayed that the government does not widen the business class further. Certainly the officials do hang themselves and many viewers will cringe, but what principle of journalism gives a government department yet another soap box without the least amount of heckling?

A second conceptual problem centres on the film's representation of the developing world, and this viewpoint reveals no knowledge of current debates put forward, for example, by the aid agencies Oxfam-Canada and CUSO, by refugee support groups, and most clearly by Africans and African Canadians themselves. Non-whites speak only in the pressured interview settings. Crowd scenes open every sequence introducing a new country, emphasizing hundreds of people (which would seem to symbolize millions) in apparently anarchic movement. Sullen faces look back at the camera – people waiting endlessly in offices and refugee camps. (Do people of any country ever look happy in line-ups?) And in Asia? The film shows intellectually striving Chinese, pathetic Vietnamese. No need for the Hong Kong entrepreneurs to learn English because real-estate deals, the marketing of Coca Cola, and wallets made from salmon skins will prove big hits in British Columbia.

After the film sets its sights on the workings of Immigration Canada it quickly becomes restricted to looking at the world through the department's eyes, from within an institution under seige: from urban crowds, misery, violence, repressive regimes, angry men, overcrowding. This is the developing world that "everyone wants to leave," the narrator says. The film's failure to provide even one personal study or visual sequence of a refugee outside the interviews with Immigration Canada follows exactly the department's goal of restricting contact between refugee claimants and Canadians. These human contacts would inevitably stir up sympathies (the dreaded "humanitarian concerns" of official parlance) to cloud the refugee determination process and make refusal of entry more difficult for the officials.

It is unfair, perhaps, to criticize the producers for not making a different film, but the strategy developed by *Who Gets In* has its consequences. Another film, with the same limited goal of investigating Immigration Canada, could easily have framed the interviews and the refugee stories differently. What gets left out of *Who Gets In* includes Canada's United Nations commitments to international refugees – commitments that set up a different context than Canada versus the scoundrels. The film leaves out the statistics on total numbers of immigrants and refugees – statistics showing that refugee claims in Canada are far below a "flood" and, indeed, well below our needs for modest economic growth. And it also fails to provide a clear delineation between the categories of "refugee" and "immigrant" – a clarity that would make it harder for officials to apply immigration criteria to refugees. All these omissions reinforce Immigration Canada's view of the world.

Conceptual problems mix freely with the aesthetic decisions taken by the producers. The pressures of mainstream topicality and the NFB's close historic ties to government departments seem to influence the film's structure, providing conceptual frames that correspond with specific aesthetic practice. Whether the conceptual frames determine aesthetic practice or vice versa is perhaps not that important here. What matters is understanding how formal decisions influence meaning. Throughout *Who Gets In*, camera position corresponds with authority, especially in the refugee interviews. And since authority in this case has defined its job as keeping the rascals out of our Canadian communities, the camera work metaphorically implies a Canadian viewing position. Camera angles generally parallel the ground for interiors and exteriors;

the exception is striking in the low-angle shot looking up on the official's mass of files, an angle that softens her callous attitude (to her case load, the applicants, the refugees seeking asylum). The framing of people by medium shot and close-up follows the standard documentary rhythm of dialogue, establishing an office interior context, zooming in for intense moments in the interviews. One striking exception occurs when a refugee claimant is first viewed by a close-up of his army boots advancing towards the camera. Since the film goes on to explain that he was turned down because of unsuitable character – he had "a few rough edges," Malloy says – and a later glimpse in the sequence shows him scowling in a line-up, the first shot seems prescient.

My criticisms of *Who Gets In* should be placed in context. I have no idea about the filmmakers' motives or political philosophy, so my critique stems solely from what appears on the screen and my analysis of the film in a particular social climate. The relations between intent and result could create an entirely fascinating, but different, discussion. In addition, several refugee-aid groups opposed to Canada's policies have used the film successfully. So it would be inappropriate to pass political judgement once and for all. A crucial and understudied area of documentary theory is the question of documentary use by real flesh and blood audiences, particularly since meaning and value rarely parallel exactly the analysis of critics. Where does meaning reside? In the film, in the interpretations of viewers, somewhere in between?

Committed films and tapes can emerge from nearly all institutional settings, and this includes the NFB. As the work of Claire Prieto, Alanis Obomsawin, and Maurice Bulbulian shows, robust, even courageous work emerges from the Film Board, and this work is of no less political value than that accomplished independently. Yet the strategies of these producers (and a few others) go against the grain at the NFB. Unfortunately, *Who Gets In* typifies the Board's approach – high on technique, soft on institutions. Other productions, which look at social problems rather than institutions, such as the Gwynne Dyer *Defence of Canada* series (1986), have caught the topicality virus as well. Picking an issue, they seem merely to drift across the sea of public opinion without compass or rudder. These productions – stuck with the old conventions of dry exposition, matched by a lack of any formal spark, yet harnessed to the frenzied pace of mainstream journalism – drive many producers away.

The Canadian Cultural Institutions

In Canada the growth of the new documentary has taken place within a particular context that is both complex and continually shifting. This context includes economic and political forces quite capable of responding to social, even artistic, demands; it impinges on all levels of social and cultural life. And under late-twentieth-century capitalism, social and cultural activities also constitute major economic activity, especially in broadcasting, film, and publishing, so no clear separation exists between economic and cultural forces. Thus even in a discussion of specific films and tapes, now more than ever the "large-scale" economic factors require attention.

Setting this materialist context for a discussion of any Canadian art begins with five factors:

1. Canada operates as a market-based economy modified by state intervention in many key sectors such as farming, scientific research, and culture – sectors either unprofitable or undesirable for big business.

2. Canadians have inherited an economy based on regions, mainly as the result of historic economic strategies centred on the exploitation of natural resources.

3. Both the market forces and the state interventions foster a class-based society, and often a class-based culture.

4. The world economic "order" is seen to be moving steadily towards a global economy, including increased competition, and for Canada, increased pressure to link with the United States.

5. The historic weaknesses of the Canadian economy and increasing world-wide competition have led to cuts in state expenditures in everything from farm subsidies to the arts.

Canadian society thus seems largely determined by three major contradictions: the market versus the state; the centre versus the regions; and the role of minor imperial power versus the role of subsidiary to the United States.

Historically, these forces of political economy have been played out across the divide of Quebec and English-Canadian cultures. Long before the conquest in 1759, Quebec's distinct economy and language nourished a unique culture. Today the economic differences with the rest of the country may have lessened but the cultural nationalism remains strong, and most Québécois define themselves as belonging not simply to another region but to a "distinct society." Quebec's language and history continue to stimulate a rich culture, at times caught up in a backward-looking politics, at other times part of a politics as progressive as any in North America.

In Canada since the 1930s there have been four major cultural initiatives aimed at "solving" problems created by these three major contradictions: the CBC, the National Film Board, the Canada Council, and the institutionalization of Canadian studies. All of these initiatives have intervened in all three areas of contradiction. They have not been designed solely to deal with the U.S. threat, for example. These are not simple, transparent, institutions or merely propaganda arms for the federal government, because they were also created through genuine public pressure from working-class and middle-class groups. They continue to be pulled in contradictory directions.

A. The CBC remains one of the best-known symbols of Canadian society both here and abroad. It was created in 1936 as a response to wildly conflicting pressures for public, non-commercial, and state broadcasting in radio. But the public, the non-commercial, and the state hardly make compatible partners. Consequently the conflicts over its mandate and relations to commercial broadcasting have only increased since the birth of television. The CBC clearly differs from its U.S. broadcasting counterparts, yet in the area of film and video documentary it joins the U.S. networks to form the mainstream, the dominant producer of images.

Despite its independence from the federal government (in legal if not financial terms), the CBC often plays the crucial and complex role of conduit, at times propagandist, for both the Canadian state and the "world view" of the market.[7] Sociologist Ian Taylor described *The Journal*, the CBC's leading current-affairs vehicle of the 1980s, as "more or less routinely engaged in a 'fudge': it constantly and predictably avoids any informative interrogation of ideologies that compete with the existing parliamentary consensus, and it constantly takes differences . . . and elides them into a consensual form."[8]

Judging by the evidence of program schedules and the experience of producers and distributors, it would seem that Canadian broadcasters believe audiences are not greatly interested in documentaries. A disproportionate number of documentaries screened in Canada carry a British pedigree. In other cases, independent work gets repackaged into the conventions of current affairs journalism. The CBC mandate is easiest maintained with Canadian current affairs content. This may or may not reflect what management thinks Canadian audiences want, yet the launch of *The Journal* in 1982 showed confidence in the existence of an audience – or at least that one could be created for larger doses of non-narrative. Apart from the distinctive brand of journalistic reportage on *The Journal* and, beginning in November 1992, *Prime Time News*, the CBC confines its documentary broadcasts to *Man Alive* and *The Fifth Estate* (both covering social issues), *The Nature of Things* (environmental topics), and *Canadian Reflections* (a hodge-podge of topics, screened well outside prime time). *Man Alive* and *The Nature of Things* both use independently produced documentaries, but many of these are repackaged to feature the programs' regular hosts as narrator, thereby fixing the CBC stamp onto outside productions. CBC Newsworld qualifies as the most timid in its documentary broadcasting, preferring packaged series such as the "best of" the NFB and the "World's Finest," which was a bulk purchase of the BBC's global issues program, *Panorama*. A senior programmer stated in 1991 that Newsworld was not interested in independent Canadian documentary. [9]

B. The National Film Board has operated since 1939 as a much more contentious institution than the CBC, and, as recent studies by Joyce Nelson and Peter Morris show, the aims of its founders were mixed, to say the least. [10] John Grierson, Vincent Massey (then ambassador to Britain), and key members of the Mackenzie King cabinet all sought an improvement in British Empire trade, creation of a propaganda arm for Canada's war effort, and an increased sense of the country by its citizens. The home-spun public aim for the fledgling institution was simpler: to "interpret Canada to Canadians." [11]

Some of this NFB history is now contested. For example, the NFB has long championed its role based on its success at building massive theatrical and non-theatrical audiences. However, Peter Morris reveals that Grierson and others "constantly fuddled NFB distribution statistics," and that "NFB audience claims during Grierson's tenure were highly exaggerated at best and knowingly false at worst." Morris states that the "considerably inflated" statistics were "based on claiming the potential theatrical release as the actual theatrical release; ie. quoting the number of theatres with which the NFB's distributors had contracts (about 600) as the number of theatres which actually showed the films." [12] Joyce Nelson takes the critique of the NFB and its audiences well beyond statistics. She argues that the NFB's much touted rural and union exhibition circuits of the 1940s, run by travelling projectionists, were developed out of fear that the "foreign-born" people concentrated on farms and in factories potentially threatened Canada's war effort. [13]

Since its founding the NFB has been praised by users, attacked by Tories and red-baiters, scorned by free enterprisers in the commercial film world, and ridiculed by many documentary iconoclasts.

C. The Canada Council was established in 1957 to "encourage the study and enjoyment of the arts, humanities and social sciences, as well as the production of related works." The omnipresent Vincent Massey played a hand in this as well, because the Massey Royal Commission of 1951 had recommended such a body, to be modelled largely on the British Arts Council, launched in 1946. The Canada Council has played a vital role in the Canadian arts ever since. In fact, the Council has proved the only reliable funding source for many artists, especially through its Media Arts Section support to non-commercial video producers. Such funding remains crucial outside Ontario and Quebec, where provincial arts funding seldom rises above a paltry level. At the same time, it is within the Council that the social-class tensions of Canadian art seem most clearly played out. Organizations from the National Gallery, the ballet, and symphonies to the smallest video production centre rely on Canada Council funds. Rugged competition prevails from one department to another, with the Media Arts Section well down the list from the heavy hitters in dance, visual arts, and (symphonic) music.

D. Canadian Studies gained institutional status in schools and universities during the 1960s. "Can. Lit." with its established canon now sits proudly as a cornerstone for the liberal arts. Yet this wave of Canadiana has been actively whipped up by the state through large incentives and subsidies. Librarians, Chambers of Commerce, and research academics can all apply for special "Canadian content" funds. Clearly this has been a popular and democratic passion as much as a federal policy brought down from above. The U.S.-Canada free-trade deal of 1989 has, perhaps ironically, spurred a resurgence of these pursuits. Yet when seen from the vantage point of Quebec history, elements of the popular *and* federal government rhetoric about Canadian studies appear less innocent. The failure of the 1980 Quebec referendum on "sovereignty association" and the demise of the Parti Québécois during the 1980s allowed English Canada to ignore Quebec for most of the decade. Today that province is as little known and appreciated as it ever was back in the 1950s.

The flawed triumvirate of the CBC, NFB, and Canada Council faced increasing hostility during the 1980s from the federal and provincial governments in the form of threats and economic cuts. Yet, ironically, in our era state patronage of high culture functions as an indicator of a mature and prosperous society. The model of the German arts centres throughout the world shows the key role that prestige arts play in international image building and hence trade. Even the most wildly anti-bourgeois avant-garde featuring Brecht, Fassbinder, and Joseph Beuys has done its bit as ambassador for German postwar culture. Canada's frenzied chase for the 1996 Olympics, with the attached "cultural component," shows in only slightly more blatant terms the same belief that trade follows cultural prestige. Given these trade and culture links, cuts to Canadian art show that the state either wants it both ways or remains immature at image building. Quebec author Marc Raboy has argued that after the defeat of the 1980 Quebec independence referendum, the federal government rapidly shifted from cultural policies based on "national unity" to economic-based cultural policies based on modern communications. [14] Within the federal government, throughout the 1980s the Department of Communications gained in status to the detriment of the Ministry of Culture. In the 1990s, with Quebec nationalism on the rise once again, the ideological need to focus on national unity could return. Yet given a free-trade agenda it is unlikely that national unity will be coupled to hearty support for the Canadian arts in the same way that those two linked arms in the 1960s and 1970s. Canadian studies will probably continue to receive strong support, especially in Ontario schools, at the same time as the federal government cuts back the smaller cultural industries of publishing and "community arts."

At the national level, economic priorities have promoted ever greater regional disparities and a continued lack of communication. Consequently, the regional basis of much Canadian art remains ever stalwart, even if the forms of expression have changed. This regional character hardly constitutes a tragedy in cultural terms, because much of the best art and literature produced in Canada has been local, with specific roots. And since economic development as normally practised tends to bring Central Canadian culture to "the regions" rather than creating a reciprocal flow, the result means a replacement of often rich and local art with the often bland "universal." For the Atlantic region especially, poverty and the continual brain-drain to Central Canada have done more to destroy the old cultures than any of the new development projects.

The changing ethnic and racial composition of Canada has fostered other doubts about the CBC, the NFB, and the Canada Council. Groups who in the past might have vigorously defended these federally

supported agencies against the vagaries of the commercial market
have begun to question the narrow demographic representation seen on
most programs. Many non-white artists as well as most activists in the
labour movement feel marginalized by the major cultural institutions.
CBC managers often lament that "public broadcasting" will die unless
the public speaks out on its behalf. Yet for many the public aspect of the
CBC has become hard to see, and every year it gets tougher to feel sympathy for its dilemma. A number of the producers interviewed in this
book voice even stronger opinions about the NFB, and some argue that it
has outlived its usefulness.

For its part, the Canada Council has maintained a fairly narrow definition of what deserves funding, and in the worst senses this definition
has been internalized by producers. Documentary has been supported
only half-heartedly, and encouragement for exploring new areas of content or new relations between producers and their subjects has been
lacking. Operating on a kind of sweetheart jury system of "peers," the
Council recruits filmmakers and videomakers who have been successful (in the Council's terms) to decide who shall receive new grants.
Although this system has encouraged young artists, and may be prefera-
ble to more bureaucratic committees, those on the outside not considered peers have little chance of breaking in. [15] Given this history and the
backlash, only vigorous lobbying for affirmative action and a wider definition of peers will change the system.

Indeed, the shifting ethnic and racial composition in both English
Canada and Quebec may soon foster a shake-up. While Canada remains
a predominantly white society, African Canadian, Asian Canadian, First
Nations, South American, and Central American artists have accomplished a great deal since 1980. Although they have not gathered enough
strength to take on the mainstream media, new producers and new
kinds of representations have certainly been felt in the independent and
oppositional sectors. However, as Richard Fung points out, "In one evening of mainstream television there is more multiracial representation
than can be found in the entire body of Canadian video art." [16] Because
documentary practice usually involves representational activity (either
in ethnographic or autobiographical terms) and has always maintained a
social conscience, it is only surprising that these issues of Canadian
racial representation did not surface earlier.

The Committed Documentary:
Independence and Accountability

The idea of the independent media producer is in some ways a U.S. import into Canadian cultural terrain, and a rather vacuous sleight-of-hand akin to "free trade" – masking more than it explains. Independence in the United States means freedom from Hollywood, and for some people freedom simply from the major studios. But using that criteria makes all documentaries independent. Independence in Canada usually means freedom from a salaried position at the NFB or from broadcast television. Yet this definition implies little more than the opportunity to work freelance. In both countries independent film and video production rarely means freedom from state funding.

All the producers interviewed for this book have at one time or another used arts council grants or NFB facilities to set their projects in motion. Also, many of the producers rely on television money for production itself (that is, not simply for broadcast sales). This need not damage or compromise the radical effect of the work. Nevertheless, the restrictions, limits, and self-censorship circling around all media production remain key factors for radical media-makers in Canada. The limits on independence are not greater here than in the United States or Europe: they simply present a different set of boundaries. Yet many artists have adopted the independent label rather uncritically, without examining the context they work in.

In both the United States and Canada, "independence" has been used as a simple antidote to the evils of commercial media. For example, in the area of high-school media education an unusual alliance has sometimes formed between groups concerned with the effects of rock videos on teenagers and those pushing for the simple recognition of non-commercial film and video. This alliance opposes the "bad stuff" of popular, or commercial, culture with the "good stuff" of art.

In contrast to the loose and unhelpful notion of independence, the concept of accountability seems much better suited to handle the new documentary. Accountability is a complex notion. It takes for granted that any media-making requires collaboration, power, ethical authority, an audience, and financial debts.

Collaboration comes into play in film and video more than in any other fine art. This is true even for persons with well-defined political and artistic goals, and it is true even at the most modest level of artistic and technical production. *Power* flows like an electric current from the

class position of most filmmakers and videomakers and from the institutional weight carried by late-twentieth-century media. *Ethical
authority* relates to power, but refers to more personal relationships of
trust or consent established between maker and subjects. *Documentary
audiences* are often more specialized than for fiction, but even when a
film or tape has been subsidized, market criteria bear down on its circulation. And the success of its circulation partly determines whether the
producer can raise money for future projects. There is also a question of
tone and assumed knowledge between the work and the audience that
plays a part in the work's creation. *Financial debts* often mount up and
remain even years after the production has been completed. Debts can
be subtle and complex, involving, for instance, promises and limitations
undertaken by the producer in order to secure funds – in colloquial
terms, the strings attached.

No producer stays completely independent; some are accountable
to the mainstream and their careers, others are linked to alternative or
oppositional "communities." The producers' relations with their sub-
jects/communities and with specific audiences form the base point for
the ideas of accountability that I will use here. Accountability should be
defined broadly. It need not imply a contractual arrangement between
producer and others. I use it more to indicate the producer's world view,
sympathies, and connections. Accountability also relates to commitment, and the result is the committed documentary.

The relations of accountability should not overwhelm a producer's
critical sensibility – the need to probe and question and the need to challenge. Too many films and tapes made by persons committed to a cause
abdicate their viewpoint in the name of "giving voice" to someone else.
That approach turns the maker into a simple mouthpiece for those who
appear on screen, flattens out contradictions, hides subtle biases, and
often leads audiences to reject the work as "propaganda." If this book
tips the balance away from the notion of the "independent creative artist" towards "relations of accountability," it is primarily to even the historical balance, not to suggest that producers abandon a critical sensibility, or analysis, or open mind.

An older series of debates in documentary concerns *ethics*. These
ethical questions pertain mainly to an individual producer and an individual subject. Anyone who has edited a film or tape knows how easy it
is to make someone look foolish. Most standard documentary texts and
interviews with working filmmakers include practical questions about

how a director relates to those they film. Critics of Flaherty's *Man Of Aran* (1934), for example, questioned his ethics in convincing the Aran islanders to risk their lives by re-creating their old fishing methods. Interviewers have often challenged direct cinema practitioners about including moments of embarrassment for their filmed subjects. This is related to Brian Winston's questioning of the media's concept of "the public's right to know" – his belief that the public "right to know" should only be applied to those persons in positions of power, and that the "right to privacy" should prevail with ordinary citizens. [17] Film-maker-journalists often present an extremely intimidating force in their questions and interventions. For many of the people being filmed, the media represent authority closely linked to the police, the government, or management, and they fear the consequences of not co-operating. So questions of ethics and power crop up throughout the entire process.

The best notion of accountability incorporates many of these older ethical issues but enlarges the terrain to deal also with group ethics. By group ethics I mean the relations between the media-makers and the larger community they are working with and documenting – and not just the people who will appear in the final product. Again, this relation need not be a legal contractual one, it may be a rough "understanding" that the maker will represent a community fairly and responsibly. These issues apply to producers working from inside the community depicted, but they become particularly acute when the producer hails from a different culture or race.

Since the demise of the organized left, both old and new in North America, the term *community* has emerged as a political shorthand to deal with coalition politics across a broad spectrum. But the term carries ambiguous, even dangerous, ideas within it. First, it parallels the liberal notion of multiculturalism in which Canadian society is pictured as a mosaic of equal groups of different cultural heritages, a notion that thereby downplays relative power among groups. Second, the term suggests a geographical contiguity that overgeneralizes. The gay population of Halifax, for example, does not all live in one downtown neighbour-hood – its members live in the city *and* the suburbs, in high-rise condos *and* within nuclear-family bungalows. Third, it suggests a political, even cultural, unity that rarely exists and that particularly masks class tensions. As a shorthand, especially in colloquial speech, use of the term "community" is understandable and usually clear enough. It carries a very necessary power of generalization. I often hear phrases such as "the

Black community believes . . ." or "the gay community demonstrated for . . ." or "the video community wants to see. . . ." But in putting these phrases to paper, we can readily see how they exclude differences and contradictions. Persons in the gay community obviously share many ideas and experiences, but many gay communities exist and at times the differences must also be recognized. In his interview in this book, John Greyson develops these thoughts by questioning the validity of describing himself as a *gay* artist.

In one specific debate over group ethics, some people argue that white filmmakers should not attempt to depict Native and Black communities, while others feel that responsible co-operation is necessary or possible. Those who argue against cross-cultural representation stress two reasons. First, that control over an "image" remains a principle of first priority for groups without much power, and this principle must be recognized by the dominant society. Second, that because funding is so scarce priority should be given via affirmative action to Native and other non-white media-makers.

In Canada these issues of cross-cultural representation and "group ethics" have been rapidly pushed to the forefront by a new generation of First Nations writers and media activists, fostered in part by the failure of the constitutional talks on Native self-government held in the 1980s (depicted by Maurice Bulbulian in *Dancing Around the Table*). The interviews with Alanis Obomsawin, Zach Kunuk, Richard Fung, Claire Prieto, and Judith Doyle all touch on the need *for communities* to control their images. For First Nations people, a lack of control over their image characterizes the entire twentieth century. In Canada, the rapid development of anthropology and museum building at the turn of the century led in turn to narrow definitions of "Native art" and subsequently to the current situation in which white producers can pull down media funding for Native subjects far easier than can Native people themselves. The question thus turns on the power to fundraise as much as on the sensitivity of the images depicting Native people. [18]

The critique of mainstream ethnography has placed serious doubts on the ethical authority of the "scientist observer." Many peoples who have traditionally resigned themselves to be the subjects (objects) of anthropology now question the authority of the observer to take pictures, collect stories, and interpret their culture to the larger outside world. The challenging films and writings of Trinh T. Minh-ha, an American of Vietnamese background, have pushed this critique the furthest: "The socially oriented filmmaker is . . . the almighty voice-giver (here in a vocalizing context that is all-male), whose position of authority in the production of meaning continues to go unchallenged, skilfully masked as it is by its righteous meaning." [19]

In many cases the producer needs to anticipate how audiences will understand the work. Will audiences see the film as representing the maker's particular viewpoint, or a view of the specific persons appearing in the film, or as a view that can be generalized to represent a larger group? For example, if a producer includes an interview with a working-class woman, will the audience then interpret that one woman as typical of all working-class women? In this way accountability and the desire to anticipate audience reactions to both content and form go hand in hand.

A change of focus from "independence" to "accountability" can reflect a partial shift from economic to political issues. The central concern is not so much the source of a producer's funds as what he or she does with those funds. Using this criteria, radical committed documentaries can emerge from salaried producers at the NFB, from the CBC, from the private sector, *and* from those working with unions or community groups. Each of these working relations brings with it gains and losses. Now, perhaps, some working situations will stimulate radical work more than others. My criticisms of the NFB and CBC, despite the many good people working there, stem from the vast power and resources that these two institutions maintain: the percentage of their truly important work given their enormous yearly output is abysmal. Yet in Canada films and tapes of deep commitment and radical vision have emerged from all sectors.

4
The Elements of Documentary Distribution

For many producers and users in Canada, the mechanics of distribution for political films and tapes are a mystery. Most commentators on the media, in articles that either bemoan the crisis in documentary or celebrate Canada's lively film and video culture, ignore how audiences discover and come to see the work. Yet distribution is the linchpin for the entire circulation of media in society.

All works of committed media have difficulty making inroads into broadcast TV. They come on as too strong, too partisan, and too innovative for the packagers. Nevertheless, these works continue to attract diverse audiences in non-theatrical and semi-theatrical settings across Canada. How do these varied audiences come to see the works of committed documentary, and what is the role played by distributors?

Markets and Audiences
Mainstream Theatrical Distribution
The dominant cinema defines theatrical film distribution in narrow terms as a managerial division of labour designed to channel the flow of products into the market – a cinema powered by capital and the agendas set by the middle class. There are the inevitable recurring battles in the mainstream over territory, percentages, block booking, and who pays for advertising. [1] But the production, distribution, and exhibition sectors generally respect each other's realm, with the distributor's job being to sell films to the exhibitor at the best possible price. In Canada theatrical distribution is streamlined considerably, because only two exhibition chains, Cineplex and Famous Players, control 95 per cent of the screens.

64

Theatrical Film Distribution

Major Producer/Distributors
Buena Vista (Disney)
20th Century-Fox
Warner Bros
MGM/UA
Universal
Orion Classics
Orion
Tri-Star
Columbia

Mini-Major Producer/Distributors
Miramax
Cannon
New Line Pictures
Concorde
AFI USA

Major Canadian Theatrical Distributors
Alliance Releasing
Astral Films
Norstar Releasing
Cineplex Odeon Films Canada
Criterion Pictures
C/FP Distribution
Creative Exposure

In Quebec
Cinema Plus
Cinepix
Cine 360
Aska
Films Transit
MaloFilm Group

Exhibitors in Canada
Cineplex (U.S.-controlled)
Famous Players (U.S.-controlled)
Landmark Theatres (Edmonton)

Non-Theatrical Distribution

The world of non-theatrical distribution remains even less well known. Here the atmosphere resembles more the marketing of industrial products than the rough and tumble, sometimes glitzy world of theatrical distribution. Whereas the hoi polloi of the theatrical distributors congregate at Montreal's World Film Festival and Toronto's Festival of Festivals, the non-theatrical types must make do with the trade-show ambience of the Eastern Canada and Western Canada Film and Video "Showcases." At these events school and public library audio-visual buyers invite non-theatrical distributors to rent space and display their most recent "product." Even in this non-theatrical "educational" sphere, the mainstream distribution model prevails. For most profit-making non-theatrical companies, distribution settles into a narrow groove. The distributor's job is to funnel product into the prearranged slots of curriculum and public library categories.

Major Non-Theatrical Distributors in Canada

Marlin Motion Pictures*
Visual Education Centre*
National Film Board of Canada*
Magic Lantern Communications*
International Tele-Film Enterprises*
THA Media*
Group MultiMedia*
Kinetic*
Omega Films*
Canadian Learning Company
Full Frame Film and Video*
National Geographic
Time Life Pictures
BBC Enterprises
* indicates Canadian ownership

Major Buyers (English-language materials)

Metro Toronto Public Library
Metro Toronto Catholic School Board
Peel Board of Education (Ontario)
Regina Public Library
Calgary Public Library
Calgary Board of Education

Calgary Catholic Board of Education
North York Board of Education (North Toronto)
University of Toronto
York University
Manitoba Department of Education

A glance at the catalogues of distributors and libraries reveals how the product and the subject categories often fit hand in glove. Subject headings gleaned from recent catalogues include: motivation, consumer education, government and civics, parenting, ethnic art. Private-sector non-theatrical distributors, such as THA Media and International Tele-Film, do carry some excellent, even left-wing, films. Nevertheless these companies operate for quick turnover profits and in no way challenge the basic market model of narrowly defined distribution.

The Four Realms of Film Distribution
  1. Hollywood (eg., Astral)
  2. Art film (eg., Norstar)
  3. Educational mainstream (eg., Marlin)
  4. Educational alternative/oppositional (eg., Full Frame)

The Five Realms of Video Distribution
  1. Hollywood, from prestige to martial arts (eg., Video One, head office, Toronto)
  2. Mainstream music video (via record companies to TV)
  3. Educational mainstream (eg., Marlin, Magic Lantern)
  4. Video art (eg., Art Metropole)
  5. Video art and alternative/oppositional (eg., V-Tape, Video Out, Le Vidéographe, Full Frame)

Video distribution matured rapidly after 1980, and the division of labour and territories will probably continue for some time. In the fifth realm of video distribution, of most importance for the new documentary, a key distributor such as V-Tape handles both high-concept video art and committed documentary – everyone from Vera Frenkel, a leading formalist, to the small women's community organizations. V-Tape sees no difficulty with such a mixed venture, because its mandate centres on publicizing video as an art form per se. During the late 1980s, however, V-Tape began to package titles by subject matter, notably the *Video Against AIDS* compilation tape. This signals a change in emphasis away from the older emphasis on auteurs and "video as a new medium," a change to be welcomed by those seeking to use video as an oppositional tool in Canada.

Since the mid-1980s video art has crept into the educational marketplace, while retaining its high-art modes of circulation based on festivals and gallery purchases. Video art gains its legitimacy through critical magazine dialogue and festival programming, so purchase of the works more often follows from the initiatives of festival curators than from the active marketing of the producer or distributor. This does not mean that video artists and distributors remain passive in the process. In fact, in the world of video art the artist's public persona is much more critical to a tape's success than it is in the educational film world or the frenzied music video realm, where directors play second fiddle to performers and remain a mere technical packaging designer – the video images a vehicle for lyrics. For the video-art market, a sector of the larger art world, subject matter remains secondary to the personal vision or expression of the artist. The intensity or originality of that expression determines the success of the work.

Film and Video Festivals
Both mainstream narrative and non-commercial film and video productions rely on festivals as a vehicle of publicity. Promotion via posters, ads, and catalogues costs dearly but publicity, especially when generated through festivals, is cheap. This is especially the case with low-budget, independently produced documentaries. Thus a festival offers one of the best means of reaching programmers, reviewers, and future audiences. A showing at one of the three largest film festivals, in Montreal, Toronto, and Vancouver, can help a new production significantly through the attention of mainstream media and the presence of national and international programmers. None of the big festivals pay rental or artist fees, because the publicity gained from inclusion is deemed worthwhile in itself. Unfortunately, the size of these events and the attendant glitz surrounding the gala presentations (usually Hollywood or Hollywood-inspired fare) tend to bury the documentaries. Only the most astute program readers notice the Canadian documentaries in the massive schedules, and the press reviewers seldom dip into this category without strenuous prompting. Occasionally, however, a review or interview appears, greatly improving the prospects for the film or tape. Later on, enterprising producers can milk a festival screening for all it's worth – it is especially a boost to their résumés when they fundraise for their next project.

Film and Video Festivals in Canada
Toronto Festival of Festivals
Montreal World Film Festival
Vancouver Film Festival
Festival du nouveau cinéma, Montreal
Yorkton Film and Video Festival
Banff TV Festival
Atlantic Film and Video Festival
Images Film and Video Festival, Toronto

A number of small irregular events, such as the Women's Film and Video Festival in Montreal, Vues d'Afrique in Montreal, Edmonton's InSight and Third World Festivals, and the Guelph, Kingston, and Peterborough international film and video festivals, have furnished good publicity for the works exhibited and have helped build audiences for all committed documentary.

The grouping of films and tapes into festival programs legitimizes work in ways that single screenings in theatres or semi-theatrical showings could never achieve. In addition, a festival program often achieves better political results through the linking of diverse audiences at the events, and it can create increased awareness about the range of groups committed to social change. Viewers see a diversity of experience and struggle.

The problem with festivals stems from the narrow range of experts who do the programming. Too often, even politically motivated festivals quickly jettison any sort of community involvement in the name of an artistically advanced program. Film "buffs" and media academics often hijack the show, narrowing its approach to the possible audience and limiting the organizational efforts. Venues that might be comfortable and neutral for the general public, such as community centres and public libraries, get overlooked in favour of downtown theatres and galleries, white entertainment clubs, and imposing university auditoriums. Advertising slips into mainstream patterns. Finally, the program itself comes to dominate, and other planning, such as setting political goals and building the event through co-sponsorships, gets shuffled to the sidelines. In the worst cases the publicity generated simply mirrors these narrowed priorities of the festival, with producers' careers getting all the attention to the detriment of issues raised in the works themselves.

Political Distribution

For political media, effective distribution should be conceived as broadly as possible and perhaps defined as "the art of finding the right audience, no matter how small, and then expanding and building on that audience." Distribution of the new documentary is an attempt to build audiences for *innovative* film and video – works that educate and prompt action through entertainment or challenging forms.

Finding and building the "right" audience seldom translate into finding the largest audience in the least amount of time. Politically, a smaller, more actively engaged audience can in the long run provide a better starting point for a film than a larger group of unconnected people seeing it on television. In distributing a new work, most politically engaged distributors first try to reach groups most directly interested in the subject; then, together with those groups as endorsers, they try to move out into larger publics. This may seem odd commercially, especially to producers anxious for royalties to pay off debts to labs and friends; but in the long run this two-step release works better financially as well as politically. Without thousands of dollars for saturation promotion the new documentary relies heavily on personal contacts and word of mouth. But with the support and endorsement of active groups who most value the work, the films and tapes have often achieved a moderate success.

Ready-made audiences do not exist for political media, and distributors must play a major role in both political and media education. Plugging films into Grade Ten geography slots may work well for the National Geographic, but it fails for works on racism, unemployment in the Maritimes, or gay washroom sex. Political distributors fight a constant battle trying to open up hardened (some might say petrified) subject categories, resorting at times to suggestions on how a "moral values" curriculum "unit" might consider a film on gay and lesbian old people, or how Lacourse and Patry's *Night and Silence* might work in geography. Media-education buyers and managers play a key role in the non-theatrical sector – a role fostered in the training grounds of mainstream library science and teacher's colleges. This "battle of the subject categories" can come into focus if we compare the subject headings used by Kai Vision-Works, an alternative library for still photos and slides in Toronto, to the headings used by libraries and school boards. Kai Vision-Works' unusual, though sensible, listings include "women in Central America," "poverty," and "union organizing." The libraries and school boards list work under heads such as "geography," "motivation," and "moral values," categories that limit the possibilities for creative political media.

Users of political media succumb to consumerism as much as everyone else, and the rather frantic desire to program only the newest work pervades many social-issue groups. Political distributors experience constant frustration when organizers and programmers reject tapes and films only two or three years old. This can create pressure on distributors to take on more material than they can properly handle. If a film or tape fails to be noticed or widely screened within the first year of distribution, it may be doomed.

The Full Frame Story
Accountability
In 1974 the Development Education Centre of Toronto launched its distribution service, DEC Films. The venture immediately took off, particularly through its South American collection. By 1979 DEC Films also carried Canadian films and tapes in an attempt to develop links between international and Canadian social issues. DEC's approach centred on action for political change, and its mandate revolved around political and cultural education, not providing consumer goods for a market. Thus, the development of specific audiences became the key to successful distribution. Today the successor to DEC Films, Full Frame Film and Video, represents a much broader range of film and video producers, but the distinction between supplying a market and building an audience remains key. [2]

In the 1970s DEC Films could afford to carry political films that would never find a large audience. Its staff felt simply that certain material should be made available in Canada, and if they rejected it no one in Canada would see it. Thus they acquired the salient but rarely used *Sarah's War* by Recha Jungmann and Lothar Spree and *Le mépris n'aura qu'un temps* by Arthur Lamothe.

Full Frame's acquisition decisions for Canadian material rest as much as possible on two areas of accountability: to find good resources for political activists in Canada, such as anti-racism groups, the women's movement, Third World immigrant and solidarity groups; and to support independent, mainly left-wing, producers to communicate challenging ideas. I joined the staff in 1981, and in my experience we have sought out artists willing to experiment formally in the development of political ideas, although we have been limited in our ability to handle too many "difficult" works. For instance, we have taken on

Brenda Longfellow's *Our Marilyn* and Sima Khorrami's *Sima's Story*
(1990), but we have turned down distribution of Louise Carré's *The Forgotten War* (1984) and many others for lack of time and resources. [3] This
narrowed selection process marks a retreat from the more buoyant
1970s and reflects the tougher economic climate all distributors faced in
the late 1980s and early 1990s.

In the first kind of accountability, the local one, we have been
encouraged or pushed by local Canadian groups to find materials. The
strong demands by Tom Waugh, Harry Sutherland, Gay Bell, and other
activists to introduce gay and lesbian work into our collection certainly
pushed DEC in that direction in the early 1980s.

The concept of use-value provides a cornerstone for this activity,
because most social-issue groups look for media according to subject
matter rather than director or genre. This approach has its detractors.
Certainly, in art circles the idea of usefulness carries a bad name and
often leads to that odious phrase, "preaching to the converted," so often
employed in the mainstream media to denigrate political films and
events. As a participant at a film showing reported:

A group of women from different organizations were screening a film on
women's music and the power of emotion and social awareness behind women's
creativity. Most of the audience was responding positively, when one woman
said, "We're just preaching to the converted here." It was a definite put-down. I
had learned a lot from the film, and felt that the discussion was helping women
from different groups discover shared assumptions. It's one thing to take up the
challenge of involving other people in the women's movement, but that was not
our main purpose. The comment stifled further discussion. [4]

In my view distribution should involve a dialogue between users
and distributors over the long-term versus short-term value of a
resource. The distributor (and the producer being represented) must
attend, of course, to the immediate needs of the user. For example, a
women's group might be desperate for a basic resource on incest that
shows facts and figures and outlines basic political strategies. At the
same time, a distributor could suggest tapes employing a more personal
approach to incest, which could help raise different kinds of discussion.

In the second type of accountability, to independent, innovative
political artists, DEC/Full Frame has tried to return as much in royalties
as possible. The basic contract with producers, adopted in 1974 following the Montreal Rencontre of political distributors and filmmakers,

sets royalties to producers at 50 per cent of proceeds from rentals and sales. This financial return has been of mixed success. Some producers have done well, yet for others DEC failed rather miserably to achieve a distribution that resulted in good returns. The pressures of having to seek ever newer resources and the need to build audiences almost from scratch have hurt the fortunes of some films and tapes. This situation will only gradually improve.

In the mid-1980s Sophie Bissonnette's *Quel Numéro: What Number?* (*The Electronic Sweatshop*), a perfect example of what I mean by the new documentary, became one of DEC's most successful films. *Quel Numéro* vividly represents the uniquely Quebec approach of cinéma direct, which lies between U.S. direct cinema and French cinéma vérité. The film weaves back and forth between observation and interviews, using staged but unscripted situations and personal testimony embedded within a tight, thematically defined structure: a film about women and new technology – a descent into workplace hell from supermarket checkouts to Canada Post. By mainstream standards this was a difficult work: a feature-length documentary (eighty-one minutes) about women and technology using Quebec examples only.

Where's the market? CBC and TVOntario programmers barely gave it the time of day. Nevertheless, we sold many prints and tapes, hundreds of groups rented it, and festivals of many kinds exhibited it. The film made money and women across Canada learned about crucial issues of health and workplace democracy. *Quel Numéro* was successful for three reasons: the quality of the film and the care taken to include both humour and a partisan point of view; the subject matter, which previously had been rarely approached from the perspective of the women affected; and extra promotional effort by Sophie Bissonnette and DEC Films.

The challenge for all independent political distributors is to remain open to concerns new to society and also to welcome new formal strategies. These new concerns and forms seldom fit easily into existing distribution categories, television slots, or curriculums. Distributors rarely create audiences from scratch, but they can work with energetic existing groups to reach a much broader public.

Principles of Representation and Production

Beyond the general principles of accountability and independence, Full Frame has developed more rigorous criteria for evaluating films and tapes. These fall into two categories: a politics of representation and a politics of production. They work as more specific criteria for acquisition decisions than "What makes a good film?" and "What makes a work politically valuable in Canada?"

A politics of representation centres on evaluating how people appear on the screen.[5] Who narrates? With whose authority? Who speaks in the third person, from what formal and/or political point of view? Who speaks in the first person? Does the editing leave a space for subjects to speak fully for themselves – as compared to television's propensity for slice-and-dice quotes – or does a tape's over-reliance on a subject's experience, particularly in interviews, become a cover for the producer's lack of analysis or lack of self-examination? These issues become acute when artists portray cultures other than their own, or when distributors judge international work through North American aesthetic values.

A politics of representation examines the types of people chosen to illustrate a thematic point (for example, a decision to interview only *working-class* men in a film about rape), or the types of people chosen as average Canadians (usually white men), or persons used to illustrate a leftist metaphorical point (for example, a woman in designer jeans chosen to illustrate the "decadence" of the ruling class). The use of specific persons as abstractions often arises as a debate about personal exploitation between filmmaker and on-camera subject and has been fruitfully discussed as documentary ethics by the writers Alan Rosenthal and John Katz.[6] But I am referring here solely to the representation of persons on the screen and how they are made to stand for ideas, concepts, and events. Representation has been most fully debated among feminist producers and users; the issue as related to class and race has not been as widely discussed. Throughout the 1980s, hotly contested debates over cross-cultural representation ripped through the field of ethnography, but the issues pertain to every creator of political films and tapes.

A politics of production centres on the producers' relations with their subjects – the third characteristic of committed cinema – works not simply *about* people but *with* them and *by* them. Some of these issues are clearly reflected on the screen, some can be inferred, and others only come to light in talking with the subjects.

- Who set the agenda for the work? Who picked the topic?
- Who paid for the production, or sponsored it?
- Did the size of the budget – either large or small – influence the outcome?

- Did technical criteria influence the outcome? For instance, a decision to use film versus video, a big crew over a small one, an insensitive crew?
- Was the producer overwhelmed by the subjects, or by some subjects to the detriment of others? In Bill Nichols's phrase, did the producers lose their voice? (Often, one or two spokespersons – usually men – try to speak for others in a community, blocking a producer's access to others.)
- Who benefits? What risks are involved for those who participate?
- Will the work receive the kind of attention that will advance the issues or advance the career of the producer?

Financial Constraints

A friend once wrote to me that distributors never ask you what your film is about, how you achieved the brilliant lighting, or how you almost got killed or went bankrupt making it. They only ask you, "How long is it?" Alas, his story rings true, but I had a comeback: one time a buyer at an educational film showcase rushed up to me breathlessly and asked, "Do you have any good ten-minute films on stress?"

Independence from grants carries its own price – an independence that pushes us towards the market-driven jaws of operating. In Full Frame's case, even minimal grant funding has provided space for important activities such as the distribution of risky, more unconventional films and tapes. John Greyson's *Urinal* and Richard Fung's *My Mother's Place* could not be handled without some assistance. Astonishingly, in the mid-1980s the Media Arts Section of the Canada Council once criticized the Quebec distributor Parlimage for its "animation" work on the grounds that Canada Council funding should only cover "distribution." Here is the narrow version of distribution internalized *par excellence* by a major cultural funding agency.

But the politics of accountability, representation, and production usually get thoroughly blended with more mundane concerns in DEC/ Full Frame's selection processes. Other factors in deciding what to distribute can include the need to maintain a balance of features and shorts, films and tapes, and works suitable for rentals or sales. These are added on to the pressures to carry ever more material in order to take advantage of the large budgets of major customers, or to help qualify for certain types of grants. Finally – unfortunately – there is the pressure to take on what seems to be mediocre work for the immediate political value in raising discussion of a particular issue.

The *Other Film Industry Report* written in 1985 to influence federal culture and communications policies stressed the crisis in spending for educational media. The authors showed how shrinking budgets for libraries and school boards had damaged profits for the non-theatrical distributors. Since then, cuts in Manitoba education, Alberta public libraries, and Ontario school boards have hurt even more. Yet, surprisingly, the Canadian market for Canadian-made educational media equals the Canadian share of the market for theatrical features. Buyers spend $12 million per year on rentals and sales of non-theatrical films and tapes, the same amount as the Canadian share of the theatrical revenues from Canadian box offices. [7]

The educational market circulates two kinds of films and tapes. First, those narrowly defined "educational" products that tie in directly to primary or secondary school curriculum. Health, science, or math films, shorter than twenty minutes, with intriguing titles such as *Head Lice*, *Plants of the Sea*, *Posture: Thinking Tall*, and *How Blood Clots*, make up the bulk of these. Second, the more general-interest works, both documentary and fiction, that Full Frame and other political distributors handle also scramble for a place in public libraries and school or university collections. The specialized curriculum-oriented product can achieve enormous success, often with sales of up to two hundred copies, and can quickly return $20,000 or so to both producer and distributor. The more general type of work reaches its best-seller status at well below fifty copies, and after the three-way split of lab, distributor, and producer, the producer rarely gleans more than, say, $15,000 over a five-year contract. The combination of tighter education and library budgets and the enormous pressures to reduce video prices with the onslaught of home video have nearly killed the 16mm market and have contributed to an even more precarious climate for politically committed producers and distributors.

Unless they receive grants of some sort, just reaching the break-even point seems elusive. When buyers and community groups bemoan the high cost of films and tapes, these are the dreary financial statistics distributors drag out. Filmmakers and videomakers, needless to say, seldom get rich on this kind of endeavour.

5
Audiences: The Ideal and the Real

"My first audience is Black. It's the reason to make the work, because we as Black people need to know and discuss what's going on out there, what our history is." Claire Prieto

"As a cinematographer I like to feel when I'm shooting that I have the whole audience in my head." John Walker

"I aim my work for audiences not used to seeing images that concern them." Richard Fung

"The bourgeoisie is not my audience." John Greyson

How do documentary films and tapes address their audiences? What do they assume? What conventions do they employ to convince viewers of their point of view, and how do audiences respond?

The simple reason for discussing audiences is that I want to promote the new documentary. Although the audience for these works remains small by mainstream standards, it is not narrow and it could grow both bigger and broader. In demographic terms documentary attracts a diverse range of viewers crossing barriers of class and race and composed of men and women, children and adults. My assumption is that high-school and university-trained adults, especially older, second-generation Canadians, make up a disproportionate number of viewers for documentary on television because Canadian television documentary concentrates on current affairs, and because these viewers have grown up with the NFB. [1] But because documentary is seen in other settings as well – in schools, art galleries, community halls – many other groups, including young children and those with less formal education, are also exposed.

In promoting this type of documentary I hope in no way to contribute another crude dichotomy between a passive mass audience and some enlightened specialized audience weaned from the mainstream. In the first place the members of both audiences are often the same people, and in addition both the products and the effects of the mainstream remain incredibly diverse. It is one thing to talk about television as a mass medium, quite another to talk of a mass audience. When I watch baseball on TV I am part of a mass audience, but the next evening when I watch *Night and Silence* on TVOntario I am part of a minority audience. True, some people only watch baseball or *Wheel of Fortune* and never get caught up in *The Nature of Things*, which is a pity. But the kind of critical language that slides easily from talking of mass media products to that of mass audience is a crude and elitist form of cause and effect that explains nothing.

Many commentaries on the media centre on the effects of various forms or specific programs. Conservatives, old-style leftists, and even the anarchist Noam Chomsky and the Canadian feminist writer Joyce Nelson tend to see strong effects and a passive audience.[2] Populists of the left and right plus mainstream sociologists and apologists for the networks talk of more limited effects and see the audience as more active or resistant. Jo Holz of NBC says, "Industry people are much more inclined to see the audience as active than critics who worry so much about the effects of television from an outside perspective."[3] But even the most advanced debates about the television audience involving sophisticated theory seldom touch on the question of improving audience literacy.[4] With so many film and television theorists working as university teachers, it is amazing that so few write about media education.

Producers need to know what works and what does not, and audiences need to be more open and better educated in the ways of the media. In both cases we can only start from where audiences are at. Unfortunately, even a basic theory of the documentary audience does not exist, and much ground remains to be broken.[5]

Why Do Books on Film and Video Leave Audiences Out?
Some of the standard excuses, explicit and implicit, for the failure to consider the role of the audience:

1. The proper domain of criticism is the film, the tape, the artwork, the text itself.
2. Discussion about audiences slides into mere sociology – empiricism devoid of theory.
3. Talk of audiences is a dangerous notion that opens the door to a chaos of interpretations, whereas the role of the critic is to unearth and enlighten us on the right meaning.
4. Discussion of audiences is unnecessary because all viewers are basically affected in the same way: all meaning resides in the text. (The text-centred view is widely held among critics stretching from *The New Yorker* to *Screen* magazine.)
5. Discussion of audiences is nearly impossible, because there is little empirical data to base theories on, and in any case few media critics have the training to develop that data.
6. Producers should avoid thinking too much about audiences lest their vision be compromised. (This old fear of "pandering" to an audience flows effortlessly into the realm of criticism.)

Drawing Us In:
From Mode and Genre to Viewing Positions

The relations between particular films and tapes and their audiences only begin with viewers pinning down the mode and genre. When we hear narration and see location photography, both of them edited according to ideas and themes (rather than characters), most of us immediately think "conventional documentary."

Yet beyond that first step of classifying those first on-screen images as expository documentary or narrative fiction, we as viewers need to participate with the sounds and images in a much more detailed manner. Film theorists have laboured for years to describe how the mechanics of narrative cinema position the "spectator in the text" and to show how certain conventions and stylistic devices guarantee how viewers will "read" a shot, a scene, an entire film even. Key elements in a film's strategy to position viewers include such narrative devices as the withholding and releasing of information and such editing devices as the point-of-view sequence. The use of music, placing familiar stars in lead roles, and the privileging of one character's point of view also help establish a limited number of interpretations.

Some theorists take this much further and elaborate the fixed-viewer position that is embodied in all classical Hollywood, with variants residing within specific genres. Some take up the idea of men's and women's genres. And while only the most theoretically extreme see all classical Hollywood in Freud's Oedipal terms, a writer as creative as Tania Modleski has fashioned theory in which the conventions of daytime soap opera only fully make sense from the position of an "ideal mother."[6] Although other feminist critics reject that sort of text-determined theory, we can benefit from applying the hypothesis and imagining the ideal viewer for documentary.

Other theorists see the viewer as more active. They argue that the conventions of narrative and more specific genres must be learned and then actively read throughout the film. Of course, even lab rats can learn to decode signals and information, so the term "active" hardly guarantees much consciousness on the part of the viewing decoder. Yet, since the amounts and levels of information in films and tapes are so complex, and we know from experience that viewers' readings differ widely, the notion of the active viewer holds some credence. We should also distinguish between literal and emotional viewing positions, because there are many instances when the work displays a scene through the eyes of a "good" character but we identify emotionally with a "bad" one – the outcast, the lively villain, often anyone trying to escape from authority.

Nevertheless, narratives usually do their best to ensure one reading (or a set of acceptable readings) of their elements by trying to force the viewer to accept specific viewing positions. Of course, the term "viewing position," if taken literally, is much too theatrical a metaphor for the cinema. From its first days in 1896 the wonder of the motion picture was its speed, its multiple time, its multiple views. Viewers could be everywhere at once, freed from the proscenium arch. We flit and fly from scene to scene, back and forth in time, glimpsing one set of characters, then another. We look at subjects from a high angle, or from below. And yet as viewers we remain one step behind the camera, even when we know more than the characters and can see multiple views. So the term viewing position should be understood as a metaphor, the result of an attempt to organize all the views and all the scenes displayed before us. Although theorists can disagree over the success of that organization and over the "effects" of film and tapes, viewers who decide to participate in the narrative must *start* from the viewing positions offered them.

Documentary also harnesses a range of devices, both conventional and stylistically fresh, to position viewers – usually working the conventions of exposition and observation. Yet viewers are never totally passive. They engage in "gap-filling" between sequences, they relate examples to their own experience and even develop counter-arguments.

None of these engagements require a special, sophisticated viewer. They are required even of those who end up agreeing with the work's point of view. For viewers to participate (whether they are naive or sceptical), they must follow the chain of logic established in the flow of the work and relate to the narrators and witnesses appearing on screen.

For the film theorist Bill Nichols, one entry point for thinking about the position of documentary viewers stems from the conventions of direct and indirect address. Direct address is typified by a narrator or character looking straight at the camera – and by implication the viewers – to communicate information.[7] Direct address can also be established solely on the sound track, especially in the classic, disembodied voice-of-God technique, but also with the more modern subdued narrators, or even with first-person testimony. The voices set up a direct relation between themselves and viewers without the intervention of other on-screen narrators or characters. Conversely, with indirect address all the information and relationships seem held on screen. Action, landscape, and collage all roll by as if the viewers were not present. Events, sounds, and images are *displayed* for observation by the audience. But the word "displayed" is crucial, because indirect address is only indirect, not absent. Characters may be speaking only to each other, but the film arranges a position for the audience to watch nevertheless: the viewer as voyeur.

This valuable distinction between direct and indirect address does not, however, let us assume that direct address is any more *effective*. With direct address we know a little more about whom the film or tape thinks the ideal viewer might be, because the narrator or characters speak to us in a particular tone with a specific set of assumptions (what can be assumed and what needs to be told). Thus we know only that the attempt to position the viewer is clearer.

Even the most conventional expository documentary employs narrative. But in the new documentary we not only find small narrative devices slipping in to bolster the non-narrative arguments, we find longer narrative sequences used to communicate on a different level or even used to disrupt viewer expectations. Zach Kunuk's *Qaggiq* sets up a loosely edited narrative sequence for a marriage proposal involving two families. John Greyson's *The Pink Pimpernel* combines narrative fiction and interviews with AIDS activists. In both cases the narrative brings out relations among people that would have been difficult to convey through "pure" observation. These sequences also set up very different tape and viewer relations and a different documentary effect: clearly this is the goal of many producers. Yet even with the more difficult genres and hybrids our attempts as audience to read the conventions draws us in. The engagement begins, whether our classification seems satisfactory or has been frustrated.

Where Does Meaning Reside?

The full meaning of a film or tape includes everything displayed on the screen and heard on the sound track *as well as* all the references leading into it and away from it in the eyes, ears, and minds of the audience. [8] The types of promotion used in attracting viewers, the off-screen lives of the subjects, the current events preceding or following what we see on screen: these all play a role. The frames of reference can be political, ethical, or aesthetic and can originate in the social world or within other media. [9] In the case of documentary they include genre expectations, the inherited and codified history of particular landscapes or workplaces, actual events prior to their capture on screen, and public knowledge of the off-screen lives of characters or narrators who appear on screen. The meaning thus does not reside in the film or in the individual interpretations of the viewers, but in the activity of viewing. Sometimes it depends on the reaction of the person sitting next to you, or on the rest of the audience in general. Some theorists use the term "supertext" to refer to phenomena surrounding Hollywood fiction. With *Batman*, for instance, the history of the comic book, the press hype, the controversy over violence, and the dolls and T-shirts all contribute to the meanings we derive from the film on screen. Who can say where the film text begins and ends – and where the audience takes over? [10]

Documentaries are just as fluid. In the months before Laura Sky's *The Right To Care* had its première at the Toronto Festival of Festivals in September 1991, newspapers had been filled with the details of a looming nurses strike. Thus the full meaning of the film text must be examined in that context. This activity recalls the performance of music, in which the written score forms only a guide to how the musicians will play. When Miles Davis performed "My Funny Valentine," meanings only emerged in the interpretation, in the relations between the score for the original pop song and his performance.

If documentaries tend to receive much less hype and the connotations of star and genre weigh less heavily than in narrative fiction, they make up for those factors with all the surrounding social, historical, and political connotations. The supertext surrounding all Canadian works by white directors depicting First Nations peoples now bears forcefully on what appears on screen. The debates over appropriation of other cultures call attention to relations between producers and Native people on screen and promote a healthy scepticism towards even the most responsible collaborations, such as Sara Diamond's *Ten Dollars or Nothing!* and Judith Doyle's *Lac La Croix*.

Documentary's Ideal Viewer

Matching documentary's ideal and real viewers certainly presents problems. If we accept that daytime TV melodrama engages the "ideal mother," perhaps documentary calls up the "ideal father." For Grierson's model of citizenship the concept strikes a rather obvious chord, not without its critical appeal. Many NFB films of the 1940s centre on work or the war and speak to viewers about their children and wives. But a more likely candidate for documentary address – an audience member that has remained constant and cuts across all genres – is the viewer as "ideal student." The ideal student as viewer pays attention to every detail, accepts the frames of reference set by the narrator, sympathizes with the testimony of victims, accepts the authority of experts called on screen to comment, picks up on the background musical themes, shares the producer's emotional feelings about the landscape, and, furthermore, knows all the newspaper background. What documentary producer, working in the mainstream or as an iconoclast, would reject such a viewer? Even those Brechtians or postmodern avant-gardists seeking to disrupt the easy pleasure of viewing would be delighted with such an active and attentive student.

A look at Laura Sky's *The Right to Care* might suggest how the role of the ideal student viewer could be played. To participate as an ideal viewer for the film:

- we *see*, close up, rather helpless patients in critical condition and *imagine* ourselves in their place;
- we *hear* nurses talking to the patients, spending time with them;
- we *participate* by feeling the tension in the mini-drama of the birth crisis, and *experience* the relief of the successful birth;
- we *accept* Sky's selection of five nurses as a representative sample of nurses in Canada;
- we *empathize* with the job frustrations and job insecurities of the nurses, *knowing* what it's like to work for a large bureaucracy and *recalling* that recent newspaper reports have shown nurses protesting cuts to health care;

- we *compare* how the medical company salesmen talk about medical products with how the nurses talk about their patients;
- we *conclude* that nurses do remarkable work centred on human contact, which conflicts with a system centred on statistics and money.

The ideal viewer for *The Right to Care* thus considers the evidence, understands the context of the anecdotes, and feels strong emotions due to the human relationships shown on screen. The concept of the ideal viewer rests on the notion that to understand and participate in the film or video text we must accept certain viewer positions, just as an ideal student would do.

Yet, just as there are problems with the concept of an ideal mother for the soaps, the concept of ideal student for documentary is so text-centred as to be elitist – it imagines only one position for viewers – and it is so far from actual viewing situations as to be laughable. Viewers for documentaries, as for the soaps, are usually either less attentive or more hostile than the ideal student. The concept of ideal viewer may help pin down how producers and their texts would like viewers to position themselves, but to assume that viewers fully accept those preconditions attempts a leap into interpretation that cannot be proved.

In the end, perhaps a balance needs to be struck between viewing the text as the solid bearer of all meaning and viewing the text as awash in a sea of "intertextuality" encouraging an anything goes of interpretation. Similarly, a balance must be struck between an audience viewed solely as "others-somewhere-out-there" and an audience viewed as completely fluid, including critic and others, leaving no room for critical distance.[11]

The Competence of Viewers
Documentaries are usually pitched to a general adult audience. Most producers want to reach the widest possible group and fear that an overly complex or specialized work will sail over the heads of many viewers. In addition, if producers want to sell their work they must pitch it to the audience level targeted by the purchasing institutions, primarily television and schools. Television is generally looking for a low common denominator. College use of documentary tends to centre in the large introductory classes, so films and tapes that operate on an introductory level prevail. Finally, and perhaps most interestingly, the documentary tradition has usually focused on the broad social aspects of a

particular topic, and documentaries have usually been produced by non-specialists: that is, people who define themselves first as filmmakers and videomakers, or journalists. Certainly, more specialized genres of scientific, teaching, and training films are commonplace in schools and business. But with the exception of visual ethnography, even these more specialized works are produced by media professionals, not the scientists themselves. Documentary could develop better-known specialized genres, but not without changes in the economics of distribution and exhibition. Perhaps the boom in self-help video documentaries distributed through public libraries and retail stores points the way.

If we return to documentary's links with other forms of cultural non-narrative, we can easily locate genres aiming for a broader audience. Television pop-music biographies, concert films, many travel and nature films, and much of the routine menu in light current affairs shows can pass easily as documentary (using both expository and observational styles). Here the level of viewing competence needed may seem to be much lower, because few references to specialized historical, scientific, or political phenomenon crop up. Any allusions stay close to the immediate frameworks of popular culture. But viewing competence should not be confused with the need for specialized knowledge, because even the simplest pop-music biography is thick with the visual, aural, and cultural connotations of popular culture. Ironically, documentaries dealing with broad social questions that operate with low expectations of the general adult audience often ignore the rich cultural allusions present in the supposedly simpler genres. Again, what is most interesting about the new documentary is the recognition of these cultural allusions: the recognition that conventions of the despised television genres might enhance the serious documentary and supply rich allusions not always possible in the old conventional forms.

So there are two aspects to the competence question. Some viewers may not know that Trudeau was once prime minister, or that Asian people live in the Caribbean, or that Eisenstein was a Soviet filmmaker who was also gay. That will make it difficult to fully understand *Dancing Around the Table*, *My Mother's Place*, or *Urinal*. Competence implies understanding versus misunderstanding in general terms. For instance, do viewers know the references to historical names and places, the geography, or the instruments being played in a music tape? Do viewers understand the general arguments put forward? In addition, the question of visual competence raises other issues. Are viewers familiar and comfortable with both rapid montage (as in *Sesame Street* and music video) as well as more leisurely paced works of observation? Some film and video producers assume that to receive the message properly, audiences need a strong narrator, a crisis structure, and sequences that follow traditional visual codes. When producers assume that kind of visual competence, is it any wonder so many audiences find documentary condescending and boring?

The Engagement of Viewers

Intellectual and visual competence allows for the possibility of more serious engagement. Viewers may accept (knowingly or not) the dominant logic of the work, but they can also engage in a negotiated or oppositional reading. [12] A negotiated reading can take many forms, with viewers accepting some of the specific arguments of a film but rejecting the conclusion, or vice versa. With Patry and Lacourse's *Night and Silence*, viewers may accept that the terrible plight of Eritreans deserves Canadian aid but reject the film's criticism of Canada's External Affairs department. Viewers of Richard Fung's *My Mother's Place* may be wholly convinced that Rita Fung is a wonderful character, but they could also feel irritated by some of the tape's formal devices. In the first case viewers accept specific arguments but not the general conclusion; in the second viewers accept the basic premise but reject some of the ways that the premise is established. The negotiation can be conscious or not – a rational difference of opinion or a vague sense of unease. As well, an oppositional reading need not mean that the viewer derives no knowledge or pleasure from the film or tape. Viewers may be able to twist the logic and the conclusions to "read against the grain" and meet their own criteria. This usually proves easier with fiction and observational documentary than with exposition in direct address, but viewers often take what they want in any case.

More complex and serious forms of engagement require viewers who are more than simply competent. I referred previously to the tension between the need to actively participate and the acceptance of a viewing position. Endorsement of the dominant, preferred logic of a film or tape is no passive endeavour; it can require sophisticated levels of competence. In the case of a negotiated reading, can we be certain that viewers are really negotiating and not simply misunderstanding the logic of the work? In using the metaphor of reading against the grain, can we be certain where the grain lies, and do we know for certain that *any* viewers only read with the grain?

Viewers reveal different capacities for comprehending and engaging with what appears on screen. The Israeli researchers Tamar Liebes and Elihu Katz, in their exhaustive study of *Dallas* fans the world over, use the terms referential and critical to discuss the viewing abilities of television watchers. [13] Some viewers may only be able to relate on-screen events to their own experience, while others may see that the program is a construction. Liebes and Katz point out that all viewers apply referential terms to what appears on screen but more sophisticated viewers may also employ judgements and comparisons about semantic issues (themes, messages, archetypes) and syntactic issues (genre, formula, the meta-linguistic).

To illustrate this range of engagement, let's look at the example of the TV host in drag in John Greyson's tape *The World Is Sick (Sic)*.

Referential: I engage with the characters and events portrayed on screen solely on their own terms or in reference to my experience in the real world.

I see a man dressed as a woman reporting the events of the International AIDS conference in Montreal.

Critical: I can step back and see that the events displayed on screen contribute to an elaborate construction by the producer.

A. Semantic:
i) *theme*. I conclude that Greyson is using comic drag as a way of satirizing television coverage of AIDS.
ii) *message*. I sense that Greyson is trying to tell us that broadcast television's repressed sexuality causes it to fear AIDS, and its political timidity rejects any endorsement of the radical actions of the AIDS demonstrators.
iii) *archetype*. Greyson's reporter in drag stands for all professional reporters and presenters who work for broadcast television. I am reminded of Lloyd Robertson, Peter Mansbridge, and Wendy Mesley; I don't know of any outwardly gay TV news personality.

B. Syntactic:
i) *genre*. *The World is Sick (Sic)* is a fake documentary, a satire combining real events (the AIDS conference) and a phoney TV reporter. It resembles a report on a CBC news program, with a professional reporter

covering a radical event. It resembles a serious social-issue documentary, but it is leavened by art-video satire and visual effects.

ii) *formula*. The reporter interviews, takes quotes, and summarizes, but manages to make his/her feelings known. I see an up-tight woman reporter shocked by what she sees. The reporter loosens up (gets turned on sexually) by covering the event (an interpretation Greyson denies in the interview). The reporter serves two dramatic functions: his/her comments and demeanour introduce conflict, and her loosening-up provides dramatic movement and resolution. The inclusion of a fictional reporter allows Greyson to comment on media coverage of the AIDS conference without having to use real television footage. The comic fiction also allows him to satirize all reporters.

iii) *intertextual*. (meta-linguistic). Greyson is using the conventions of drag comedy to lampoon the reporter's naiveté. I see elements of misogyny in Greyson's employment of the rather clichéd up-tight woman. (He disputes this reading, remarking that he deliberately used "bad drag." There's no mistaking the reporter for a real woman, he says.)

These thoughts about the reporter in drag in *The World Is Sick (Sic)* thus illustrate a range of possible responses – in this case, my own responses – to the video.

A comprehensive theory of documentary has to address whether documentary as a genre within the expository mode engages different faculties among viewers than narrative fiction. Can we distinguish educational frames of reference that differ from the frames of entertainment (without setting the two in opposition or as mutually exclusive)? With documentary, do we settle into an educational frame of argument, logic, action? Are the viewer emotions stirred up on screen of a different calibre than the emotions engaged by narrative fiction? Are we more apt to encounter guilt if we fail to engage seriously with a program on a serious issue? Is anger towards real social actors who appear in documentary a different sort of anger than that directed towards fictional characters?

The types of engagement listed above as dominant, negotiated, oppositional, referential, and critical work best as a model for single viewers. But documentary in particular seems to immerse audiences in more socially defined viewing habits. How do viewers engage with the text in domestic and group settings? Do influential viewers steer the engagement of others in particular directions? Recent studies of television viewing show how domestic power plays itself out in household program selection, program validation, and the interpretation of meanings. Men, who generally work outside the home, tend to see television viewing as a form of relaxation, separate from work. Women, whether they work outside or not, are more likely to see the TV as an extension of domestic work. The English writer David Morley, perhaps the leading theorist on TV audiences, shows in his book *Family Viewing* how women use television viewing as a means of holding the family together, as a means of communicating. Shared enjoyment of a particular program can allow openings for other discussions and expression of feelings. [14] Decisions over who selects the programs and how the programs get interpreted may well reflect the power of husbands over wives and parents over children. Because men see themselves as actors in the outside work and political worlds they may feel more equipped to choose and comment on news, current affairs, and documentaries. They may use commentary on documentary programs to assert a greater knowledge of the outside world.

When people watch documentaries, they seem more apt to see themselves as part of a social or cultural group than they do when viewing fiction. [15] This is especially true for social-issue media that focus on a group in society. For viewers to fully engage with the film or tape they need to define their relation to that group: are they part of it, opposed to it, in sympathy with its aims or plight? Hundreds of films and tapes look at victims of the social order or natural catastrophes. Those with inadequate housing or psychiatric problems, members of ethnic or racial communities, and victims of war, famine, and typhoons have all been presented. Ethnographers have displayed the cultures of Bali, New Guinea, the bush, desert, and forest. Documentary viewers are often addressed as a group that contrasts sharply with the people on the screen: the watchers are well housed, healthy, secure, modern, and Western, for instance.

This group identity seems much more insistent than in narrative fiction. Certainly fiction usually assumes a white male perspective on the world, and with some crime and social-problem films the implied audience clearly functions as the norm in contrast to the deviance being shown on screen. Even so, in narrative fiction the pitch seems delivered in much more broadly defined terms. The audience is addressed as a mass of free-floating individuals.

Judith Doyle's film *Lac La Croix* addresses Ojibwa land use in Ontario's Quetico Park. It demonstrates how the documentary engages viewers in terms of audience groups. Am I viewer as environmentalist, as canoe tripper who uses provincial parks, as supporter of Native land rights, or as member of another First Nations' community inspired by the events at Lac La Croix? Am I viewer as cottage owner threatened by Native pressure to curtail Northern development, or viewer as a B.C. Tory or Quebec ultra-nationalist worried that Native land claims will go too far? *Lac La Croix* seems to encourage viewers to set themselves within this range of options. It raises issues that reach beyond abstract questions of moral rights and national definitions. It engages specific controversies and current conflicts hotly debated by well-defined groups. At issue is not some easy form of sympathy with the Native people against the RCMP, but a much more specific alliance such as, "I belong to a group that also uses the park," or "I voted for a party that has taken a stand on Native sovereignty."

The phenomenon of documentary viewers seeing themselves as part of a social group occurs most often for direct-address social-issue works. It seems less likely with indirect address and for biography, portraits, or works on the boundary of narrative and the poetic. For example, John Walker's biography of Paul Strand, *Under the Dark Cloth*, may certainly challenge us to examine our lives in comparison to Strand's, but we are not encouraged to relate to Strand as part of a specific group of viewers. And yet to the extent that the film holds up Strand's life as an example of a political artist, it does present a challenge at least to artists as a professional group.

Settings and Medium

The meanings that audiences derive from documentaries and the uses that audiences make of them are determined by the medium and the exhibition situations. There are four basic settings for documentary audiences: in theatres, on television, in educational spaces (galleries, museums, schools), and for special events in public non-theatrical spaces.

In addition to shaping the size and type of audience and the kind of documentary effect, the settings also shape how viewers actively use what they see and hear on screen. Each setting seems to encourage varying levels of attention, including the levels of competence and engagement. The same documentary shown in different settings may be perceived differently (even by the same people). Television audiences engage in a very different set of viewing patterns than do audiences in theatres – television viewing usually takes place within intimate but power-laden domestic relations. An audience for a film in a church hall or basement may well set up its own viewing dynamic; a general public audience at a repertory cinema quite another.

Audiences also shift dramatically in relation to the medium of exhibition. The audience for a particular film or tape may be minuscule for its theatrical run and huge for its television broadcast. A museum exhibition of a video-art program that includes documentary may generate considerable controversy but get lost in the program shuffle on television. TV audiences are notoriously fluid. My own shift of viewing from baseball to *Night and Silence* gets repeated with millions of viewers every day. The use of remote-channel zappers to sample two or more programs at once only complicates the search for a TV documentary audience.

Many students of cinema and television have tried to define the unique characteristics of each medium and the differences between the two by referring to audience attention. Marshall McLuhan's famous contrast between cinema as hot and TV as cool rests on the supposed levels of attention in viewers. [16] Horace Newcombe's stab at defining a television aesthetic includes the criteria of intimacy. [17]

The prevalent belief that television viewers float passively in and out of attention (a cool engagement) is now being hotly debated by both apologists and critics of the medium. This makes it difficult to generalize about the levels of attention in television viewing as opposed to cinema viewing. [18] Other types of comparisons defy easy generalization as well. The television audience for documentary vastly outnumbers its cinema audience, yet the critical authority of the theatrical cinema still carries greater weight. [19]

Canadian art galleries and museums have exhibited documentary video since the 1970s. Obviously the cultural and historical power held by these institutions lends a credibility and meaning that could not be achieved through television or community exhibition. John Greyson, Sara Diamond, Richard Fung, and Zach Kunuk have all benefited from gallery and museum exhibitions. Conversely, the rather less popular atmosphere inhibits broader effects.

The screening of documentaries as special events turns the discussion of audiences in a radically different direction, away from a concentration on single viewers and from documentary consumption. Films and tapes exhibited as special events are the result of programming and exhibition decisions. Rather than asking why individuals *choose to watch*, we need to ask why and how groups of people *choose to show* specific documentaries. A partial answer lies in tracing how a group sees itself in relation to the dominant culture, and how it is depicted in the mainstream. Documentaries are shown in small-group settings for internal education, initiation of new people, inspiration, and specific, practical examples of what it means to be a member of the group. Documentaries are used in public settings for general public education, attracting new members, giving background about the group and its members, fundraising, and making links with other groups.

Viewers know that broadcast TV and festivals need new "product" to maintain their existence. A public exhibition can lend credibility and new meanings to work in ways that a showing at a gallery, in a festival, or on TV could not. The decision by a non-commercial, non-arts group to show a work publicly carries the weight of endorsement. This is a form of educational programming that hopes the audience will become better informed (even active) around an issue through attending the screening. The audience will be inclined to view the work as important and authentic, with its meaning partly determined by the "spin" engineered by the exhibiting group.

Where Are the Documentary Audiences?

Any theory of how documentary addresses its viewers and how it makes assumptions about viewers will remain inadequate unless it is complemented by empirical study. How then should we look at "real," socially specific, historically situated audiences?

Canadian Audience History

Canadian audiences have been exposed to a range of documentaries in many settings, including the following.

1897-1914: Canadian Pacific Railway promotional travelogues
1900-present: government training and travel films
1935-present: film club showings of international hits [20]
1920-1960: documentaries as introduction to theatrical features
1940s-present: film festivals
1940-present: NFB non-theatrical activity in schools and communities
1960-present: widespread use of documentaries in schools as part of curriculum
1950-present: documentaries on television
1970-present: community video documentary on cable television
1970-present: video-art documentary in galleries and festivals
1970-present: combined video *and* film festivals organized by issues or themes

The history does not fall away like dead skin, it becomes part of our memory. It bears on today's audiences, determining size and colouring perceptions. Controversies over past NFB audiences, generated by the research and analysis of Peter Morris and Joyce Nelson, should cast doubt on present claims among all parties about audience size and might lead us to rethink the belief that documentary audiences have shrunk in relative size since the 1940s. The increased ability of television to reach new audiences combined with more modest figures for viewers in the past might show that documentary is by no means in decline. Scepticism about NFB effectiveness during the 1940s and 1950s should lead us to rethink what Canadian audiences perceive to be typical documentaries and standard conventions. If we no longer know what audiences perceive as standard conventions, how can we make work that will challenge conventions?

Today's Audiences
Some of the more cynical observers of documentary have developed a litany of negative assumptions about who watches documentary:

i) Documentaries are watched only by teachers, egg-heads, people who have to, and the already converted.

This is clearly false but often perpetrated by the mainstream culture apologists. We might just as well say that narrative fiction is epitomized by Rambo movies and watched only by simple-minded people escaping from reality. Documentary is watched by single viewers and viewers in groups, for specific and general learning and pleasure.

ii) Documentaries are produced by and for a minority elite, not the ordinary viewer.

Certainly documentary, like other complex industrial art, is produced by a minority with training and access to money. It may also be true that most serious social-issue documentaries seem pitched to an influential middle-class audience. But the belief that "ordinary," working-class viewers have no taste for exposition is patently false. We know that the total "non-narrative" audience is huge – this includes the audience for news and current affairs programs, self-help tapes, "infotainment," game shows, talk shows, nature shows, and dozens of segments on children's shows.

iii) Documentaries are old fashioned, so they don't reach entire groups of people brought up on *Sesame Street*, interactive video games, music video, and high art: therefore they are ineffective. If you want to be effective you need to work in popular (or avant-garde) genres.

Certainly, much documentary drifts in the doldrums and relies on the stalest of conventions, but can we say that these forms have no effect in education or even in stimulating action? I suspect that these assumptions originate with artists tired of working the old conventions. More and more audiences want livelier documentaries, but to say that narrative fiction or experimental hybrid forms are the only means of effective communication cannot be proved. Community, ethnic, and cultural groups often program documentaries as a means to other cultural and political ends, such as reaching out or informing other groups in the society.

iv) Documentaries are disliked because they're impersonal and carry no emotional charge.

This statement seems correct for a large proportion of work, but the distinction between the neutral communication of information and the striking of emotional chords can be drawn too sharply. Many documentaries shun emotion at all costs, but many others, even those of the most conventional bent, derive power through key, moving interviews, or through music and other non-verbal elements, and they manage to draw in and captivate their viewers because of those elements.

v) Documentaries are scorned by sophisticated, critical viewers because they pretend to be objective even though they are not.

This statement is also true up to a point and has led to great doses of healthy scepticism among viewers, schooled and unschooled. The standards for documentary evidence and the rigour in making an argument remain much lower than for books and good journalism. Viewers have come to know that. In addition, many people maintain a sensitive bullshit meter when looking at any media. For instance, union members who have seen their struggles covered by the press certainly know the power of the media and have become all too familiar with a supposedly objective language that reports how the company *offered* and the union members *demanded*.

Yet there are plenty of sophisticated documentary viewers at festivals, people tired of Hollywood, European, and Canadian fiction formulas, viewers whose only demand, to paraphrase film critic Tom Waugh, is to "Show Us Life."

Canadian Audiences for the New Documentary

The committed documentary has often aimed for a specific audience. The Soviets directed their efforts to the industrial working class; solidarity films aim for an educated, sympathetic public; films and tapes on social problems seek opinion leaders; works on the arts usually target the style-conscious middle class. The producers often strive for a specific audience effect, such as consciousness-raising, muckraking, fundraising, changing policy, or recruiting to a group or movement – a more closely targeted audience than their counterparts in the mainstream. They presume that a smaller audience need not mean a diminished effect. They look for different, often more specific effects. A politically defined use normally centres on a politically defined audience. Apolitical producers seem to chase topics that interest them without thinking much about the audience. And except for a few producers at the NFB, the idea of building an audience for new kinds of work or new issues rarely surfaces in the mainstream or alternative film and video-art circles.

In most cases the match of a work's subject matter and interest on the part of a social group seems obvious – a tape on nurses being shown at the YWCA, for instance – although the decision to show an innovative work over a more conventional one (when there is a choice) cannot be explained so easily. The ways that individual viewers interact with the films and interact with the larger group that initiated the exhibition remain even murkier. Without empirical studies on theatrical audiences and TV viewers, we cannot know whether the new documentary has tapped a new audience or the same old one. We do not know whether these viewers also watch conventional documentaries, or whether they are new viewers who never had a taste for, or gave up on, the conventional forms.

Prospects for the New Documentary
There seem to be large and glaring gaps in the audience for the new documentary. For instance, with the exception of Alanis Obomsawin, new documentary producers have ignored young children, and perhaps most surprisingly the labour unions and the NDP almost never program innovative work. [21] For the NDP I would assume the reason lies in the party's narrow goals, which place little value in the more broadly defined issues treated by the new documentary. But these gaps may also reveal an unconscious boundary for new documentary producers. Although they may feel more comfortable making politically motivated films and tapes than their mainstream peers, the tension between independence and accountability persists. And the right to choose one's subject matter remains a key, although usually unspoken, factor in the kinds of work produced. Perhaps they feel that work directed to children or specific unions, for example, would force too many compromises. [22] So, for now, a large and rather obvious set of audiences for the new documentary is not being reached.

There is no simple match between the new documentary and its audiences to compare with the rise of the novel and the new eighteenth-century urban middle class; modernist writing and painting with twentieth-century European intellectuals; rock 'n roll with white teenagers in the 1950s; rap with black youth in the 1980s. The new documentary does not represent a youth culture, or a class-based phenomenon. Certainly there is a match between feminist works and a feminist audience, but the new documentary is broader than that, and not all feminist films and tapes would qualify as new documentary in the way I am defining it here. The same holds true for the rapidly emerging "non-white" media – some qualifies as new documentary, some does not.

Yet the new documentary appears in all settings, and convincing evidence from non-theatrical use suggests the appeal of this work for women, gays and lesbians, and people of colour. The use reveals a strong thirst for women's and non-white points of view. At the very least people want their faces reflected on the screen – want their experience acknowledged and their analysis considered. Films and tapes that match "local" on-screen subjects with a "local" audience – the home-movie effect – provide the first step. Works based on a woman's or non-white analysis are still so rare that they are always greeted with the utmost intensity. This audience will continue to grow.

PART TWO

6

Interviews with Film and Video Producers

"When I talk with
people I talk as a
Québécois."

Maurice Bulbulian was born in Montreal in 1938 and grew up in the city's working-class neighbourhoods. In university he studied science and afterwards worked briefly as a teacher before he was recruited by the NFB in 1966 to create film strips for high schools. By the early 1970s he was fully involved in the forefront of Quebec's committed documentary movement and a pioneer in Le Vidéographe's community television experiments.

While Bulbulian says he is not an innovator, he has been a key figure in Quebec's unique movement of cinéma direct, pushing much further than many of his colleagues the practice of genuine collaboration and interaction in the making of documentaries. His work always focuses on groups with the least power, those pushed to the side by the dominant society: Quebec's Native peoples, mine, forestry, and fish workers, Mexico's squatters and the homeless, Burkina Faso's rural villagers, and most recently British Columbia's Kwakiutl people.

Bulbulian's films of the 1970s formed part of the documentary movement created by Michel Brault, Gilles Groulx, Pierre Perrault, Gilles Carle, and Arthur Lamothe that developed the most militant and sustained analysis of North American capitalism yet seen on film. The work, which was carried out sometimes with the blessings and sometimes against opposition in the French Section of the NFB, was closely aligned to unions and various left-wing movements for Quebec independence, though it cut a much wider swath than the politics of the Parti Québécois. [1] Many of those directors left the NFB for feature fiction, or freelance documentary, or a milder politics, but Bulbulian stuck it out.

Richesse des Autres (1974), Bulbulian's best-known work of the 1970s, compares the situation of mine workers in Quebec and Chile. The title seems representative of all his work, and the film features many scenes with groups of miners standing outdoors or huddled in cabins talking to each other, or directly telling the camera about working conditions and the industry. These are strong, articulate voices, many belonging to veterans of the United Steelworkers of America – workers with a tradition of militancy and class analysis. The film contains no voice-over narration and no music. The scenes with the miners are punctuated by long pans over Northern Quebec's winter landscape of mining towns and forests. The political centre of the film hinges on an interview with René Lévesque, which is later juxtaposed with a speech by the Chilean president Salvador Allende to a visiting delegation of Quebec miners.

During the 1970s Bulbulian also completed a major trilogy on the forests of Quebec. *Dans nos forêts* (1971), focusing on work and working conditions, is an investigation in the style of cinéma direct, while *La revanche* (1974) takes a more essay-like, less observational approach to examine the foreign control of the forestry industry. Then in *Ameshkuatan: les sorties du castor* (1978) the focus shifts, in a mix of ethnographic observation and social documentary, to examine life among the Montagnais of Eastern Quebec, especially their relation to the forests and traditions of trapping for beaver.

After completing *Land and Liberty* (1978) in the squatter shanty towns of Mexico, Bulbulian returned to Quebec to begin a cycle of films on the First Nations of Quebec and Canada. *Our Land, Our Truth* is a matter-of-fact unromantic essay on the family life, economics, legal affairs, and most centrally the language of the Inuit communities of Ivujivik, Povungnituk, and Sugluk of Northern Quebec. It was followed by Bulbulian's most influential and widely seen work, the two-part

Dancing Around the Table (1987, 1989), which examines the four conferences on aboriginal rights mandated in 1982 during the repatriation of the Canadian constitution. The films begin with the conferences, showing the provincial premiers, the Native leaders, and Trudeau at his most belligerent, but they quickly branch out to follow key Native negotiators back to their communities; we see where they are coming from. Incredibly, these extraordinary and important films have never been aired on the CBC.

Bulbulian's work with Native peoples enriches an already strong tradition among Quebec's left-wing filmmakers willing to probe the contradictions of the distinct society by highlighting Native struggles. The most important work in this tradition is undoubtedly Arthur Lamothe's twelve-film series *La chronique des Indiens du nord-est du Québec* (1973–79). At a time when Quebec nationalism runs high, these directors have had the courage to look at tough questions and potentially embarrassing situations.

When our interview took place, Bulbulian was editing *Salt Water People*, a detailed examination of the Kwakiutl and their historic fishing economy in British Columbia – a subject first introduced through the lives of Bill Wilson and his mother Ethel Pearson as shown in *Dancing Around the Table*. This new film takes us much deeper into the traditions and economic life of the Kwakiutl nation. The film's strength, like many documentaries in this oral history style, lies in its mix of seeing and hearing the analysis of a people and a way of life foreign to most of us.

Tell me about your new film, Salt Water People.
Maurice. It deals with the vision that the West Coast Native People have of the sea, plus the relationship between the sea resources and the Native culture – between the sea and their spirituality and their own definition of looking at things in a holistic way. We decided to follow the marine life cycle over a year. We also deal with the traditional Native calendar. This film has been a few years in the making.

After the European settlers came into B.C. in the mid-nineteenth century, one of the first things they realized was the richness of the sea. In order to get involved in that they had to push the Native people around. They didn't push them with guns but with laws and regulations – a whole series of laws since 1872. A people who were living along the sea coast and along the rivers in an intimate relationship with the sea resource were simply pushed away from that. One hundred years later those people are still clinging to that special relationship and their vision of how to live with the sea. The film compares what's left of that vision with the past, present, and the future. How were they pushed away? How did they survive? How is the sea presently exploited? The same industrial structure as in the forests and other resources also applies to the sea.

Over the past thousands of years the Native people have developed a management system, which is inside them. You can't separate them. You don't meet a Native person and ask them, "What is your management system? Show me page twenty-two." They're going to talk to you about all kinds of things – the seagulls, the mountains. And you think to yourself, "I don't want him to talk about that, I want him to talk about the sea." But the mountains are the beginning of the whole cycle. It's where water accumulates, as snow. You only realize afterwards that they've been talking about management all the time. It's not the same language or the same parameters. It's the other way of seeing it.

Today, at the same time we are destroying our forests we are emptying the sea. A major biological collapse is going to happen in the Pacific. It's harder to see. You see it negatively. I met an old man who travels all the time between Hawaii and Alaska – had been doing it for many years. He says that what you can't believe is the total silence today in that stretch of sea. You wouldn't imagine that there's noises in the sea but there is. Drift-net fishing, with nets fifty kilometres long, in a fleet of two thousand vessels, is literally strip mining the sea of everything. The drift-net is not selective. It takes in whales, porpoises, sea gulls. All kinds of birds get caught.

Consider the harvesting of salmon. Around 1911 the catch was about thirty-two million from the Fraser River alone. At one point it was down to two million and today it's about twenty million. Then there's the herring. You know about the cod on the East Coast. You'll hear about the herring on the West in the next three or four years because they are going at it in a terrible way and the herring is the key to the whole cycle of fish. It's the fish that the bigger ones feed on – the salmon, the whales. When the herring come, they come in such a great number that, the Indians will tell you, they shit so much that it provides all the nutrients for all the small creatures. Try to talk about that – that the stocks are going down – to scientists and they'll say, "Well maybe, but it hasn't been proven." The day after the herring is gone they'll say, "Well yes it's been proven."

I felt after making *Dancing Around the Table* that we should film in

B.C. and stay with the people: to see what we only heard about in that film. *Dancing* focuses on the Native politicians so I wanted to deal more with the people.

Is Bill Wilson [who appears in Dancing Around the Table*] working with you on the film, or does it involve a broader group of people?*
Maurice. I use the same approach as in my other films – when I was in Monterrey, Mexico, I spent a good three months living there, discussing the film and all kinds of ideas with people. It was the same in B.C. I spent nearly a year in research, meeting people, talking to them. I always present my hypothesis for the film: "So far my ideas are like this." They tear it apart or they add something, and I go on like that until the moment we start filming. But at the moment we start it becomes my film. There's only one person running a film. It has to be this way.

That doesn't have to mean that I don't transfer to video and show portions of it as I go along. I show it to many different groups. A village here, four or five people there. Some people have a broader knowledge. I got a group of elders together at one point. So there's a constant back and forth.

One of the most striking features in all your films is the scene of a group of people gathered together to discuss an issue, or one person standing facing the camera giving testimony with other people present. I would imagine that setting up those kinds of scenes – those opportunities for people to talk – is a crucial part of your planning.
Maurice. I never have one principle character in my films. It's always between forty and two hundred principle characters. With these public and collective issues I find that the best situations, when ideas and feelings really come out, is when people are together. Now it's not cinematographic per se. But there's always moments when you get the basic statements and feelings coming from people wherever they are. If they're around a table, which is not an easy thing to film, and it happens there, so be it. You don't run away from it. More important is to be with people when they are together and things are happening. That's what I'm trying to do most of the time.

Are there disadvantages with filming people in groups?
Maurice. Well, technically there's many problems. But you always discover things when there is a group. People often become themselves when they are in a group; they come out with their emotions in a very

distinct manner. You can meet people on a one-to-one basis and things will go okay and nothing special comes out. But in a meeting you sense something more – the others around know it and share that feeling. Then you know why others have said that I should talk with this person. You understand the reputation. Often after a group session I shoot follow-ups with individuals. In *Salt Water People* I attended meetings and afterwards asked two people if I could get together with them for some filming. It happened that they were in the right mood. They were together and they just let themselves go. Another person had interesting things to say and a special way of saying them, but it didn't work at all with him.

For another film I was in meetings with the Inuit. I don't know if you've ever been in such a meeting. Because of the consensus system they seem to last at minimum five hours. Everybody talks, everybody expresses their ideas. Then they start all over. After listening to all the others, the first one who spoke has now modified his own way of thinking. So he speaks again and his ideas change. It goes on like that until everybody says the same thing. It takes a lot of time.

These are sensitive issues you're dealing with. You want to make sure that the film crew is not just a technical group. Do you have any general principles about working with your crew?
Maurice. More and more I worry about how the crew is feeling, how the subjects are feeling, and all these relationships. The entire crew has to work well together. Because if you have trouble working together don't expect to see any magic on the screen. There is something which is not what the camera sees, and not what the sound records, and not the intention of the director; it's beyond that – the something which is magic in film. Like everybody drinking from the same bottle of wine.

What did you want to do with documentary when you joined the NFB in the sixties?
Maurice. When I was a young kid my idea of cinema was Tarzan and war films. Then in Grade Ten I joined the ciné-club: I hoped to see more Tarzan. But the first time I went they showed Flaherty's *The Land* and Ford's *Grapes of Wrath*. I'd never seen anything like that in my life. And afterward people started talking about the films, analysing how they felt about them, etc. I was very struck by that one screening. And I said, "This is what I'd like to do." I was very taken by the documentary of *The Land* and at the same time by the people in *Grapes of Wrath*, who are absent in *The Land*. Somehow those two things had to come together.

Since then I've been wanting to make documentaries. I probably sent twenty applications to the Film Board, which were all refused, so I went into teaching.

The first thing I did as a teacher was start a ciné-club. Then one day the Film Board contacted me and said they're into multi-media and they need somebody for the educational sector: "Are you interested?"

"Well maybe. Is there any way to make films?" I said.

"No, It's film strips. One frame at a time."

"Okay, I'll start one frame at a time." A year and a half later I was in French production.

What about the influence of your parents?
Maurice. They were very hard-working people. My father had a sort of half-restaurant, half-pastry shop. Seven days a week. Up at five, closing at midnight. My mother worked there too. We never, ever took vacations. One day, though, they had to do some repairs at the store, which had to close. So my father said, "Well, we're going on a vacation." I was all excited. We took a train from Montreal Central Station to Trois-Rivières and right across from the station there is a park. We went to the park, had a lunch, spent a few hours, then rode back to Montreal on the train. That was the vacation.

My father was an Armenian who fled the genocide there in 1910. My mother was Ukrainian and fled when the Cossacks were killing half the people over there. They both immigrated to Canada and met here on the French side of the city. My father didn't speak Ukrainian and my mother didn't speak Armenian, so I was brought up in French.

I guess because of the hard life of my parents I feel the whole question of social justice, if you want to use those words. It's something beyond ideology, beyond politics in the life of people who should be born to have at least a minimum decent life. What's the use of the human race if that is not an attainable goal for everyone? Thinking of the lives of my parents, working like slaves, to me it wasn't fair. There has to be some kind of social justice.

Were the executive producers that you worked under at Société nouvelle different than the others at the Film Board?
Maurice. Very definitely. It was something special because of the collegiality. Société nouvelle worked so that all kinds of people had input – directors, producers, and a major contribution from people in distribution. The distribution people had relationships with all kinds of audience groups – testing, etc. We were working as a group and we came

under attack because of this. As opposed to the act of creation by a single individual who is called the director, we were trying to help ordinary people communicate directly to the government. So we had to work that way.

We made some major errors, especially in the area of community television. Our idea was to put the equipment in the hands of the people and they would express themselves. That was good in theory but the quality of the image was poor, especially the low definition of the VTR. What we should have done is give them the equivalent to broadcast quality, which was not possible at that time because that equipment was not portable. We were enthusiastic about the portability.

How have your films fared on TV?
Maurice. *Dancing Around the Table* was refused by the CBC and Radio-Canada. They don't like films with a point of view. All my films are like that, so I'm on the permanent blacklist with Radio-Canada. CBC don't even know that I exist. But to the last day of my life I'm going to fight for my right to film with a point of view. I'm completely opposed to the so-called balanced journalism of Radio-Canada. Refusing a point of view is censorship. Within *Salt Water People* there is not one single item which is not true. Everything which is presented as a fact has been checked. An opinion is an opinion, but a fact is a fact. You don't fool around with them. On this whole question of the fishing, I decided that the point of view should be that of the Native people. Canadian Fisheries and MacMillan-Bloedel spend hundreds of thousands of dollars on commercials to promote their point of view – all shown on the CBC. CBC doesn't say to Coca Cola, you can't show that because it represents your point of view; it doesn't say you have to be fair and show Pepsi, and Seven Up, and Canada Dry. So it's one rule for one kind of people and one rule for the others.

I'm still hoping. It should be shown on a national network.

There is a sense that documentary about Québécois work and workers was something you pursued actively in the 1970s but left behind in the 1980s. Does that ring true to you?
Maurice. Yes, it does. Absolutely. In that sense the Québécois documentary as a whole reflects what is happening in society. In the seventies, social issues were very much in the forefront and the dream of becoming our own country was equated with the dream of also becoming a *different* country. It was not just the question of separation. What it boils

down to now is that the rich people have French names instead of English names.

The eighties were a time of the individual talking about himself/herself, even in documentaries. If it wasn't the filmmaker in front of the camera it was somebody they identified with on a personal basis. Very closed. I guess the whole of our society has been going through that. And what is coming next? I don't know, some kind of nihilism. We don't know because we are with the society as it happens, we don't precede. We only follow a current.

The other change is that many documentary people got involved in Quebec's new commercial industry. There you have to compromise just to survive. I have a friend who's a freelancer working on a documentary and he's dealing with six government institutions. All of them have their rules and regulations, each wants things presented in one fashion or another. He's going crazy. One of those institutions is a TV broadcaster, who has its nose into the content. He has to clear everything in his script with them. I managed to keep away from all that, by being at the Film Board and being a stubborn old son-of-a-bitch, so nobody wants to talk to me, nobody dares. They're happy when I'm away filming. But I feel very lonesome, because I kept those dreams of the collectivity.

But I guess the pendulum will swing. The downfall has already started somewhere. The whole question of the common sense of the people is going to come out. Where and in what form I don't know. How can Canadians put up with so much abuse day-to-day and still manage? I just can't figure that out. And it's worse in the U.S. Thirty-four million people below the poverty line, yet where are the leaders or the community people? Are they all into other pursuits? It's a mystery to me.

How did you come to make the film Ameshkuatan? *What led you to deal with the Native people in Quebec?*
Maurice. That began way back in the 1970s as part of the Société nouvelle. There were many components to that – community television was one. We had decided to spend one year in the Lac St.-Jean area. I left Montreal with a complete crew, including a production manager and an editor. We lived collectively (at first, anyhow). Organize community TV, work with young people, and make a film: that was our plan. The hypothesis was to look forward ten years to 1980 and see what the region would look like. Once there I decided that forestry was the most interesting subject, but I realized soon that the film couldn't focus on one small region – it's the entire huge area of Northern Quebec and Ontario.

The first people who dealt with these forests were the Native people, first called savages or *sauvages*, from the Latin *silvatico*, which simply means people living in the forest. So we decided to produce a film about the Native people and their relationship with the forest. Another film was based on a circular voyage around Quebec in order to grasp the general situation of the forest and the workers in forestry, and in the third we asked what would things be like if the workers got together to manage the industry, in workers's co-operatives, etc.

But even before coming to the Film Board I was interested in the question of the Native people. When I arrived at the Film Board to make film strips they already had a list of things for me to do – one strip on cats, one on aeronautics, one on physics, and I did all those. But I had a project – to do something on the Native people of Canada, and the film *Ameshkuatan* was my first opportunity.

Later I got involved making films outside Canada, but as soon as I came back in 1982 I started work with the Inuit. At my first meeting with the Inuit Council, they said, "So, you want to make a film with us, huh?" And I said, "Yes, if it's okay with you." But they weren't very impressed – weren't very impressed at all, because a few years earlier a filmmaker had promised them all kinds of things. As happens very often when people go to faraway places, he didn't give a shit after he left. They were apprehensive that I was simply another one. I was recently back from Mexico where I had been working with youngsters who were sniffing glue. So they asked me what I was filming in Mexico: "Probably filming Indians over there?"

"No, I stayed in the shanty towns, living there for three months." They asked, what is that? I thought, how can I explain that – people living in the country who have to leave and move to the outskirts of the city. Then I told them about the film of the youngsters sniffing glue. Well it turned out that glue sniffing was a major problem in their community, so we found something in common, and they understood the kind of film I was interested in making. I was not interested in going out and filming the caribou or the whales if it was not to show the relationship of these people to these animals. So that's the way it started with the film *Our Land, Our Truth*. Of course the Inuit length for a film is two hours. They have their own conception of time – people around the table – consensus. If you are three around the table or one hundred it goes the same way. And I wanted to respect that sense of time. Now, when I showed it to TV executives they said, "Your film is beautiful, we want it, but can you make a one-hour version?" They wanted a white man's version. I said yes to that shorter length. But when they asked me to remove comments about Inuit land made by Tadousie, the Inuit linguist and the central character, I said, "Never."

I would imagine that a man like Tadousie, who is a linguist, so concerned about the survival of his language, would strike a particular chord in Quebec.
Maurice. This man was a personal friend of René Lévesque. He has received many decorations from universities, etc. He's probably one of the greatest living Canadians because he has written a dictionary for the Inuit people – the words and their usage. He did this over fifteen years on the CBC Northern radio service. Every day he had an open line. He'd start by saying, "Today the word is such and such and in my opinion the word means this." Then some old person would phone up and say, "Tadousie, I think you're wrong," and this went on for years. So Radio-Canada asked me to cut him out of the film or they wouldn't show it. I said, "Over my dead body."

So the motive for cutting him out was purely political? The parallels were too close?
Maurice. Absolutely. You know Quebec has now become "our land" and this guy is talking about a part of Quebec becoming his land. If *we* say it, that's okay, but if *he* says it, no way, it's nonsense. That coincided with the second, more extreme government of Lévesque, where the whole social project was set aside, and where power became the main issue. It was after the 1980 referendum where the bitterness started.

At what point did you decide on the structure of Our Land, Our Truth? *Did you work with an editor?*
Maurice. I seldom just leave a film to an editor, but in that case I left it to Fernand Bélanger, who's probably one of the great filmmakers in Canada – we talked about it and I was so close to it I said Fernand, you do it. We had a basic canvas. The structure of that film is simple. We follow time and once in a while people talk in relation to what we see, and in relation to the season. It's linear. But the main problem was how to edit these people. We worked with people in Montreal who are fluent in Inuktitut, who created a word-for-word translation. It wasn't translated into French, it was translated into the Inuktitut way of talking, the structure of their way of speaking, so we could follow the equivalent in French. At the end we had Tadousie and others come in and view it. That was

extraordinary because at first they didn't understand the idea of cutting the film. When we showed them part of the film they simply said, "Yeah, that's okay." I knew they weren't getting my message. So we made a demonstration of the changes that could be made by cutting. Some playing around. It took about a day and after that it was glorious. They were saying, "Why not cut here?" They now understood that in cutting it one way you say one thing, doing it another way you say something else: one kind of emotion or another kind of emotion. So we had fun for about a week. The film satisfied them.

Do you have a particular audience in mind during the making of your films? Is there a Québécois audience in the back of your head?
Maurice. Mostly it's a Québécois audience, for the Mexico film even. I can't do otherwise. But I have other audiences in mind also. This is why when I go out to the West Coast I go there as a Québécois filmmaker. I don't go there as a Canadian filmmaker. I hope you understand the difference. When I talk with people I talk as a Québécois. And the way they talk to me is because I am a Québécois. *Salt Water People* would have been completely different if done by a Canadian. I don't say it would have been worse. Just different. The dialogue between people would have been different. Since I'm perceived as a Québécois, the last time I went there I was starting to get problems because of Oka and because the attitude of the Quebec government towards Native people sets a new context.

I was getting flak. But I'm giving it too. When Ovide Mercredi comes here and says the Québécois nation does not exist, I say that's bullshit Ovide. Your lawyers are telling you that as a strategy – that if you identify against the Québécois it will be easier to get sympathy from English Canada. You're starting to play politician games. You know that the cause of the Native people and the cause of the Québécois are identical in the reshaping of this country. It has to be that way. It's not one or two against the others. It's a rearranging of the people living in this country. And there's also the forgotten, newly arrived people to take into account, because this is a country in the making. It's not a country of the past.

But yes, my films are intended primarily for the Québécois people, and each time Radio-Canada refuses one of my films it hurts me very much. I know that people won't see it.

Are you consciously trying to challenge the audience?

Maurice. I don't think so. I'm proposing something for them to think about, to agree or disagree. If somebody comes to tell me that they don't agree with my film, I say good, let's talk about it. Why don't you agree? I present things that are not "The Truth" but on the road to the truth. But that truth or that way has to be confronted with other truths in all cases, so that some kind of consensus comes out.

Salt Water People deals with the relationship between nature and human beings, so I hope it will interest the farmer in Saskatchewan, the dairy farmer in Quebec, as well as anybody living in a city. The issue isn't reduced to fishing and to the specialists. I took the greatest care with that because there's a whole vocabulary. I spent a year researching and for a while I was lost. I couldn't tell the difference between a chub salmon and a chinook – between a trawler, a seiner, and a gill-netter. I was concerned that viewers understand this, because if they lose touch too often they just go away. With *Dancing*, since there was so much constitutional language, I held forty test screenings when I was editing. Then I could go back to the editing table and ask myself why is it that they don't understand that? In *Salt Water People* I knew that viewers might be learning as many as fifty new words. If somebody says, "I went on the seiner," and at the same time you don't show the seiner and establish the connection between the word and the boat, you have trouble. The same with spawning. Not everybody will know about that. You have to show it and establish that spawning is more or less a sexual act and that the eggs of the female are fertilized by the male. Always keep the didactical thing in mind if you want to keep the audience with you. If you do that you can open up to the large issues of pollution, spirituality, and the difference between being in harmony with nature and controlling nature.

In Dancing Around the Table *your sense of enthusiasm and your sense of learning really come across. To me there's a real excitement in learning where those people who are sitting around the table actually live. You go back with them, literally, to where they're coming from.*

Maurice. There is a pleasure in learning. At the same time you can reconcile that with having a point of view. Often with so-called balanced films the facts are not straight and you can sense it. You may not know why but you can sense the manipulation going on there. And that's because they have to show issues as black and white. They can't show them with tints of grey. If you have a point of view you can go into all the shades you want to.

That was one of the things I set out to do in *Salt Water People*. I knew nothing at first but I learned all kinds of things in the research. So at minimum I can give some of that back throughout the film, so that people can learn about these things in a pleasant way. I get pleasure in that. Viewers will learn how the Native people think about the sea. It's a real knowledge. I would replace scientific with another word, but as valid. It's one road towards knowledge as good as the scientific one. One Native man in the film looks out and says there's a bank of fish out there. How did he know? Well, there was a bird that came and gave them a message that the fish were there. These are ways of learning based on the spiritual connection, which I know nothing about except that it exists.

Some say the documentary is dying. Do you feel a pressure to experiment with the conventions of documentary? Do you try to challenge the audience in terms of style?
Maurice. I'm not an innovator. There are those who are concerned with transforming the language or the style of cinema and those who are concerned to use the language for expression, and I would rather fall into the second category. If the audience is not taken by your film, you're not doing a good job. That's putting it very simply, but I'm not willing to experiment. I don't think it's in my nature. The key element is that the people are there throughout, expressing themselves. That sets your parameter – your limits.

With *Salt Water People* we've got the people, the ocean, and the traditional calendar. I have to find a way of marrying all these things. When we're under the water I have to find a way for the fish to speak their mind. A film is like a problem to solve stylistically. I think I have solved these things and it's a good film, but stylistically I haven't invented anything. I see lots of films and I've used things that I've seen here, there, and everywhere. I remember seeing Michael Snow's *Région centrale*, with the camera revolving, revolving in the arctic landscape. Well, I've used that. Thank you, Michael Snow for doing that film. You were trying something at the level of style and I was impressed – it stayed with me. I guess I'll use all kinds of things that I see, but I'll never come down to the little things in the video clip – flit, flit, flit – never.

There's another aspect to that question. Too many filmmakers think anybody can be a documentarist. They think, "We will go out with a film crew, and stick the mike under somebody's nose. Okay, and when they're talking about this we'll do a shot of that, and to explain the relationship we'll add on a commentary." People think it's easy to do because many have done it. That's the reason you see so many terrible films. On *The Journal*, for instance, they have a little reportage and they call it a documentary. Well, they're wrong. It's not a documentary.

"Here we are in Rio de Janeiro," they say, "and while we're here we'll do a little piece on the people in the shanty towns." I'm sorry, that's not a documentary. So I guess too many people have been doing that. You're dealing with people, with life: if you show people who are homeless it's dramatic already. Right away you have something. If you ignore style you do that subject a disservice, and if you see too many of those films you might reach the conclusion that the documentary is dying. But it will never die. Filming with people and creating this relationship between the camera and real life will never disappear. It's impossible. But it will always be devalued, that's for sure.

When you ask me about style, I don't even know if I have a style in my films, but I'm not too worried about that. It's a difficult question because I'm eclectic by nature. I was recently in Lithuania and saw many films made by Baltic people – most are stylistically close to the Russian cinema. One I saw treated a serious subject but in a humorous rather than a cynical way. After seventy years of oppression they have all the reasons in the world to be cynical, yet there was a place for humour. That touched me very much. It may seem simplistic, but I just want to make the next film as good as the last one. Maybe a bit more interesting. I like the formal beauty of the French school, and I always say one day I'll make a "nice" film, probably just about a flower.

"Spaces
for
women ..."

Sara Diamond has worked in video since the late 1970s, doggedly creating from scratch a history of women and work in British Columbia. Her tapes explore daily life and political life, often in juxtapositions never before considered. Born in New York City in 1954, Diamond grew up in a family steeped in radical politics and harassed by the U.S. government during the anti-Communist 1950s. They moved to Toronto when she was five, and later – like so many political and cultural rebels of her generation – she gravitated to Vancouver. She has worked as a teacher of media and women's studies, including stints at the California Institute of the Arts in Los Angeles and Emily Carr College in Vancouver. She is now the director of the video and TV program at the Banff School of Fine Arts.

Diamond's first works, created within the Amelia Productions video collective of Vancouver starting in the late 1970s, focus on women engaged in radical political actions. The best known are *This Line Is Not in Service* (1981), on a strike among women operators at the B.C. Telephone Company, and *Concerned Aboriginal Women* (1981), about an occupation of the Department of Indian Affairs office in Vancouver. In *Concerned Aboriginal Women*, during the occupation a number of Native women tell their life stories directly to the camera, providing a chilling context and rationale for their current actions. The tape achieves a level of intensity that lifts it far beyond a simple documentation of the women's political action.

After the disintegration of Amelia Productions, Diamond's work shifted dramatically in style and approach to embrace the preoccupations current in video art. *Influences of My Mother* (1982) is personal and inward-looking, a biographical sketch based on photos and letters combined with staged scenes of Diamond dressed as her mother. The tape is tightly structured as an investigation in six parts, with titles such as Denial, Judgement, and Heroic Mother.

Keeping the Home Fires Burning: Women, War Work, and Unions in British Columbia (1988) marks a synthesis of Diamond's earlier social-issue documentary with conventions drawn from theatre and video performance. The tape constructs a rich compilation of historical footage on labour in the 1940s, but interrupts this actuality footage with staged scenes of popular theatre as it might have looked in the shop floors and union halls of the time. The scenes allow Diamond to raise issues of conflict within the labour movement, specifically the role of women in the wartime workforce.

Perhaps more than any producer of the new documentary, Diamond's work brings together some of the most diverse traits of conventional documentary and an anti-realist aesthetic. For instance, in *Ten Dollars or Nothing!* (1989), a short tape based on the reminiscences of Josephine Charlie, a Native woman from Lake Cowichan, Vancouver Island, the sound track presents Charlie talking about her days working in fish-canning plants and her attempts to lead workers to strike for better conditions. Dense rapid-fire images culled from historical footage of the local First Nations are reworked, slowed down, coloured, and reversed through optical printing. At times they illustrate the commentary, and at other times they carry a more poetic relationship to Charlie's stories.

The Lull Before the Storm Part 1 (1990) and Part 2 (1991) show Diamond's continued struggle to make effective, popular tapes that will contribute to social change as well as integrate sophisticated concepts of film and video theory. Produced for the Knowledge Network, British Columbia's educational television, *The Lull Before the Storm* embarks on a history of Canadian women's work – in the paid labour force and at home – between World War II and 1960. Part 1 (two tapes, *The Forties* and *The Fifties*) is primarily a drama centred on the work and domestic tensions of one family, although it also integrates footage from documentaries of the 1940s and 1950s and CBC television. The two tapes of Part 2 are structured as a more conventional documentary essay about women involved in the B.C. logging industry. The first tape, *The Women of Wood*, concentrates on home life; the second, *Community Acts*, focuses on women activists. Both combine interviews and historical footage.

Other interviews with Sara Diamond have implied that theoretical concerns always take precedence for her, so I was interested to probe for a more direct political motivation to her work. As with many other producers interviewed for this book, Diamond's early family life continues its strong influence. During the interview she often referred to her parents' political commitment and the role of Jewish culture in her work – reflections that for me helped to bring home the roots of her theoretical analysis.

Have politics and art always gone hand in hand for you, or did you have an engagement with one before the other?
Sara. I was a red-diaper baby but didn't know it until I was a teenager. My parents were political refugees who came to Canada because of McCarthyism, so they were pretty closeted. Political ideas circulated in the family, but not very openly. My parents were damaged by their experiences, and I believe my mother died partly from the anxiety. My grandmother was very open about their past, but also disillusioned. I reclaim her tradition, I suppose. I read the Marxist economist Ernest Mandel in a study group when I was seventeen. That was a really formative experience. I believed I understood the world.

I dabbled in theatre and drawing classes, and then got caught up in the hippy counterculture. Before I joined the organized left I worked in women's agit-prop in Toronto, and in Vancouver I participated in "The Working Theatre" and *May Day* magazine.

I participated in the famous Artistic Woodworking Company strike in Toronto in 1974. Then I went to Latin America, came back to do union work, and was active in the Revolutionary Marxist Group and Revolutionary Workers League. The RWL was a major part of my life: five years' total commitment. The left taught me to think and read critically, to think on my feet, and to organize politically. The organization encouraged me to go to university, so I went and studied history. I read Gramsci, critiques of advertising, theories of consciousness. At the same time I was frustrated by the new left's inability to break out of print media, and their scepticism of using film and theatre.

How has your teaching of video and women's studies influenced your video work?

Sara. It's easier for me to think about that the other way around. My work influences the teaching. The need to make theory accessible, and manageable, to relate it to practice, led me to teaching – to create a more sophisticated basis for curriculum. I started doing workshops at Video In in Vancouver and tried to develop what was offered into full-length courses. Then, at the "100 Years of Marxism" Conference in Vancouver, in 1983, I gave a paper on the absence of women's labour history and challenged ideas about the efficacy of the Communist Party and social democracy to address women. After, I started teaching labour history at Capilano College and noticed the lack of Canadian audio-visual resources on labour, especially women in labour. That teaching did affect my art work.

Can you tell me about the formation of Amelia Productions? What was the context for video in Vancouver during the late 1970s? Were you reacting against particular currents in video, extending a tradition, etc.?

Sara. It started haphazardly, from a few directions. Three of us had studied in the Simon Fraser film department and were dissatisfied with the focus on structuralism. We wanted to work in documentary and try something more instrumental, especially in relation to the women's movement. Amelia also developed through cable TV. Cable provided a way of doing a counter-news practice and gaining access to an audience. We weren't naive about finding a huge audience, we worked with material that was geared to specific groups, in the way AIDS cable programming is happening now. The Vancouver Rogers Cable station was particularly good at the time. There was access for independents and a self-generated practice. Rob Carver was very helpful, and he's still there at Cable 10, but the cable industry doesn't allow that openness any more.

At the time, Women in Focus was studio-based and issue-oriented; it didn't tie itself to current events. At Amelia we wanted to get out there as social activists. We laughingly called it "occupational video," since the tapes on the B.C. Telephone offices occupation and the Native Affairs offices occupation were successful. These were shot and edited quite quickly, re-edited, and seen shortly after. Another tape, on VDTs, took longer to shoot, but had immediate value nevertheless. Many unions used it.

But there were limits to that practice at Amelia. For instance, we didn't go very far with our debates about theory; we simply agreed to put aside our differences. It was one of those 1980s' experiments – people sleeping with each other, etc. – that eventually went kaboom. It was good we stopped, but it was valuable for then.

In talking previously about Influences of My Mother *you've mentioned your mother as a personal source for your interest in history. Is there any fiction involved in the screen biographies of you and your mother? If so, do you worry about whether audiences will pick up on it?*
Sara. Contradiction in the tape stems from my memories and lack of material. I sought corroboration from other oral histories, photos, etc., to place her in a field of actuality. My father's and grandmother's versions of her life have a parallel. I know, for example, that she was really "liquidated" by McCarthyism – everybody says that, and I try to imagine what that was like for her. The tape centres on myth-making and fiction-making about our parents, though it does have a foot in what actually took place, in "events."

My work deals with the way subjectivities get produced and transformed. So the issue of becoming more truthful doesn't arise.

My new installation *Patternity* is the next stage. I'm tremendously like my father, who's still alive, and he's very similar to my grandmother. My work with him for the tape established that connection and also made this work different from *Influences.* Because of the *Patternity* show people now feel very intimate with me. They think, "We know you." In both tapes I do these messy personal, rather neurotic, revelations. They're partially included to help people have access to their own feelings, to not fear their own processes. But you know I don't take these revelation sequences very seriously. I don't walk around in that state. They're a construction. You write those sequences for a particular reason and in a confessional form so that they stand as testimony that you've been through something.

In Keeping the Home Fires Burning *you show the first results of your extensive research into archival materials. Was there any footage that particularly surprised you? What was your best find?*
Sara. My best find was the NFB film *The Proudest Girl in the World,* which opens *Keeping the Home Fires Burning.* I was excited about it since it was so amazingly of the time, you could say. But archival research is such a huge territory to cover, I now have researchers to work

with me. In *The Lull Before the Storm* I use sequences from the 1950s' CBC program of Ashley Montague talking about women. It was priceless. I fell off my chair laughing. Yet it was interesting since it shows the liberal-masculine perspective of the time. I've also used the old CBC footage on the Lake Cowichan area, which is full of racial stereotypes and fictionalized images.

I really get in there and research. That CBC research depends on personal contacts that you make. The National Film, T.V. and Sound Archives is terrific, though understaffed, but they have been partially privatized, which is criminal. The NFB stock-shot archives are very well organized, but expensive. It can be hard work searching for a specific image.

When you say search, does that mean that you go in looking for material to illustrate points in the script, or is it a more open process?
Sara. I'm open to what I'll find. I love archival research. I get seduced by it and could live in an archives. I'm open to what I'll find because I often use the material ironically. The irony is by way of deconstruction, à la Jacques Derrida. It's not negation or illustration, but more in a standing side by side way – with the script, etc. Even the Ashley Montague material, as used in *The Lull*, doesn't always reinforce the stereotypes about the fifties.

Were you familiar with the U.S. film Rosie the Riveter *when you made* Keeping the Home Fires Burning? *How would you describe the differences?*
Sara. I was very familiar with it. I couldn't have made my tape without it. *Rosie* was very tight and well made. It allowed me to make something more discursive and fragmented and less heroic; also to look at the failure of women in industry. I wanted to deconstruct the truth value of documentary, by building the agit-prop sequences – which in fact recall the workers' theatre of the time. I wanted to undercut the idea that all women shared the same experience of factory work during the war, without falling into the trap of saying this is what actually happened, rather, "This is subjectively the truth." I don't think the first option is possible any more. That's a basis for much of my work.

Nor am I making reflexive anti-documentary. I'm interested in documentary's relationship to writing, through voice-over and the "other" (edited) direct voice of subjects. Then there's documentary's link with commitment to a social project. The historical debates and fluctuating

definitions are interesting. For instance, Joris Ivens and the U.S. movements in the thirties integrated fiction into documentary (though their
reasons often stemmed from hoping to reach a deeper inner truth from
the subjects). The shifts in documentary conventions certainly continue, including TV advertising's ability to use documentary techniques
to convince.

Do the staged scenes in Keeping the Home Fires Burning *stem from your
background in video performance art, or theatre, or something else
again?*
Sara. I can honestly say that they come out of both traditions. The workers' theatre of the thirties and forties was only partly Brechtian, especially on the West Coast, due to its volunteer, popular nature, without a
developed aesthetic. Video art has consistently refused to draw on standard theatricality – it is anti-narrative, anti-catharsis. It attempts to
challenge people. I also draw on the strain in radical performance art
that's agitational and echoes Brecht's idea of social characterizations
rather than characters.

*What's your view of feminist media theory in film, television, and video
at this point in their evolution? For example, are the discussions about
women viewers and "reading against the grain" parallel or convergent
with your work?*
Sara. The way we view and watch is complex. In my work I script in
order to create spaces for women to take up different viewing positions,
and to feel confident about those positions. This fits with reading
against the grain, in the forms of irony and humour. It's a survival skill.
My work is always ironic and coupled with a social context. I hope it
reinforces people who are organizing resistance: part of a culture to create a field of resistance.

*You've talked about humour as a useful cultural strategy, and all your
works use humour in various guises. Is that a conscious strategy or just
part of your general outlook on life that creeps in?*
Sara. In *Patternity* I refer to the traditions of Jewish humour, especially
in the radical left. Despite the patriarchal and hierarchical elements of
Judaism, the oral culture uses slippage, and so many jokes that turn on
language. I was raised that way and later had it reinforced through the
women's movement, which thrives on irony. In *The Lull* I tried to invert
everything, to take the jokes further.

Are there times when you regret using humour?
Sara. No. I feel comfortable with the humour. The thing I don't want to do is serious, unmediated narrative. Parts of my work, like *On to Ottawa*, do that, but it's not what I want for the whole. That's the culture that surrounds us, so I'm trying in my work to treat my addiction to our culture: those narratives that you can get totally submerged in, yet walk away from. I want to create work that is difficult, though accessible, where the audience says, "What's going on here? Why is there a problem?" In *Patternity*, for example, viewers might ask "Why are her hands always moving? Why is she always present even though she doesn't speak?" One guy wrote a very funny review of the installation – he obviously didn't get it – where it really bugged him that the hands were moving all the time. He couldn't concentrate on the "main image." If anything my work is always about a peripheral vision. In *Ten Dollars or Nothing!* there's a frame around a central image, and by the end you wonder whether the central image or the frame is more important. In *The Lull* there's always something else happening, working against. Historical footage cuts into the narration and the text is inverted for its humour.

Is there any danger of taking the complexities of the past too lightly?
Sara. The past is always a construction – the issue is, what kind? In writing the family scenes for *The Lull* I realized that those scenes were not only about the past. I wanted to make a piece about the 1950s because for me that's when the nuclear family, which is now in deep shit, was constructed. I couldn't possibly write only about the historical family. I wrote about relationships I know now, relationships predicated on how we were constructed then. I wanted to write a piece that had no resolution and was full of pain. [laughs] You know when you're having a fight with somebody and in the middle of it you say to yourself, "This is so stupid, why am I in this addictive mode?" One part of you is laughing, and yet the fight carries through to its full drama. You know those scenes when people rush out of the room because their cooking is criticized. It's the horror of the domestic structures that we all inhabit. I wanted to capture that.

Soap opera gets produced out of that, but I wasn't doing pure soap opera. I was aiming for humour and pain in the same moment. Even though I'm not trying to make positive images, at times it ends up that way. *Heroics*, for example, was a critique of positive images, but an endorsement as well. In *The Lull* I didn't want that. I wanted something that was difficult for both men and women to watch, difficult to identify with.

The Lull Before the Storm *works for me as a fascinating hybrid where the documentary discourse and the staged scenes take turns holding precedence. Did you develop both sides of the equation at once?*
Sara. I set out to integrate the drama and the documentary, and the first version, which I showed at the Toronto Images 90 Festival, worked that way. But I didn't like what I'd done. Mixing all the interview material in with the drama seemed like a ploy. So I went back and separated much of the documentary and drama into two complete works. Knowledge Network broadcast the two versions separately.

What was your working relationship with Knowledge Network TV for The Lull Before the Storm? *They seem quite proud of their involvement.*
Sara. They were excited by the project. It was beyond their usual levels of production but went stunningly well. I had a free hand. At first one of the production people wasn't confident that I could pull off the technical and directorial aspects, but I think he really changed his position. The crews loved the work since it was demanding and managed to escape many categories. We were very well organized and came in well prepared. We knew what we were doing and rehearsed a lot. I have to say that the technical directors helped me pull it off, and without their commitment it would have been very hard. But I knew what I wanted, in terms of look and lighting.

Was this your first time working with professional actors? How did you cast and prepare them?
Sara. Yes, my first time. I had done theatre, which proved really helpful since I had that knowledge in the back of my brain. I had taken acting classes from the time I was six or seven, then again in my twenties. So when the actors would say "I really need to know my motivation," I would know how to talk about Stanislavski and explain that my way of working is different.

I cast properly. I worked with the union, ACTRA, who were supportive and interested and taught me how to handle the bureaucratic aspects. My past union work helped me understand contracts. I went through all the top casting agencies in Vancouver, and we spent about ten days taping many, many people. It was demanding for the actors, since they had to move between styles but they loved working on it, since they normally do all this American shit.

Let's move on to Ten Dollars or Nothing! *How did you meet Josephine Charlie? Did the taped conversation come first as a project of oral history before your ideas about the visual style?*
Sara. I met Josephine Charlie through Reg Bullock, who had been adopted into Josephine's band many years before. Reg's wife, Ruth, was in *Keeping the Home* as one of the women who worked in agriculture during the war; I'd known them for a long time. In the late seventies when I was doing B.C. labour oral histories, Reg said that I must talk to Josephine. She'd worked in the canneries for years and was a leader in the union and the Native community. She was ninety-one in 1979 when I interviewed her, and she died in 1985. I had no images of her, and that set up a difficult problem for doing the tape. It's part of an experimental series about the thirties. There are two other companion pieces, one about domestic workers in both the country and the city, and the other about the urban political scene. 29/92 was released in 1992 and *Fit to be Tied* in 1993. Each tape is treated differently, through the way I use text, diaries, and fictionalized images versus raw material.

How was Ten Dollars *funded? I didn't see big agencies listed in the credits, but you obviously did extensive research with many assistants?*
Sara. I got a small grant for a research assistant and funded the production myself. I've also had help from the NFB for stock footage.

How did you decide on the rapid pace for the imagery?
Sara. Josephine Charlie's reminiscences had a certain flow on the original audio tape, but I changed that. I only used segments referring to cross-cultural experience. The structure of the completed tape works on three levels: as description, description with narrative, and full narrative. I wanted to cut against narrative – based on current theory about the problems of history, especially the different perspectives on understanding history. I wanted viewers to see the tape as a representation. None of the material was shot by First Nations people, and not much by women. So I wanted to produce something that was obviously edited and manipulated, dramatized, colourized, etc. This gives more weight to her voice.

*I'm interested in whether you feel a tension between your position as
an independent producer and a sense of accountability to the women or
communities depicted in your tapes. How does that play itself out?*

Sara. I started *Ten Dollars or Nothing!* a long time ago, before the debate
over cross-cultural representation erupted, and I don't know whether I'd
make that tape now. I want Native peoples to get pleasure from it and
draw from it. My audience isn't just a white one. But if the tape is interpreted now as an appropriation, I would understand and feel a responsibility. I really respect the arguments being made about who has the right
to represent and the problems of appropriation. Still, I think it's important not to end up in an essentialist position over issues of race, where
race becomes the only issue that defines identity, where we lose the
notion of how complex identities are, and where solidarity is not possible. To create working-class history where I can only represent white
women is a terrifying thought to me.

The Women's Labour History Project has always tried to be inclusive – even when being very specific about histories – to not fall into the
racist hierarchies that mainstream history perpetuates. You can't talk
about B.C. labour history without talking about Japanese workers, for
instance. We've tried compiling elements that together will show a fragmented but diversified history of women in the province. We hope that
the histories in the tapes are specifically tied down and the subjectivities clear; this is what these women thought, this is where they were
positioned. Things did happen in history, even though there's not one
position on them. The Japanese were interned, women did go into industry. Our job is challenging because we want to work independently and
critically and yet have reference.

For another new project, which depicts the On-to-Ottawa Trek of
1935, we were contracted by the On-to-Ottawa Historical Society to
produce a tape based on their play. Although it's their version we're
working on, I'm adding dramatic material to the play; they have the
right to challenge what I write. It makes for a really interesting negotiation, and to be honest, I have had mixed feelings about it.

*The traditional discussion over documentary ethics deals with how
you treat people you are filming, how you get them to agree to be
involved in your project, and how the filming can have future consequences for them.*

Sara. I care about the people I interview. I often have a history with
them. I've known the women in Lake Cowichan for fourteen years.

They treat me like an aberrant member of the family. I feel responsible to those I interview, but I often try to capture conflict and difference on issues. I have said to people, "There's going to be others in the tape that you won't agree with." So I don't have ethical problems in setting up situations to challenge people.

This relates to our discussion on theory. Poststructuralism has despite itself reinforced notions of objective practice, since postmodernism in practice is so analytical and distant and therefore no different from the false traditions of journalistic objectivity.

How do you feel about the current state of documentary?
Sara. In the art world and within broadcast TV, documentary carries a peripheral status, which relates to both economics and critiques of realism. And in the U.S. the economics of documentary is worse than in Canada. Documentary remains such a contested term. So many definitions are used, often based on ideas from the 1920s of essential truth and attempts to evoke the "real."

On the other hand the current economic restraints have prompted people to defend the genre. I think there's a place for work that functions in an instructive way about representation and yet also functions in an instrumental, socially motivated way. I'm not as cynical as many people about representation. I think there's merit in trying to understand historical forces from the subjective positions that you construct in the work, and what facts are meaningful to those "people" – how events took place from those perspectives that allow us to understand historical process.

How necessary is it to develop a "profile" for yourself and your work? Is it necessary to sell yourself and your ability to be reasonable and responsible? Are you ambitious?
Sara. People say I am. It probably appears that I promote myself well, but I hate that part of it, despise it. I feel cut off from money and feel that some of the work should have more broadcast potential. It's really the problem of not living in Toronto. I've worked hard to create an organizational infrastructure where things take care of themselves, but it doesn't really work that way. I'm always behind in my fundraising – to make sure I'll have an income six months from now. I've built a personal profile by speaking, writing, and teaching, and by explicating and contextualizing the work. There's no space to rest. I feel it as I get older.

"What do they want, a theme park?"

Since the mid-1970s **Judith Doyle** has been actively involved in the Toronto art community centred on Queen Street West. Doyle, who was born in 1957 in Toronto and studied creative writing at York University, first made a name for herself through performance art and in her role as editor of *Impulse* magazine. She is a key figure in the new documentary – someone who moved into documentary from the more fine art-based experimental film world without giving up the desire to innovate.

As Doyle herself stresses, there is a solid continuity between her earlier "art" films and her later "political" work. *Eye of the Mask: Theatre Nicaragua* (1983), her first full-length social documentary, was shot during the beginning of the Contra war against the Sandinista government. The film shows the last flowering of revolutionary popular theatre at a time before the war made such activity in the countryside impossible. In addition the film also highlights traditional Indian-Catholic religious festivals as well as the still-popular cultures of U.S. pop music and fashion in Nicaragua. Doyle edited the film to show the strengths and complexities in all three cultural strains.

Eye of the Mask seems best described as a kind of portrait film, based on loosely organized sequences showing various facets of Nicaraguan culture. Unlike many observational films it does not rely on a narrative structure, and unlike works in the style of classic exposition it uses little voice-over narration to tie up its thematic threads. The result is a demanding and rich one-hour plunge into another culture.

In 1986 the Lac La Croix Ojibwa community near Kenora in Northern Ontario asked Doyle to produce a video document of their fight with the provincial government. The dispute centres on the right of the band to use outboard motors for guiding on lakes that are part of Quetico Provincial Park. The completed informational tape led to a much more wide-ranging film, eventually titled *Nequaquan: Lac La Croix* (1988), in which Doyle, in close collaboration with elders, band political leaders, and a cross-section of the community, examines both the political fight with the government and the traditional and present-day Ojibwa culture.

Like *Eye of the Mask, Lac La Croix* is a loosely constructed mix of exposition, observation, and engagement with the people who appear on screen. Compared to more conventional documentary, particularly of the television variety, *Lac La Croix* is slow paced and makes few concessions to a narrative drive. Several key people, including the traditional healer Ron Geyshick, appear throughout, but the film develops primarily as a portrait of the community. The film also sets up the complex interactions between southern white culture and traditional Ojibwa culture, showing the Lac La Croix people engaged in blending the two. It reveals that Ojibwa culture, contrary to most impressions, has never been static. Scenes of a Johnny Cash impersonator belting out his music in the community hall dissolve into scenes of traditional wild-rice gathering. Neither seems out of place.

After completing *Lac La Croix* Doyle continued to work with Ron Geyshick, editing a book of his short stories entitled *Te Bwe Win* (*Truth*).[2] These stories, which complement the film, elaborate, often in fantastic form, the remarkable blend of modern Ojibwa culture and art. Two shorter commissioned tapes also deal with First Nations traditions and the dominant white world. *Whitefish Bay: Self-Government* (1991) looks at constitutional law and the attempts of a small Native community to gain economic independence. *Seventh Fire* (1992) portrays traditional healers working with the Anishinabe Native Health Centre in Toronto.

In the interview Doyle talks about the kind of "negotiated representation" needed to produce these kinds of work. Her concern for proper collaboration follows a line of thought close to Laura Sky's ideas of "informed consent."

How did your first two films, Private Property, Public History *and* Launch, *come to be made?*

Judith. They stemmed from my interest in performance art during the seventies and from recorded and transcribed conversations. *Private Property* documents the lives and stories of women in the Creemore area of Ontario, and *Launch* deals with shipyard union organizing in Collingwood, Ontario. They share the same visual strategy – a sequence of still pictures and voice-over derived from edited interviews. Performance art as I practised it then at the A Space Gallery was based on art-community collaborations.

I was also involved with The Funnel Experimental Film Centre, and I got my technical training there, rather than at film school. Though my background was in writing I wanted to present the texts with slides and tape, in collaboration with visual artists and musicians. Performance was more complex and challenging than just reading texts aloud, and more affordable and responsive than film. Our relationship with an audience was direct. One piece I did with Fred Geysic at A Space in 1978 featured us reading statements while Super 8 film and slides were projected simultaneously behind. A Space ran performance and video regularly; mine often involved projection and juxtaposition of sound and text. Later it made sense to integrate those elements in film.

In the seventies some community centres also had video production programs and artist-run centres; for example, the community-based TV produced at Trinity Square, which involved many artists. This direct connection was severed with the Canada Council's and Ontario Arts Council's decision to stop core funding of centres, and a switch to project funding, putting pressure on the artist centres to carve up their work and predetermine their programming.

In *Private Property* and *Launch* I wanted to show what gets acted out and what gets repressed when people take photographs, and I felt that a clear, explicit structure was appropriate to deal with this issue. I had a small budget so I shot on Super 8, using an animation stand. I was influenced by the feminist works of Chantal Ackerman. From her films I felt that it was important to give things their own time, and to pare down.

What turned you in the direction of the Nicaragua project, which later became Eye of the Mask?

Judith. I had gone down to Nicaragua a couple of times for artists and writers conferences and had been really compelled by the way

Nicaraguan artists saw their relation to the larger community. It made me wonder what would happen if those activist strategies were imported here. I began to think about our cultural work in Canada – who watches it, what are its effects, and what role art can play in bringing out problems and contradictions that have been repressed. The arts scene down there had problems, certainly, but I felt that Nicaraguan art had something to offer to my community in Toronto. I had no idea what I was getting into with 16mm production on this scale, but I went ahead and gambled in spite of our shockingly low budget.

I wanted to make a type of experimental film that also addressed political documentary issues, and this was controversial at The Funnel. I needed to move out into a larger context and reach broader audiences. A third factor was my interest in liberation theology. I had been raised Catholic and my cousin in New York was a Maryknoll monk. The seventies were an energetic, optimistic time for the church, and I had done a lot of reading on the theology of liberation, also partly related to my interest in Paulo Freire's theories of education. Going to Nicaragua had encouraged me to come to terms with my own lapsed Catholicism, I suppose.

The original idea was to do a broad survey of many arts, but we realized immediately that we would have to be flexible. The decision to focus on theatre evolved in the process of pre-production in Nicaragua. We were there during the U.S. invasion of Grenada [October 1983] and the country was very tense. I saw some film crews just sitting around the Intercontinental Hotel waiting for interviews with government leaders; others packed up and went home out of fear. I think the film was successful because of our willingness to be flexible. No one could get vehicles and gas. Even the major Nicaraguan cinema collective at INCINE dropped a project on popular theatre because they couldn't get any trucks. We hitchhiked and took buses. We used faster film stocks since we had to abandon our light kit. We shot with an Arriflex BL camera and Stephen Deme, the cinematographer, dissembled it every morning to get the sand out. Nicaragua was not a country where you could schedule. It was also very confusing. There were no street signs in Managua.

Your films seem like classic cinéma vérité in the French sense, where the camera works as a catalyst. Jean Rouch says, "The camera deforms, but it has the possibility of doing something I couldn't do if the camera wasn't there: it becomes a kind of psychoanalytic stimulant which lets

ings they wouldn't otherwise do." Were there situations in
there the presence of the camera prompted increased open-
ur subjects, or the opposite?

Judith. Those ideas about recording instruments as a stimulus had played a role in fine art circles for us in Toronto during the seventies, and certainly informed my first two films. But in Nicaragua the reality of that situation affected us all on the most primary levels. We had little control over many situations in Nicaragua. In fact we were shot at, and after we had left one rural area the owner of a location where we filmed was ambushed and killed.

In the long run I think the only people really changed in these extreme situations are the participants. Now to a certain extent the people in Nixtayalero, the theatre group we travelled with, were challenged to work through their ideas about popular theatre because of the filming process. The filming may have exacerbated tensions in the group. The process of filming some plays triggered analysis of how those plays worked or were ineffectual for some audiences. They had a lot of responsibilities, and they were all in their early twenties. Unfortunately the war soon made this kind of rural theatre too dangerous, and the popular theatre was consolidated in the cities. Many of the theatre people shifted into radio work around 1986.

Eye of the Mask was considered quite a break for you and your work,
wasn't it?

Judith. Yes, unfortunately it was. Yet I don't see the big break between *Private Property* and *Eye*. The big break was in the response of the art community. That indicated to me the acceptable limits of filmic behaviour. When I look at my work – the performance, the publishing, my curatorial activity, and the films – I see continuity and an interest in a series of ideas to do with voice and the politics of culture. With *Eye* I ran up against political walls, a fear of confronting issues in experimental art, and an almost institutionalized attempt to marginalize political art into some kind of genre.

Nevertheless, your work has moved steadily towards a more conventional documentary style and away from experimental modes. Does that indicate a frustration with the experimental film world?

Judith. A number of us who had been working at The Funnel were moving in that direction, and a split developed between those of us interested in feminism, gay activist concerns, issues of representation, and explicit sexual politics, and those more attached to the punk, anarchist, structuralist, New York schools. There was also tension among film and video artists over strategies of dealing with the Ontario Censor Board. So by 1986 many people had left The Funnel in search of projects in a different context and on a bigger scale. That history is very complicated.

I find your work challenging in its structure and what you assume the audience should know. It works on a more sophisticated plane than the average documentary. Do you see it that way?
Judith. I know my films are different from what people are used to. TV documentaries use voice-over and narration to explain the substance, combined with a kind of visual wall. My films don't work that way. I hoped the film could still play on TV, which was a naiveté on my part.

In *Eye of the Mask* I wilfully skewed the conventions, experimenting with text and narration, contrast editing, and scene order where scenes deconstruct previous ones. For example, we wanted to show that the overall culture is mixed and contains contradictions of three cultures: the Miami pre-revolutionary culture shown in the nightclub scene, which is both elite and popular; then the traditional but skewed Indian-Catholic festivals, also mixed in themselves; finally, the fledgling revolutionary culture shown in the plays we filmed. None of these cultures could sustain dominance. So we set up sequences that emphasized this layering. For instance, we cut from the nightclub sequence but kept the singer's drawn-out ending to the song to play over famous wire-service photos of Nicaragua during the Somoza years – the street fighting, the atrocities, the National Guard. That certainly undercut her performance. So, through editing, I focused on the way these cultural elements interacted.

In *Lac La Croix* I couldn't afford to shoot film during all my interviews, but I wanted the narration to come from the community, so we quickly developed a method of showing a speaker, then fading into voice-over. Neither of the films follows a conflict-resolution structure that makes so many documentaries work like drama. Although *Eye of the Mask* is sort of a road movie, it's basically structured around ideas and the development of themes. Nicaragua has usually been treated in terms of conflict, but I wanted an antidote using storytelling and popular fiction – theatre, parades, costume, and music. *Lac La Croix* has a basic conflict between the community and the provincial government, so there's some satisfaction for the viewer, but you don't see the adversaries at each other's throats. The antagonist is displaced.

Perhaps it's a feminist structure, because I focus on connections on many levels rather than reducing the narrative to one main conflict. I'd rather work in an associative, playful manner. The structure of *Lac La Croix* takes the story from morning through a day into evening, then repeats this in another season – winter. Movement takes place between work space and personal space, and you see the tension for the guides between their identity as "Indian guides" in the resort and their lives in the community, which are also influenced by the mass culture.

What was the relationship between you and the Lac La Croix community? And how did the film come to take on its final form? For example, when you were shooting was there a tension between documenting the immediate fight about the provincial park and explaining more long-term issues?

Judith. The community hired me and raised a good portion of the money, with the original idea of producing a videotape to be used in arguing their case with the media, the government, and the larger public. Of course many people in the community didn't understand what we were doing at first, and some thought we were from the CBC. In doing the video sketch we compiled hundreds of hours of interviews, initiating a process of speaking with the community, then playing back and continuing the discussion. At first people didn't seem to think there was much of interest to say about the community. For the film we made VHS transfers of several rough cuts and played these in schools, band offices, and homes, and the speaking became easier. People realized that the tape and film interviews set up a little distance and that you could say things to the camera that you might not say in a meeting. It opened up a different kind of social communication. It broke down some long-standing divisions based mainly on families. In the end, even after the film version was finished people felt amazed that there was so much to say, and they wanted more than the one hour. They're now involved in developing local TV programs.

The other reason for pushing ahead to make the film after we had completed the video sketch was the way in which the community had been treated in the media. The video sketch drew attention to the community's fight concerning the motor ban in the park, but people felt appalled at the CBC coverage and the way Lac La Croix was represented. The TV reports featured ministry officials, U.S. tourists, and muscular Native guides in the background.

The people in Lac La Croix usually take a holistic approach and don't see a division between the motor-ban fight and other community issues. They want an economic and cultural future and, to use a government term, they see the need to develop a "community profile." I believe that this process of self-representation and the making of it into an object is usually positive. It works as a marker to look back to in the future.

Were you satisfied with the working relationship that developed between yourself and the Native community?
Judith. David MacIntosh, my editor, worked closely with me on the film, and right from the beginning we were very conscious of our role as non-Natives in the community. We tried to analyse our own expectations and preconceptions about the community; we knew how important it was to take people at their word when they told us about sensitive material; and we had to keep in mind the power and authority attached to the media. The mythology of cinema is so pervasive, and people's fantasies about how they will appear allow potential for great abuse. It's nothing personal. It's the institution of late-twentieth-century cinema. In Lac La Croix they put this tape about their community into the same VCRs as World Wrestling Federation tapes.

We approached the filmmaking and our role in representing and documenting the community as a process of negotiation. There had to be a process of building consent and correcting mistakes in stages. I personally believe that process is very important. In Lac La Croix we had many discussions about the basics of filmmaking and the realities of the mainstream media. For example, I talked about the principles of sound and picture editing, the drawbacks of a straight talking-head format, and the fact that this film was being produced in a context different from the CBC. I saw this as a transfer of knowledge and skills and a way of broadening involvement in the film so the community could participate in developing structure and refining content. We recognized that people would not necessarily be immediately critical of a particular sequence in the film as we played it back to them, but that criticism might only get back to us in a roundabout way. So the process of reviewing took a long time. Although we were concerned about our role, we didn't want to slavishly follow directions or act like robots. Naturally we saw contradictions in what people said, or times when people were not at their best, and we had to respond to raise our concerns.

The issue of white people documenting Native communities has been hotly debated in Canada in recent years. Did you talk with the people in Lac La Croix explicitly about these kinds of cross-cultural issues?
Judith. There have been ongoing discussions about community control in that band for a number of years, including control of the "community profile" and control of their representation in the media. After completing the film I worked at Lac La Croix on more technical projects such as giving workshops on video and putting together proposals for Native self-government, and I collaborated on a book of stories. To the extent that Native people need to develop skills, collaboration is necessary, as long as the representation on screen develops through negotiation.

I don't think that a one hundred per cent separatist approach is realistic or desirable at present. Yet the dominant society has always used the excuse that Natives don't have skills. Native media production won't happen unless Native directors are put in the driver's seat. There's great strategic importance in making strong statements about Native control over how they are represented since the general situation is not good. Although one can't generalize about these questions, I believe that collaboration and mixed crews are viable or at least necessary now. But as an immediate goal, Native people should hold the key creative positions and determine the voice of the film.

In both Eye of the Mask *and* Lac La Croix *you reveal a tension between U.S. popular culture and an older traditional culture that is being developed in a consciously political manner. Did you see these similarities when making* Lac La Croix?
Judith. Oh yes, absolutely. The two films almost share the same structure: the fly in and the drive into the countryside, the scenes in the Managua disco and the Johnny Cash performer in Lac La Croix. I'm concerned with the relations between culture and politics. In both Nicaragua and Lac La Croix, as everywhere else on earth, the culture is mixed. Furthermore, people at Lac La Croix don't want to go back to living in teepees, as the chief says. They want to maintain traditional understanding in the context of the modern world.

Those cultures need to be celebrated for what they are, without trying to disguise, transform, or erase the contradictions. Both cultures employ a complex feedback system that needs to be recognized. Lac La Croix's culture is a hybrid that at times has reinvented or reconstituted U.S. culture. Ron Geyshick's book *Te Bwe Win* shows this too, since his stories are about his dreams of deer spirits, flying ships that look like

Cadillacs, and shaking tent spirits who look like Ivan the wrestler. Some music in Lac La Croix is country-western in structure, but with traditional Ojibwa language.

Some white audiences find this cultural hybrid difficult. What do they want, a theme park? The notions of wilderness with Natives in it and the temptation to see these people solely as victims need to be addressed and deconstructed for the audience. Victims and heroes don't interest me, but that seems the norm for most audiences.

As filmmakers we need to examine and recognize pleasure in our culture. Political filmmakers in particular need to look at the potential for pleasure in our documentaries.

I found the film challenging to my notions of wilderness parks, and at first it seemed ironic that the Native community would be the one fighting to use outboard motors.
Judith. It's not that the Lac La Croix community hasn't changed over the last few years either. They are also more aware now of the need to maintain wilderness areas, it's just that the terms they use are different. Awareness of environmental issues such as the need to put restraints on fish resources has developed there. In fact, environmental concern is growing much faster in Native communities than in the South.

With the production of the tape Whitefish Bay: Self-Government, *was your relationship with the Native community the same as in Lac La Croix?*
Judith. No. *Lac La Croix* was a long-term project with a tremendous amount of travelling back and forth, which resulted in the video sketch, then the film, and finally the book I did with Ron Geyshick, *Te Bwe Win.* Each of the community-based projects I have done requires a different structure for negotiating representation. We worked out many of these issues in making *Lac La Croix*, where we had a larger budget and lots of time. Lac La Croix is a more traditional community, and we were making a more generalized portrait. We showed a rough cut in the community gym, made videos to circulate, and waited for comments to filter through in subtle ways. We talked to the elders about handling particular subjects. In Whitefish Bay we were working with the Native self-government negotiating team, and the purpose of the tape was to make the band members aware of the team's work. The primary audience was the two thousand band members of the Whitefish Bay reserve – it's not far from Lac La Croix, near Kenora. The secondary audience was other

bands now considering self-government, who would use it as an information tool. The Assembly of First Nations uses the tape. The Whitefish Bay self-government team have been at this a long time – at least four years – and we were drawn in near the middle. It will doubtless be four years before the negotiations are completed.

The community took a very strict negotiating approach for the production of the tape. Everything was discussed and tabled in written form before we did anything. We delivered a detailed script to them, we discussed narration, and we showed a rough cut. Some elements seemed problematic and they were changed. So in the end we were absolutely certain the band got what they wanted because of their involvement and negotiating.

Why were the Whitefish Bay people more formal?
Judith. Maybe because their negotiating team does this all the time with the federal government. Precision is the absolute centre of what they're doing. The negotiations must hold up in court, and any mistakes could have long-term consequences. The last thing they need is a video that contains different wording from what they want. That can be difficult, because interview subjects are not so precise.

The tape had a minuscule budget. And because of that there's more narration than I'd like, though we tried to keep it under control and we used less than is conventional. Since many lawyers, ministers, et al. have been involved in the negotiations it was important to me and to the chief that you see and hear band members speak.

This is an unusual tape. Nothing I've seen discusses these issues, certainly not at the band level. Maurice Bulbulian's *Dancing Around the Table* was inspirational, but it concentrates on the national issues.

It's good to see Native people on the screen who are dealing with law and cooler, unemotional, technical subjects, since the predominant media image of Native people is hot emotion and spirituality.
Judith. The Whitefish Bay negotiating team have extensive legal experience and are very articulate. So yes, there's not much emotion. You're right, there's a heavy leaning in Native materials to a defensive approach, talking about the problems of the past or presenting alternative visions of social structure, perhaps as a way of compelling hopefulness to the changes that self-government might bring about. Whitefish Bay wasn't interested in that kind of tape. They weren't trying to ratio-

nalize for outsiders what they were doing; they were trying to explain to their own people what's going on with this very complicated stuff.

It's a very cool tape. It doesn't even deal with what they're negotiating for. It doesn't provide details on specific goals, for instance the goal of self-managed health and social services, a tribal court, or specific plans for economic development. They are careful not to say exactly how these would operate. They don't want self-government to be judged on whatever specific structures they have in mind at present. Rather, they talk about the negotiating process. They want control over the land, in order to open the possibility of direct investment. Talking about law is almost as dry as reading it, so we were challenged to find a concise interesting form to present intricate legal problems.

Did the community feel any pressure to make something jazzier to compete for the attention of young people on the reserve?
Judith. No. And they also wanted to avoid any comparison with the high rhetoric associated with the Oka situation that was happening then. They didn't want to lose sight of their goals, and nobody knew what the impact of Oka was going to be. They're quite hard-boiled in Whitefish Bay. I don't think they cared whether anybody enjoyed the tape. It was for adult education – the voting constituency. They knew not everyone could read, or would want to read all the legal stuff, and it's a large reserve with two towns. They didn't find the tape boring. I'm sure they would have been dissatisfied if the tape was whiny in any way, or if it focused on pain or atrocities.

Did the Whitefish Bay band raise all the money?
Judith. Yes, and I was paid from those funds, based on a set budget. So when the Trinity Square Video equipment costs went higher, I had to absorb that. I have no economic relationship to the tape now. They are handling all the distribution and doing just fine. I sometimes have a rather dichotomous relationship with clients. It can feel like a hired gun. On the one hand the community is actively involved in shaping the tape, on the other hand they say, "You do it. You figure it out."

When you use the expression hired gun, does that mean that your relationship is the same as between the band and their lawyers?
Judith. It's not that much different. The lawyers are there longer. It's the "white technician" model, though it doesn't matter that you're white.

Since I've been working on these kinds of community-based projects for
some time now, and since each one takes at least six months, I focus
now on developing a more formal idea from the beginning of what I want
on the table and what they should put on the table. Both sides need the
representation to be as fair as possible with the roles clearly spelled out,
for example how editorial decisions will be made and how my own pref-
erences can be tabled quickly. You acquire a knack for it. Most people
don't have forever to participate so you must use the time effectively.
Lac La Croix was intensely pleased in making a community portrait,
which had room for imperfections, questions, and contradictions. Their
isolation was a major part of their political problem, so a portrait was
important politically in gaining visibility. Conversely, in Whitefish Bay
they are playing hardball in specific negotiations. It was a very different
kind of work.

*You've received a fair bit of attention in the press from art critics, and a
cover on* NOW *magazine. Do you work at that? Do you see yourself as
ambitious?*
Judith. On the one hand I do have influence since I sit on arts council
juries and I've worked as an advisor for the Ontario Arts Council. But on
the other hand at times I feel like an outsider in the art world. I'm not on
their planet or part of their beat with these films. Community-based
films and tapes are still given only marginal consideration, which is
understandable to a point, but I've written on this type of work to try and
redress the lack of critical consideration of it. With *Lac La Croix* I
wanted accessible language rather than a high-theory gloss; clarity
rather than inside remarks directed to my filmmaking peers. In terms of
form and structure I took a middle road and the film was criticized for
that. Kass Banning wrote in *Cinema Canada* that my film and Midi
Onodera's *Displaced View* looked like they were trying to get aired on
PBS. [3] I found that off target and short-sighted.

The teaching I've been doing at the Ontario College of Art has been
very rewarding and has allowed me to work through many issues. Students have an incredible appetite for the real and for films that deal with
politics and show contradictions. I could show documentaries all year
long. In my opinion documentary is not by definition an unexperimen-
tal format.

In making these films I've created permanent relationships that
don't end when the editing's completed. And that's one of the most

terrifying aspects of making this kind of film. I'm working on a drama-documentary hybrid set in Wasaga Beach, a resort community where my family has had a cottage for thirty years. At Wasaga the contradictions of present-day political realities are impossible to escape. In this film I'll be representing a community, but taking a more personal and local approach, with fiction elements and imaginative structures. So this will be an extension of my experiments with form and documentation.

"The names have been changed to protect the guilty."

Richard Fung, born in Trinidad in 1954, attended school in Ireland and immigrated to Canada to study architecture at the University of Toronto. Since the mid-1980s he has written and lectured extensively on the representation of race and of gay men in cinema and video art. Fung's tapes, like those of Sara Diamond and John Greyson, explore new ground in their merger of an art-video aesthetic with the more traditional concerns of social-issue film documentary. His work has been eagerly taken up by Asian, Caribbean, and gay audiences across North America, and his programming and distribution work and public lectures have made him a well-known figure.

With his first tape, *Orientations* (1982), Fung revealed the lives of gay and lesbian Asians to a larger public, at the same time encouraging both testimony and self-validation within that particular community. Structured as a conventional string of talking heads, the tape allows each of the people interviewed ample time to relate experiences and analyse their own situations. Yet even with this rather loose storytelling quality, Fung manages to impose a more formal thematic structure on the material, allowing him to concentrate on the relations between gender and race.

Chinese Characters (1986) works in many ways as a commentary on *Orientations* and shows Fung's growing unease and suspicion of conventional documentary. The tape is a tightly constructed essay using documentary footage, staged scenes, and "fake documentary interviews" about pornography and gay Asians. Rather than presenting "actual" interviews, Fung sets up a parody of a gay testimony, with himself on camera revealing explicit sexual fantasies. Viewers are often unsure whether to take the character seriously. Where *Orientations* seemed designed as much for a straight audience as a gay one, *Chinese Characters* speaks primarily to gays. Not surprisingly, the tape drew hostile reactions when it was shown at the National Gallery in Ottawa.

The Way to My Father's Village (1987) and *My Mother's Place* (1990) continue Fung's movement of placing himself on centre stage. These family biographies make him a subject and a real character on screen. In the tradition of expository documentary, the tapes are organized to examine his family history – China, to Trinidad, to Canada – and the various ways we can attempt to gain historical knowledge. *The Way* reveals most clearly the tension in Fung's tapes between a loose structure in which people are given time to speak and tell stories and a much cooler, formal structure that forces viewers to think critically about history and individual memory. As he states in the voice-over narration, "The names have been changed to protect the guilty."

My Mother's Place, which deals with Rita Fung's life in Trinidad and Canada, is both the most accessible and the most sophisticated of his work. Rita Fung talks about life as a Chinese immigrant in Trinidad, ideas about raising children in the 1940s and 1950s, running the family store, and relations with her parents and husband. The juxtaposition of his mother's anecdotal stories with a chorus of feminist experts achieves a precarious balance between the voice of experience and the voice of theory. This is a balance rarely attempted – much less achieved – in conventional documentary, which usually places short clips of experience in the context of heavier evidence from white male experts (doctors, lawyers, sociologists, and the like).

Like many video producers, your first experience with the medium was in art school. Was your education at the Ontario College of Art a fruitful experience?
Richard. I wanted to be an architect and was studying graphic design, but I gradually became more interested in film. In 1975 I discovered some good film and video teachers at the college. Sylvia Spring in particular was doing a course in guerrilla TV and her aim was to get us out into

the community, so for example we covered the University of Toronto library strike. What we were doing in that class set us apart from the video-art students. In general OCA was an alienating place and the emphasis was on capital "A" art. Yet I met many students who were interested in politics, some of whom I'm still in touch with.

After completing art school you worked in community-access cable TV. What sort of work did you do there?
Richard. I got a job in the Lawrence Heights community as a video animator. The idea among community leaders was to use video to improve neighbourhood morale, especially by working with kids. We did all sorts of things, like taping day-care activities, local plays, etc. My supervisor at Keeble Cable was Pat Dewey and she was very creative. It was an exciting time for cable video and she was intent on stretching the medium to include people not normally represented on TV. Keeble was later taken over by Rogers Cable, but Pat and I both continued even though at Rogers there was a slackening of vision.

I learned a lot in community cable. As well as covering religious shows, we taped Black parents' meetings, the first gay and lesbian TV show, and the big *Body Politic* benefit. [4]

Much of what I picked up in cable I still carry with me. Pat used to say, "This is not TV. The program should be as long as it is," or "The media should be a catalyst." We also felt a strong responsibility to the people we were shooting, and developed notions like "process over product," and the importance of "giving people a voice." Now I know that some of these notions can become patronizing, but they reflected my experience of being gay, and being Chinese but not typically Chinese.

What prompted you to make your first tape, Orientations?
Richard. John Greyson convinced me that I couldn't become a theorist, I had to do work. He encouraged me to start a project on the Asian gay and lesbian group I was involved with and he loaned me his home video-camera.

The group thought that a tape for internal discussion would be useful, and because we'd been doing consciousness-raising since 1979 I knew everyone quite well. Since there were no films or tapes on gay and lesbian Asians I wanted to expand the original idea. From my experiences in cable I put a high priority on setting up a good process, so I listened carefully to people's concerns about what they felt safe in talking about. Some of the people had not come out to their families, for example, so I allowed them a say in the editing. I explained carefully how the interview shooting would work.

One reviewer said that Orientations *was too much centred on Toronto and should have included people in small towns.*
Richard. True, but that wasn't the scope of the project. There aren't many gay Asians in small towns – it tends to be an urban experience. I wanted to include older people and working-class people, but I came to realize that would not be possible. Class power became very clear to me, and I realized why gay liberation in Canada had started in the universities, where people have fewer responsibilities, a strong sense of middle-class rights, and feel willing to take risks. Working-class people and immigrants had much more to lose, so I found it too difficult to get those people involved.

Are there particular conventions in mainstream documentaries that really bother you?
Richard. You mean that male voice-of-God narration, I suppose? [laughs] *Orientations* has no narration, which I later found out was fairly common, but I didn't really cut it out for theoretical reasons. It's the rhetoric of truth in documentary that bothers me. My aim was to include contradictions and viewpoints that I didn't agree with in order to open up questions for the viewer. With the more recent work, however, I'm more subtle about questioning this rhetoric of truth, so for instance I now prefer much longer interview segments. In *Chinese Characters* my concern was to take apart and dismantle conventions.

Political documentaries use little cliches that bother me. There's the romantic hero and then there's that macho filmmaking practice of the European boy's movie, where everything works as a kind of voyeuristic adventure with the down and out. Political journalists especially like to pretend they're part of the oppressed group when obviously they're not.

In some ways your work has become more staged and more personal. Does this mean that you're moving away from documentary?
Richard. I've been concerned with truth and the representation of truth, and it's depressing that in documentary people tell different stories in their public selves than in private. Also, when working closely with people it's difficult to represent contradictions and include varying versions of stories without undermining people. I've tried to question the

rhetoric of truth in subtle ways by giving viewers hints. For example, in
The Way to My Father's Village I talk about myself and about my relations to these other people and events. But I'm not sure audiences get it
all the time.

If I were making *Orientations* again I would use the same structure,
only I would make it slicker. But I wouldn't be as afraid of using long sections of talking heads, so I'd only use cut-aways when absolutely necessary.

In representations of people and communities that have been excluded
from the mainstream, how do you balance the need for positive images
and the need to represent contradictions?
Richard. The questions surrounding positive images and contradictions
are part of a long and complicated process. The first tape or film that is
made by a particular community often takes the form of a survey.
There's a need to develop basic representations, show variety, and establish a groundwork. Claire Prieto's films are very important in this regard
since they document an entire history and experience of Black women
in Canada that would otherwise be lost.

Something slightly different is the very strong pressure to tell what
I call "essential stories": to define the typical and the essential experience. That can be problematic. Wayne Wang's films *Dim Sung* and *Eat a*
Bowl of Tea reveal that to a certain extent. I enjoyed his films a lot, but at
the same time there's a way in which they retell history in fiction that
leaves out contradiction.

If you eliminate the difficult stuff, like in my tapes the drag and
raunchy sex, you end up using terms that are not yours. So I want to
move away from the large mainstream audience to specific ones. My
experience was never the typical one – neither Chinese, nor Trinidadian,
nor Canadian – so even when I saw films about race they never seemed
to be talking to or about me. My interest is in working from within a
community. I want us to tell ourselves our stories.

What prompted you to make Chinese Characters?
Richard. It grew out of a community debate about pornography and my
feeling that neither the sexual libertarians nor the pro-censorship people
reflected my experience as a person of colour. For us as gay men, porn
often gives the first sense of affirmation. This is especially true in rural
areas. Yet I also saw porn as problematic racially, with its complete
absence of non-white men, and yet interesting in the way gay Asians
would relate to it.

The making of this tape also stemmed from my desir
position in the video-art terrain – to introduce these expe
lery settings. But I wanted people to laugh as well; at P
orgasm with the sock on his head, for example. It's interesting that
white audiences don't come prepared to find it funny, but I tell people
they can laugh. Part of the plan was to do all sorts of stupid tricks,
although I'm not sure I want to have that kind of relationship with an
audience.

At what point do you decide on the structure of your tapes?
Richard. I've always liked triptychs and panels in art, as in Japanese
panel painting. It's a question of getting a total sense from the different
parts. My tapes work like that. I start with a grid, listing what I want to
accomplish and what I don't want the tape to do. After making *Orientations* and *Chinese Characters* I sensed my work was a bit blocky and
tight, and I was attracted to trying something more organic, but I
couldn't do it. My partner Tim is my nemesis and he always wants more
clarity, probably because he uses tapes for anti-racist education. With
My Mother's Place, two big problems arose. First, how to include even a
fraction of her information and stories, and second how to include other
contextual information about Trinidad and the women's movement in
the tape without making it look like my mother is being interpreted by
experts. I decided to segregate the other women in a section titled
"Reading Instructions" that gives the viewer some tools for understanding the piece. The tape as a whole flows along more smoothly than my
other work, but it is still segmented. One possible solution is to create a
sound environment within the tape in order to change moods. So I'm
trying to think about sound as an element of structure.

*The original proponents of cinéma vérité such as Jean Rouch talked
about the camera as a catalyst in drawing out certain truths, whereas
the Americans practising direct cinema wanted to minimize the presence of the camera to establish what they considered a more natural
situation. How has it worked for you?*
Richard. Well, in making *My Mother's Place* I immediately noticed that
my mother spoke differently in public, with her dialect suppressed and
with a more "correct" English. So I had to make a space for her to feel
comfortable on camera. I was very careful in choosing the crew and only
used people she would consider "nice" young people. I brought Lloyd
Wong along for her to talk to during the taping because I felt that would
work better than her retelling me all the same stories; she'd be trying the

whole time to figure out what I wanted her to say. She was very direct with Lloyd. He was a particular person, not just a generalized someone in an audience. My mother is pretty honest, which was a characteristic of her generation. She was not a Victorian. She told dirty jokes at home.

Having the camera there made her stories more concise, and she was less inclined to ramble. She's very tied up in her own history and finds it interesting herself, partly because she changed her class position. So this tape gave her a chance to say things for the record, which others aren't always interested in. Her memory is incredible.

Do you see any tension between working as an "independent" producer and accountability?
Richard. There's no conflict for me. Although I never end up as brave as I want to be. In my communities of gay/lesbian Asians I see contradictions and different points of view, for instance between Canadian-born Asians and immigrants, and sometimes an unnecessary "you versus them" situation. But in *Orientations* I stressed difference rather than problems. The priority centred on organizing and on the belief that no matter what the differences in the community the important task was to work together.

I feel accountable to my mother in her tape. That means taking a lot more time and trying to find a structure for including other material in the tape, information introduced by more educated people that will add to, but not undercut, my mother. That's something in documentary that annoys me: when you see a division between voices of experience and experts. In *My Mother's Place* I didn't directly juxtapose those two discourses.

Would you say you have censored yourself in your tapes?
Richard. Oh yeah! I say, "The details have been changed to protect the guilty." With my mother there's a way in which she tells the truth and doesn't tell the truth, and with my father in *The Way* I had to figure out formal strategies to hint that everything was not perfect in our family, without hurting my mother. In the gay-themed tapes I don't censor myself around politics or sex.

How much do you try and challenge audiences?
Richard. As much as I can get away with. I tend to work with so-called marginal audiences who are very much in need of seeing images that concern them. But since a certain amount of content is there I feel I can

make people work a little more. Trinh T. Minh-ha's writings and films have influenced me, in the films especially by the way she has combined different voices all carrying specific kinds of knowledge that don't contradict each other but fly past. Yet I could never make work like hers. She doesn't want to make any concessions to the audience: I'm much more gentle on them.

Experimentation for its own sake doesn't appear in my work: it's always trying for a specific effect. *The Way* consists of five parts, and to me that represents the five ways that children of immigrants acquire knowledge. I include oral history and memory, and I use a male voice-of-God for communicating facts and figures of history, which is valid to a certain extent. The voice-of-God is not deconstructed completely. Sometimes the narration comes first, sometimes it follows the images. So the five sections fill in different spaces, and I hope to get people to think about form.

For *The Way* and *My Mother's Place* the West Indian audiences come first for me. I was scared to show them the tapes at first, but they turned out to be the warmest audiences. They laughed at all the little gestures that I thought were subtly funny. The discussions after screenings have led people to think about their family histories and come up to me to tell me their stories, often filling in details about communities that haven't been documented. There's an incredible amount of narrative in that Trinidadian community. My experiences with the Caribbean audiences have been good because they appreciate subtlety, although in some ways people simply jump past the experimentation and into the "content."

I know that Claire Prieto wants to reach broad audiences and she correctly judges the priority of getting the basic information into schools and seen by children. I used to be much more negative about that, but now I think different films and forms carry different strengths. I usually try for both.

On the other hand, with *Chinese Characters* I was depressed about the effectiveness of the experimental aspects. Even people who are supposed to be sophisticated missed the subtleties, like the reviewer in *Cinema Canada* who didn't realize that the staged interviews were acted by me.

Have you been influenced by film or video theory?
Richard. I already mentioned Trinh T. Minh-ha's writing, and Bill Nichols's *Ideology and the Image* was useful for me. Peter Watkins's

film *The Journey* I found immensely interesting – his pacing, use of black, and the way he constructed an environment with sound. But the producers I feel closest to are the Black British people, especially Issac Julian and Kobena Mercer.

How would you evaluate the status of your work? Are you ambitious?
Richard. I don't push my work enough, and it's probably something in my family, which I don't feel happy about. It's a fault. I see some people who are ambitious and don't have anything to be ambitious about. After the controversy over *Chinese Characters* at the National Gallery and all the hate letters that were sent to the programmer Susan Ditta and myself, I sort of wished that I had been a better "hype-er." But on the other hand the gallery was very supportive and stood by the tape so I didn't think a real issue existed.

Documentary video doesn't get taken up like the experimental work. The arts councils are mainly interested in video art, which is a contentious thing to say but I'll say it anyway. Since ethnicity forms the main topic of my tapes, people in power aren't interested. On those arts council juries, artists support each other, which perpetuates the cliquishness. John Bentley Mays in *The Globe and Mail* would never write about this stuff. Most galleries find the tapes too long, but I'm certainly not interested in making them shorter just for them.

I can see a resurgence of interest in documentary and somewhat of a convergence between documentaries and video art, but I'm not sure how widespread that is, maybe just in Toronto. Judith Doyle, Betty Julian, Glace Lawrence, and Midi Onodera certainly come to mind. Documentary has somehow become fashionable again, like World Beat music. Internationalism and "Others" are fashionable. But that's cynical maybe.

Most producers don't survive on their work. I see Kim Tomczak and Lisa Steele who are at the top of the video world and they have to teach and work in distribution to live. Others seem able to operate in mainstream TV and not lose their souls, and there's people I respect working there. But mostly I'm completely depressed when I see TV so I don't feel I could do it.

I *could* do another tape on sex and race and I know that would be hot and it would get shown – sex is trendy too. But I'm more interested in producing the West Indian material, partly since that audience *doesn't* represent a power block in galleries and museums. I started out three years ago planning to spend only one year on these tapes about my father and mother, but it just got more and more interesting.

"The bourgeoisie is not my audience."

John Greyson, born in London, Ontario, in 1960, has become one of the most active and well-known video producers in North America. He has worked frenetically on a number of arts and political fronts since 1980, as a producer, curator, promoter for others, writer, distributor, and agitator. He has taught video at California Institute of the Arts in Los Angeles and attended the Centre for Advanced Film Studies in Toronto. His most ambitious films, *Urinal* (1989) and *The Making of Monsters* (1991), were enthusiastically received at the Berlin Film Festival.

Greyson's tapes and films centre primarily on gay and lesbian experience, but his formal strategies swing wildly between direct cinema documentary and the highly constructed and layered conventions of art video. Greyson also represents a second generation of Canadian videomakers intent on subverting the dominance of cinema by stirring the conventions of video art into cinematic fiction and documentary.

Even Greyson's earliest tapes revealed his iconoclast's bent. *The Visitation* (1980) is a pseudo-documentary combined with performance sequences on gay life in Toronto, as narrated by a fictional gay radio station. *Manzana por Manzana* (1982) and *To Pick Is Not to Choose* (1983) function as much more conventional documentaries, on Nicaraguan and Ontario farmworkers respectively. Both tapes were created in close collaboration with the local farmworkers organizations. Yet even with these tapes Greyson inserts striking, often humorous interventions into the talking-head testimonies – singing intervals by a young Nicaraguan and by 1960s TV-style corny farmers.

Moscow Does Not Believe in Queers (1986) is both a "construction" that uses documentary sequences and a documentary frame that uses constructions. The tape is based on Greyson's trip to a Soviet youth conference, but also employs performance and staged vignettes mixed with liberal doses of Rock Hudson submarine movies. The film *Urinal* (1989), his best-known work, takes the documentary/drama equation into even more complicated realms – a true hybrid based on the arrests of gay men in Ontario public washrooms, yet featuring analysis by Sergei Eisenstein, Langston Hughes, and other historical figures from the gay and lesbian communities. These characters, most meeting for the first time, then proceed to interact in ways all too human for such exalted, deceased figures.

The use of comedy provides a common thread in all Greyson's work. Mainstream criticism usually stumbles over a political artist with a sense of humour and can barely contemplate art and political responsibility in one sentence. For the left as well, humorous art, especially of the camp and tacky variety, never seems quite proper. Another basis for Greyson's work stems from the productive tension between his role as independent artist and his obvious *and specific* accountability to political movements. The videotape *The World Is Sick (Sic)* (1989) focuses on the Fifth International Conference on AIDS, held in Montreal in 1989. It features analysis by members of Toronto's AIDS Action Now group, a CBC-style narrator in drag, Pink Panther cartoons, and a dizzy array of cheap video effects. In 1989 Greyson also completed *The Pink Pimpernel*, a mini-drama in which the lead character plays a dandy activist smuggling AIDS treatment drugs into Canada. His escapades jostle with documentary and performance sequences. Greyson certainly operates within a political discourse and has no trouble defining his art in that way.

Was there anything in your background that led you towards comedy, art, and being a provocateur?
John. We got a lot of encouragement at home to paint, write, and do plays, and I went to a technical high school rather than the university route. It was when I came out into the gay community in Toronto that I started to put art and humour together. In the late seventies there was an incredibly well established gay community, so the humour in the tapes

and performance pieces was partly a way of taking that on, and to a certain extent laughing at some of the arrogant aspects of gay culture. You always reject your elders, I suppose. But I want to emphasize that the humour in my work is always fond, never vicious or mean, in relation to the community.

Are there particular conventions in mainstream documentaries that really bother you? Have you been able to challenge these in your work?
John. Voice-of-God narration is pretty high up on my bad list. At the same time I can think of good reasons to use it, as a way to shape content and capture information, etc. I'm most interested in taking conventions and playing with them – not rejecting them. I think that's more useful. In *The World Is Sick (Sic)*, for example, I use an authoritative CBC-type narrator to provide lots of information, but at the same time that narrator is critiqued and the immense bias concerning AIDS is exposed.

Conventions should be kept in historical perspective. If you look at *The Journal* or at music video you see that the mainstream continually appropriates and there's plenty of flux. It's not quite as fixed as some formal theorists think. This year's bourgeois conventions are sometimes last year's cutting edge. The extent to which TV advertising appropriates the underground is phenomenal. But I'm just as interested in how people take chances with content.

How do you see your role as an independent producer working with community groups? For instance, do you feel accountable to a particular sector of the gay community?
John. Before *Urinal* my work broke into two camps, the gay-themed work and the more conventional documentaries. Most of the work I've done comes out of committees (including the non-gay work for Nicaraguan solidarity and with the Ontario farmworkers), and I see my role as part of a dialogue with these groups. For the gay work I see myself as a speaker in a roomful of people. I try to propose a set of ideas and challenges. With the gay-themed work I've felt that I could cut loose much more, but I would never dream of working that way where I wasn't centrally involved – for example, with the farmworkers.

In social-change documentaries there is often a divide between the maker and subjects, and the trick is to try and erase that divide. I'm more and more uncomfortable with that. In fact, I'm not sure I'd do another tape on Nicaragua or farmworkers or any other subject so far outside my experience. I feel that discomfort even with gay themes, because my own specificity hardly "speaks for" any gay community, so for example in *The World Is Sick (Sic)* I set up a parallel discourse about the narrator, which I hope suggests an internal criticism. Also, at the beginning of the tape I say, "This is a Toronto-centric version of the conference, proceed with caution."

The struggle to define one's own image is most important, and yet I think it's too simplistic to prescribe what people can or can't do or say. I think in the recent controversies [about cross-cultural representation and appropriation of voice] there's been an assumption that everyone is working with realist forms. In fact, many artists are trying to deconstruct assumptions about realism, about truth, about identity. The indignation of certain loud-mouthed white writers in the Writers Union, for example, has distorted what the real issues of the debate actually are. A much more productive dialogue is happening between a newer generation of artists and critics, interrogating how representations are constructed and who constructs them.

When you were making The World Is Sick (Sic), *did you discuss the structure or the politics of the tape with people in the AIDS committees? Or did they give you a free hand?*
John. It wasn't a formal relationship, since I was a member of AIDS Action Now working inside the group. I spent a lot of time talking to other people in the group, working on the campaigns, and doing interviews to find out about the group's priorities, trying out ideas on them. Sometimes Tim McCaskell and George Smith would just roll their eyes and say, "Oh god, that Greyson, he's going to do his own thing no matter what we say."

The World Is Sick (Sic) leaves out the struggles that went on behind the scenes among the activists at the Montreal conference, especially the conflicts between the New York ACT UP delegation and everyone else. It was of little importance compared to the immense success of our collaborative interventions that week.

Did you consider that self-censorship?
John. Censorship is such a buzzword. In any case I much prefer the notion of strategic compromise. It's a question of engaging and negotiating with your subjects, since you share their subjectivity. Making tapes like *The World* involves a social contract of responsibilities, of respect for differences within a group. Imposing a particular political or artistic vision is inevitable, and can't be erased, but it can also become selfish.

To me anyone who "stays true to their vision" at the expense of their subjects is a pig and ends up walking all over people!

With *The World* I was very much involved in the committee and wanted to capture all the work we had been doing – the experience and the overlapping agendas. Yet obviously some of what's in that tape were my concerns, particularly the critique of the CBC and the attempt to show international activism in AIDS work.

The Pink Pimpernel was done at the same time and to some extent uses different artistic strategies for dealing with similar issues.
John. *Pink* was meant to be a propaganda tape for AIDS Action Now, whereas *The World* was designed to be a broader overview. *Pink* was designed to focus on the struggle over treatment drugs, so I was looking for a metaphor about those issues. During 1989 the media were full of the French Revolution bicentennial, which suggested the Scarlet Pimpernel to me and a humorous way to deal with my subject. AIDS Action Now wanted a larger audience, and we needed to give people a sense of what activism can mean in concrete terms. Of course, I inserted my own concerns into *Pink* as well, including a critique of the sweeping authority of safe-sex campaigns, the stuff about dandies, and the other in-jokes about filmmakers and lost gay history. It hasn't worked that well as a recruiting tape for the group. They need something shorter, more pragmatic and introductory.

Your latest work has adopted or played with the conventions of TV and music videos. That contrasts somewhat with your first tapes, which came out of video performance and social documentary. Does that change stem from the more advanced technology now available in the community access production centres, or do you feel that TV style should be the main discourse?
John. Early video history is all about the back and forth between high art and community documentary, and it's important to remember that some of the most interesting challenges to cinéma vérité came from video. Nowadays, music video is the only place where there's any visual innovation in the mainstream – I'm referring to their layering of images and uses of abstraction. Of course, the formal experimentation only takes place because everything is firmly anchored to the image of the lead singer and the logic of the format.

I'm interested in expanding my audience, making the work fun and engaging, and producing new content. I'm interested in taking images apart and putting them back together. I love special effects, particularly the *meaning* of special effects, as counterpoint and as an opportunity to expand how we look at the world. I often think of Vertov's *Man with a Movie Camera* and his immense commitment to technical innovation in getting across new ideas.

You say you don't want to separate technical effects from content, that you hope to get people involved. That's also related to the humour in your work, isn't it?
John. The dominant tradition in humour assumes a position at a mythical centre, like the mainstream stand-up comic. Then there's community humour that speaks in the vernacular, and speaks for all those people who weren't in the stand-up comic's audience, of disenfranchised audiences. My work differs slightly from both. My victims are institutions and conventions. The humour isn't witty repartee contained in dialogue between the characters. It grows from the construction of the scene – like making fun of cheap tricks in music videos.

I've never liked the arrogance of the straight white avant-garde film tradition. For me, if the subject proves difficult or demanding I try to use humour as a bridge over the tough spots. That way audiences are more likely to stick it out. It comes back to accountability. Artists have an immense responsibility to communicate and respond to their audiences. That's what I mean by strategic compromise – negotiating that responsibility.

I like the surrealists. Magritte's a good example. He was both incredibly philosophical and playful. He knew that his audiences weren't going to follow too far with scientific theories of perception, etc. so he made his paintings engaging and popular.

Why don't more artists use humour?
John. Humour has been one of the central strategies of video and performance art for the past decade – look at Tanya Mars and Marg Moores, for example. Social-change documentarians have often been terrified of humour, since it only seemed like laughing at their subjects who were oppressed; there's nothing funny about oppression. It's almost been taboo. Work coming out of oppressed communities seems more likely to use humour as a fight-back, empowering mechanism, helping to get people through. With AIDS, it's a way of getting us through this immensely horrible time we're living in.

One aspect of The World *that bothered me was the use of a man in drag for the on-screen TV reporter. That device of the woman in authority who's repressed but gets turned around by being sexually liberated seems pretty stale.*

John. Well, I think a man in drag is always an overdetermined image. I'd like to live in a world where a man in drag is only a sign for a man in drag. The lousiness of the drag was deliberate. Sometimes she or he looks like Harpo Marx. I wish I'd taken it much further and found a more constructive way to skew the position of the narrator. Of course drag history has different streams, like the incredibly bitchy tradition of straight drag in England. What you see in *The World* is different from that. The women I've talked to don't find the narrator in drag offensive, just weird and distracting. The issue has come up with audiences and it may detract from the more central issues in the tape, such as the focus on international grassroots activists. By the way, the CBC reporter is not "sexually" liberated in the tape – he joins the demo for reasons of political solidarity.

People in the CBC *are* repressed. They don't take chances and they're incredibly threatened by the spectre of video artists and independent producers. The thing that keeps our work off the air is their concept of editorial control – they haven't had their dirty paws all over the work from the beginning, and so as a result they don't want to air it. They know the importance of the issues we deal with, but they want to do it themselves and repackage it into their own boring and depoliticized formulas. We're threatening because we do things for ourselves.

How do you see the NFB in all this?
John. I have little hope for the NFB, and it's not just because they won't let gays in. They seem threatened by innovation and addicted to mediocrity, like the CBC. I would prefer the whole thing go under and have the money go to independent artists. The arts council system of arms-length funding and peer juries creates a more productive and equitable situation. That system can be lobbied and the community can have much more say in its structures. Also, it provides an entry point for first-time artists. Every other structure tends to perpetuate itself at the expense of artists.

Has your work been influenced by film or video theory?
John. Obviously. I can use *Urinal* as an example. I was interested in exploring why the issues of washroom sex weren't being taken up in the

gay community despite the efforts of Courtwatch and The Right to Privacy Committee – two groups that protested police surveillance and entrapment of men in washrooms. *Urinal* addresses the incompatibility of various intellectual discourses and refers to academic segregation. It attempts to de-centre the author's voice, by having the six characters serve as six narrators. I did a lot of research for *Urinal*: looking at Toronto crime tabloids from the fifties, analysis from a civil libertarian point of view, and I discovered Leroi Jones's play *The Toilet*. Foucault's analysis of the construction of sexuality in society became privileged in the film. I felt there were fundamental contradictions between these sources in approaching this complicated issue. The gay and lesbian characters embody those complications and contradict each other.

You are one of the best-known video producers in Canada and incredibly well connected. Cameron Bailey in Toronto's NOW *magazine put* The World *and* The Pink Pimpernel *in the 1989 top ten and called you "video's bad boy." Do you work at that? Would you consider yourself ambitious?*

John. It's inaccurate to call me video's bad boy. Lots of people are doing it. In Canada, Marc Paradis, Colin Campbell, Joe Sarrahan, and Paul Wong are some of the queer bad boys. Their work may not *appear* to have as obvious a political agenda as mine perhaps, but we have a lot of other things in common. For myself, I want dialogue with gay audiences. My work has never attempted to convert an uninformed or hostile public and bring them over to the wonderful world of gay liberation. The tapes wouldn't really recruit anyone. My work tries to invite people in. I want to engage with feminists, start a dialogue, such as, "Here's what gay men are up to, what do you think?"

Ambition is a word we're not supposed to think about. I always get defensive. Perhaps my work is known for a few reasons. I've produced eighteen works in ten years, so people can say "This guy must be doing *something*." Also, my work is fairly topical. Perhaps most important has been the very supportive infrastructure of gay and lesbian festivals that have brought out huge audiences. I want to reach a larger audience.

When I started working in the early eighties, artists were giving up on the notion of video as a discrete practice. They fell off the high modernist horse, started to re-engage with documentary issues and the dominant media, and began the rebirth of a much more engaged avant-garde. I was really lucky to start working in the eighties as a gay man. There's been a strong, confident gay community that keeps growing even in the face of AIDS. I've felt free to experiment.

"I want to show people who are not worrying about money."

Zach Kunuk is a small man, intense and direct, with a marvellously infectious sense of humour. He was born near Igloolik, Northwest Territories, in 1957, and before throwing himself into videomaking he had made a name for himself, and a modest income, as a sculptor. Although he describes carving and videomaking as very different activities, it seems that documentary patience was well served in his case by an apprenticeship in sculpture.

Kunuk clearly embodies the two major themes of innovative documentary and accountability to community. He speaks with passion about the need to record his people's life, past and present. Since 1983 he has worked in the Igloolik Production Centre of the Inuit Broadcasting Corporation and has produced more than fifty programs on culture, current affairs, and community entertainment. Since 1981 the Inuit Broadcasting Corporation has funded production in four regional centres in Northern Canada, with the programs shared by satellite reception. In January 1992 the IBC became part of TV Northern Canada, a broadcasting consortium of six aboriginal broadcasters plus the Northwest Territories and Yukon governments, the National Aboriginal Communications Society, and the CBC Northern Service. These institutions share programs on Native issues in several languages.

Walrus Hunter (1985) follows a group of men far out into open water and ice flows to record the details of a modern hunt. In voice-over an elderly man describes the action. The hunters navigate solely by the light and the sea current, and as part of a younger generation Kunuk was learning as he videotaped. "They don't use compasses or radios. I found that amazing."

The program *Inuit Life*, from the series *From Inuk Point of View* (1985–89), weaves material from *Walrus Hunter* plus fascinating sequences from an ice-fishing expedition into a complex portrait of Igloolik through four seasons. The tape begins with a long pan of the town, showing modest snow-covered homes on the edge of a lake. There is stunning northern light and long winter shadows. And on the sound track . . . the 1970s country-pop hit "Cover of the Rolling Stone." As in all Kunuk's tapes, children often take centre stage. One sequence begins with a series of close-ups on masks, then dissolves into a shot of a parade, obviously staged for the camera, moving into a Halloween party at the community centre. Summer sequences show the drying of fish and skins, community work, and festivals. These are punctuated by sequences created from close-ups of plants, flowers, and dried bones. A number of shots begin in close-up and zoom back to wide angle, revealing the landscape as context. Sometimes this works as a visual referent to hunters with binoculars.

With *Qaggiq* (1989), Kunuk managed to reach a much wider audience, and this celebrated work has travelled to festivals and museums all over the world. Produced in collaboration with the Montreal documentary producer Norman Cohn, the tape explores Inuit life near Igloolik around the turn of the century. It re-creates the gathering together of several nomadic families, the building of a communal igloo (*qaggiq*), and the celebrations that follow: games, singing, and drum dancing. Although the story-line was carefully scripted, the dialogue and interaction among the characters were improvised throughout. *Qaggiq* includes a set of marriage-proposal scenes between two families. Using non-professional actors, the scenes capture the complex ties of community custom, parents, and children in a culture now rapidly changing.

Most non-Inuit audiences (myself included) rarely understand immediately that *Qaggiq* is set in the past. It seems like a present-day, partly staged, ethnographic documentary. Perhaps this confusion is somewhat deliberate on Kunuk and Cohn's part, because there are no explanatory titles or narration. In fact *Qaggiq* feels like something close to the older documentary tradition made famous by Robert Flaherty in *Nanook of the North* and *Man of Aran*, the tradition of documenting a past culture by using local people to re-create their ancestors' lives and work. Before World War II, documentary readily accepted this level of staging and re-creation for the camera. But with the observational rhetoric prevalent after the 1950s, this type of re-creation fell out. A return to this level of staging certainly marks these works as new documentary.

Kunuk and Cohn plan a complete cycle of life in the Igloolik area, as it might have been ninety years ago. *Nunaqpa (Going Inland – Summer Hunt)* (1991) re-creates the lives of three families during the summer. As in *Qaggiq*, Kunuk sets up a situation, asks his actors to re-create, then observes. After pitching camp on the first night a woman elder says, "It's been a long time since I've been in a seal-skin tent. I feel like singing a song." Everyone seems relaxed and unfazed by the camera. Sprinkled throughout the tape we hear elders in voice-over talking about hunts like this they remember from the past. Kunuk also sets up a modest amount of parallel action by cutting between those out on the hunt and those back at camp waiting for their return; yet the dominant feeling remains one of observation – a demonstration of how things used to be done.

To southerners our interview may seem laced with ironies: the irony of using the U.S. soap operas *All My Children* or *The Guiding Light* as artistic models in a culture so far removed from New York; the irony that the Inuit find it easier to produce their own work than the more southerly First Nations; the irony that a man in his thirties and born "out on the land" could be producing such remarkably sophisticated media. Kunuk visited my hotel room in Montreal a day before the interview. Shortly after arriving he looked out the window on the eleventh floor, picked up his camera, and started laughing as he taped the long line of cars coming down the mountain on Crescent Street. "I only have one car in my settlement," he said. "Up there it's mostly trucks."

What connection do you see between your sculpture and your video work?
Zach. I see them as very different. Sculpture takes a lot of time – handling it, turning it around, creating an image, which will speak for itself. With video you're trying to make a point, to get your message across to viewers, to get understood. It's a very useful tool.

Most sculptors are very patient people. Is that useful in video work too?
Zach. Not really. Video is rush rush all the time. Going back to that same cut, doing it over. Playing it all back to see if it fits. In sculpture you

take time. If I'm really working at it, a carving will take two days, but one piece I worked on for two years. You do it because you enjoy doing it. That's how I see them differently.

The communication with the audience is not as direct.
Zach. Yes.

All the children who appear in your tapes seem to have a ball – a great time. How do you talk to them, to prepare? How much explaining do you do?
Zach. I notice that they act differently out on the land than in the settlement. When you take them out of town they're always happy. When we shot scenes for *Qaggiq* I just told them to go sliding, and when you see them playing ball, they're just playing ball. You don't need scripting for that.

Do they sense that they're going to be talking to or communicating to a larger audience?
Zach. When I start a production I make it clear what the story is, what I'm trying to deal with. My people are very co-operative, because they want to get the message out how they fit in. It's a recording, but from our point of view. I have no problem.

When did you get interested in video?
Zach. We had voted twice against TV coming into our community. But I travelled to other communities and saw TV. Then in 1981 I did some carving and flew to Montreal, to the [Inuit art] gallery on Sherbrooke Street. After, we just went around the corner and I bought a Sanyo colour camera. The guy in the store showed me how it runs, how to recharge the battery and everything, then I flew back home.

I wanted to record hunting scenes. Men go out hunting, come back at night, and sit around to tell stories. I wanted to go out with the hunters, record them, and come back and see it in the VCR. I started shooting, but every time I put the tape in playback it came out black and white. I couldn't understand that.

The following year, the IBC was created and they were showing a half-hour a week of programs and starting to show Inuit culture. They set up a base in Igloolik, with only one person, Paul Apak. There I was, I'm already doing it. So he hired me to be a camera operator, and then I really learned how to get the colour.

I was still carving but I got more and more into media programming.

I wanted to do it for real. We had to do a weekly program – meeting dead-lines every week. Then in 1985 I started my first independent produc-tion. I didn't really know what I was getting into. I got a small grant, then I took my camera out onto the land to shoot the summer hunt. But I didn't realize that for this much money they wanted a finished product.

In 1986 we were having a twenty-four-hour sun and Norman Cohn was in Igloolik. We were sitting around at four in the morning and we started writing a script. The following year we got a grant, we shot *Qag-giq* in 1988, and we finished editing in 1989. I first met Norman in 1985 when he came up to Cambridge Bay as a trainer on contract to the IBC. We get along pretty well. He shoots and I direct the actors. The only time I had trouble with him was when he tried to direct, then we had some arguments. But we both want the Inuit playing the lead role.

You're still working with IBC. What's the nature of that relationship? Are you an independent or a staff producer?
Zach. I run the station in Igloolik. Since I've worked there since 1983 they allow me to have my pick of material. I do my own productions on my holidays.

Have there been any tensions between you and the IBC over the approach to certain subjects? Do you have freedom?
Zach. They're pretty open with this because they understand what I'm trying to do. IBC doesn't have much money. So when I go to them with my plans it's pretty open.

Tell me about your family background, and the community you grew up in. Were you always interested in art and sculpture?
Zach. It goes back to my childhood days. I was born out on the land in a sod house. When I was five years old I saw my first white man and my first airplane and snowmobile. All these things were new. The govern-ment was moving in with its settlement program. Health and schools were big issues. All the people out on the land had to move into these communities, to sleep near the health centre. When I was nine we were still living on the land.

On one trip to Igloolik, I thought we were just going in to get sup-plies. But the next thing I knew my parents were leaving me.

It must have been a shock.
Zach. Well, I was with my brother. There I was to learn English. That was 1966. I started going to the community centre where they showed

16mm movies – it cost a quarter to get in – and then I started doing sculpture so I could go to the movies. I was always interested in movies.

So there's always been a connection.
Zach. Yes. I always wanted to create. So now when I go out onto the land I take the camera and I just love it. But it's a lot of work. A lot of takes. But it's worth it. It's there forever.

When you started making video, were there conventions in mainstream documentaries that particularly bothered you?
Zach. I later learned that there are lots of movies about the Inuit. There's the Ansen Balicki *Netsilik* series and Flaherty's *Nanook of the North.* I've seen those. Just before we made *Qaggiq* I had watched a lot of *All My Children* and *Guiding Light*, but especially *All My Children*, and it's great. They never leave the house and it's never boring. I wanted to create something like that. After we made *Qaggiq*, the southern media started saying that it's in a line from Robert Flaherty. But Flaherty did his film eight hundred miles from me, about a very different people. Netsiliks are close to us but they don't come near us, so they too have a different culture. We can understand them to speak, but they do their kind of work, we do ours.

In *Qaggiq* we have costumes of real clothes the way my ancestors looked. The Netsiliks are so many miles away. But I've been told that I'm copying Flaherty. What I wanted to do was record how my ancestors had lived, from the Inuit point of view.

Do you feel a pressure to make fiction or to make more dramatic work in order to compete for the attention of the younger viewers in the community? If the kids are watching the soaps or action films, is it necessary to develop that kind of highly dramatic style?
Zach. No, it's not. You see I'm not into any competition. What I want to do is record history that has never been recorded visually. It's not going to be the same, but it's going to be close to what I show. The Inuit were out on the land, not worried about money. All they worried about was the food that they were going to bring home and feed the family. Now it's a different issue. How to make a buck. Down the road I want to make a big one about today's issues. So right now I'm trying to get video images to do a year's circle, each season, in the area around Igloolik.

In the tape The Walrus Hunter, *which so far has no English translation, what's the gist of the narration?*

Zach. The narrator talks about how they hunt. How sometimes they have bad luck. How they cut up the walrus. And you know I've been on several of these trips and you just go out on to the open water – you get so far there's no landmarks. On the first trip I thought for sure we were lost. It's a lot of work, cutting, making bundles, then we still had to travel home on open sea. They knew how to get back using the light and the sea current. They don't use compasses or radios. I found that amazing – using their own knowledge.

The photography and editing of these tapes are quite intense, both the landscape and people. Do you feel that intense way of seeing the land is something that's common within your community, or is it a heightened sense that you develop as an artist?
Zach. A lot of people from down here say I have beautiful landscapes. But it's like that up north. The light is different and we try to show that.

There are a number of scenes where you draw attention to the land; where, for instance, you start with a close-up of a corner of a boat and then you draw back, emphasizing the context. Also for me it's a question of the pace in the editing. You don't rush.
Zach. I've noticed that southern filmmakers like to get a shot, then in the next two seconds a reaction shot – bang, cut, bang, cut, bang. We like to show it slowly, just run the camera. It's more real. The North and the South are two worlds. Many filmmakers and photographers come to the North but they never seem to change their style. I've seen books where the photographer just drives from community to community and snap, snap, snap. Of course whoever is doing something like that has to make it interesting, so they just add a little. What I wanted to do was *not* to add a little. Just show it. The way it is. My culture.

Qaggiq was included in a tour organized by the Museum of the American Indian in New York. Have you had any response from other Native audiences?
Zach. Inuit people are very open. And things are finally opening up after all these years. Even for the Mohawk at Oka. I couldn't believe that these events at Oka were coming from our own country. But I was getting angry watching the CBC news. All you saw was a map of Oka and the reporter's face. I didn't want the CBC-sided view. I wanted to find out the Mohawk point of view.

So much of that coverage was journalists talking to other journalists.
Zach. You know I was in Montreal in August 1990 and there was a demonstration of supporters at the Oka peace camp and we drove out there,
but the police wouldn't even allow us to get to the peace camp. So we
demonstrated at a park nearby. I pay tax and I see what they're spending
my money on – the wrong side.

*There are many Native filmmakers and videomakers starting to make
work who'll be heard from soon.*
Zach. Two years ago I flew to Vancouver and I sat down with the Native
producers in that area. But some were working in VHS and they'll be
lucky if their work ever gets broadcast. I saw we were lucky, because up
north we're broadcasting every day. The IBC could be a model, I think.

With Qaggiq, *how did you choose the actors? Had some of the older
people experienced those situations themselves?*
Zach. I know them all. I know everybody in my community, and I
picked those families especially for this tape. I went on the community
radio and said I was looking for young actors and anybody who's interested in acting can come. I needed three young boys and one girl. But
when I got to the community centre more than twenty girls and twenty
boys had showed up. So it was hard to choose. We had an audition where
we told them the story and then lined them up and told them to pose in
their "best shots." I videotaped their faces. Later that night at home we
watched the tapes to choose our actors.

*Did the kids have a sense that they were re-creating life from the past –
behaving as they imagined kids in the past would have behaved?*
Zach. Well I didn't have to worry about that. I got these kids out of
school, out of their everyday clothes, and put them in the caribou
clothes, which are very warm. They just ran around. They were happy
and that's all we wanted.

*How much did you explain or consult with the families or the commun-
ity at large? Was everyone aware of the purpose and the structure you
were going to use?*
Zach. We came up with this idea in 1986. I thought a lot about it, I drew
pictures, working towards it. One of the reasons everybody was so
co-operative was they wanted to show the culture. My people wanted to

dress up and show it. The actors in my tapes do a lot of their own research by talking to the elders about the old days.

Were there any disagreements about what to include?
Zach. No. When we started doing the takes – and they know we always have to do second takes – they knew they were going to act. But it was all so real some were scared. A proposal for marriage is a big thing for my people. So that scene was very important to me. It was not a game, and it seemed almost that the real thing was happening.

There's a great sense of spontaneity in the tape. You never see that in All My Children.
Zach. I know, I know. [laughs] They're acting. We're acting too.

I realize this question often comes up, but was there a sense when you were making Qaggiq *that southern audiences would not understand the time period that's being depicted? Were you concerned that people might not understand?*
Zach. The actors don't use modern tools, they use saws. But this was very low, low, low budget. If I had a million dollars I might have got it right. These people in the tape are 1990s people. I can only try and take them back to the time when traders just started coming. Also, what they remember.

Did you ever consider, for instance, putting a title at the beginning saying, "This is a re-creation of the way things were in the 1920s"?
Zach. No, I'm trying to record how my people have lived from their point of view. I thought about doing that at first. But after we shot it there were things that I couldn't change. My actors have seen trucks go by, they've seen money. I don't know how to explain it. I tried to take it as far as possible, as far as they could remember.

So it would have been misleading to say this is the way it was.
Zach. You see an image, especially today, of people way out on the land, probably doing the same things as people a hundred years ago, but they don't *think* the same. You put a guy out on the land, dress him up and get him cutting blocks, the igloo that he builds looks like one built a hundred years ago. The image I was trying to get probably looked like way back, but you know we are in the 1990s.

*Can you see yourself returning to more conventional documentary that
doesn't use such a mix of staged and unstaged sequences?*
Zach. In time I will, but I want to focus on the past first while we still
have our elders. There's always planning in documentary. And when
you apply for grants they want to see a script. Of course, I'll come up
with a script but when I go home [long pause] I let the people speak whatever they want to. They have to do it. So when you get down to the but-
tons of the editing, that's where the trick comes in.

For example, I was shooting the kids playing soccer with their Caribou ball and they were saying English words. So we just had to cut all
those English words out. It's all in the editing.

When you were making Qaggiq, *was there a sense of dissatisfaction
with your earlier work? Were you trying to get away from a more conventional documentary form?*
Zach. This was the first time for me. I'm still learning. When I created
Qaggiq my goal was for people to act in their own language – just like
their ancestors. If we're going to sit there on our sofas watching TV every
day I want to put something in that screen, all speaking Inuktitut, acting
in their own language. I want children to see how their ancestors looked.
I might as well bring their culture right to them in their homes. That
movie *Dances with Wolves* made me angry. I was really pissed off when I
saw the First Nations in the background once again.

Has Igloolik had any second thoughts about television?
Zach. From my understanding the half-hour a day will make us realize
that we have a culture we're going to hang on to. Now this year cable is
coming into town and we're going to have a choice of twelve channels.
First Choice, for example, and a lot of Detroit stuff.

Who wanted the cable?
Zach. You know, we voted for TV yet we only got CBC's channel. But
there's a lot of switches on a TV. [laughs] People realize more is possible,
so cable is great. It's not going to damage our programs. Because we're
already there.

*Are there Inuit producers in other countries that you have contact
with?*
Zach. I've met people from Alaska. But there's four IBC production sta-
tions in Northern Canada. We don't even have much contact with them.

What are the central issues facing Inuit producers?
Zach. Strictly money. The Secretary of State cut the IBC by half a million dollars this year [1990]. And I know that things have been very hard for Native producers down here. But from where I come from in the Northwest Territories the government is just getting into new programs, so having the right proposal should do the trick.

I'm doing this for my people, and for the South to understand. It takes a lot of time to make a program, and you put yourself on the line.

I'm interested to know to what extent you have to create an image for yourself as an artist, to hustle for money, etc. Are you ambitious?
Zach. I don't want to play the role model of independent producer. Other people should try. I would like to live too. I like to hop on my Ski-Doo for the weekend. I want the South to understand our culture. It's been manipulated and it will be manipulated in the future. It's never going to stop, but we're trying to get the information out, record, and act our way.

The reason I ask that question is that everyone I'm talking to is known to some extent.
Zach. This whole system is a game, you might as well play. You cannot win. You might as well join them. I'm after success. I am destined to go out there and bring it back. I want to create an understanding that we can play this game. In our organization I know people who get on the screen a lot doing current affairs, and when they go to another settlement people know their face. But they don't necessarily know the person. It's a temporary thing. When we make a program I stay behind. I don't show my face. So I can walk down the street. I'm not a star. I just want to be understood, that's all. I've never seen it – the way things were for my ancestors; my children have never seen it. I want to show people who are not worrying about money. People sharing. That's not much, I guess. I'll do my part.

This summer I shot another series, *Nunaqpa*, almost a sequel to *Qaggiq*. And to see the actors playing my ancestors, coming down the hill, in the traditional clothes, carrying things on their backs, children on their backs, women carrying packs. That last scene when they were crossing the river was real. Now we can all see these tapes.

"A medium with impact ..."

Brenda Longfellow was born in Copper Cliff, Ontario, in 1954 and studied history at Carleton University before taking up filmmaking. In addition to her three films, made in close collaboration with Glen Richards, Longfellow is well known in the Canadian film studies world for her writing and teaching. Her best writing employs a Canadian perspective on questions of international cinema theory.[5]

Breaking Out (1984), Longfellow's first film, set the tone for what was to follow. In it she mixes documentary-style testimony about women who have struggled to leave violent husbands with a written script and dramatic scenes that exemplify (rather than re-enact exactly) incidents from the women's pasts. In the manner of Bertolt Brecht the film also pulls the viewer back and forth between emotional identification with the women on screen and a more distanced analysis of the violence. The film is based on the stories of many women in Ottawa who had survived violent husbands and gone on to build lives as single mothers. Their stories became a composite testimony told in direct address by one woman, who was not an actress but another such survivor. *Breaking Out* also experiments with on-screen text – a strategy more often used in video work – which supplies general statistics but also comments on the story and the issue. The comments reveal the filmmaker's point of view in a direct, sometimes ironic – even sarcastic – form.

Our Marilyn (1989) takes many of the same techniques into an investigation of Marilyn Bell, the Canadian marathon swimmer of the 1950s. On one level the film juggles a complex theoretical argument about the representation of women in the media and the similarities and differences between Bell and Marilyn Monroe. Using TV footage and radio commentary along with the text of newspaper reports scrolling up or crawling across the screen, plus gallons of optically printed Super 8 swimming and water imagery, Our Marilyn recreates Bell's famous 1954 Lake Ontario swim during the annual Canadian National Exhibition (CNE). The fictional narrator, who is also named Marilyn, describes the highlights and the agonies of such a marathon, complete with hallucinations of monsters at the bottom of the lake; she remembers as well the difficulties of growing up in the Canada of the 1950s, as a girl caught between the icons of the two Marilyns.

Longfellow followed Our Marilyn with another film focusing on a Canadian woman from the past. Gerda, about the "Gerda Munsinger affair" that rocked the normally staid halls of the Canadian Parliament in the 1960s, had its première at Toronto's Festival of Festivals in September 1992. The film freely mixes documentary photographs and film footage with dramatizations.

I interviewed Brenda at her home in the east end of Toronto when she was seven months pregnant. Hence our conversation near the end of the interview about birth imagery in her film Our Marilyn.

What pushed you towards film production?
Brenda. It was in Ottawa in the early eighties. I was finishing an M.A. in labour history but getting really bored with academia. Then I started working with the Ottawa Tenants Council, a wonderfully vibrant group of women living in public housing doing all sorts of anti-poverty political activities, including a lot of government lobbying. We felt we could fulfil some of our educational goals by producing a series of videos, working with Ottawa Cable Vision. But from there we moved into higher-budget productions. For instance, we produced a video cabaret with other groups in the Ottawa women's movement, called Red Rose Revue. For me it seemed like a way to combine politics and a very interesting medium. A medium with impact.

After, I left for Montreal and worked as an assistant editor, trying to learn as much as possible about film production. When I moved back to

Ottawa, the Tenants Council had raised enough money to do a film on domestic violence, and they asked me to direct it. That became *Breaking Out*.

How did you find Carol, who plays the central woman in Breaking Out?
Brenda. Carol had always been involved with the Tenants Council. She had worked on the Cable Vision shows. She's a very dynamic character. But at first we weren't sure how Carol would fit into the film.

There were originally sixteen interviews, but many of those women didn't want to appear on camera. For example, there's one story embedded in the film of a woman who lived on the army base, and the only thing her husband would let her do was rifle practice, until one night she came back with the rifle and pointed it at him. But that incident was twenty years before, and the woman had re-established herself so she didn't want to be on camera.

So we decided to script and use Carol as a kind of archetypal figure. Most of the women's stories were similar. They had all married young and started having children. They didn't have a chance to experience other life. Seventy-five per cent of them had lived with violent men, then found themselves single and having to deal with all those complications. So it was easy to draw out the common features and script around it. Since Carol had lived it herself, she was quite willing to become a spokesperson for all those experiences.

Did she have apprehensions?
Brenda. Oh sure. She'd never done anything like this before. It was a huge challenge for her – for us all, to that extent. Carol and I spent two weeks just talking before we shot – talking to work through stuff and rehearse. At the end I was very touched because she came up and said how much the experience had meant to her and how she had grown. It had been very demanding, especially with the short shooting schedule. After all, she wasn't an actor. She had to appear reasonably relaxed on camera. The film succeeded partly because we used a lot of her dialogue as voice-over. That allowed her to refer to the text.

I think she works very well. There's a fruitful tension between knowing she has rehearsed to some extent but also knowing that she's not an actor and this is not a professional rehearsal. I think that's fascinating for an audience and probably makes it easier to deal with the ideas and issues.

Brenda. Yes. I think she's more believable. Early on we had worked with actors from the Great Canadian Theatre Company who were middle-class women trying to act these roles of abused working-class women. There was always something lacking in their presentation: the way they use language, use their body, a whole number of factors. It's very diffi-cult for an actor to project herself into such a working-class person, who's had to deal with the brutal reality of poverty.

So we knew from the beginning that we wanted to work with Carol. She had that kind of edge.

Were there any other more formal discussions or negotiations regarding consent?
Brenda. Because there was a script, Carol and the other women knew what we would be doing. She liked appearing on camera. Since she'd been an activist in the organization she knew why we were doing it. Carol understood the power of the medium and the role of film. She had been active in producing other tapes. Although she didn't work on the script for *Breaking Out* in general, she was a collaborator.

What was the role of the Tenants Council in the making of the film?
Brenda. They had instigated it, raised the initial funding, and had carried out extensive interviews. The centre was employing me in a sense. It was very much a collaborative process working with those women. They stayed directly involved. But the film took five years to complete, and during that time my partner, Glen Richards, and I raised money our-selves from the Canada Council, etc. It took a long time. We applied for funds and were rejected, then applied again and were successful, and we finished the editing in Toronto.

The more difficult and interesting collaboration centred on my rela-tions with the two activists, Aline Atkinson and Dorothy O'Connoll, the most prominent anti-poverty activists in Ottawa. We showed them the cuts. It never boiled down to a question of editorial control, but we certainly had disagreements. For instance, I wanted to cut the church scenes – I'm an atheist, we live in a secular society – but the church did play a role for some of the women. It was a very limited shooting ratio, mostly scripted, so there weren't a lot of surprises for people as we went along.

Aline and Dorothy had started the film with a whole list of ele-ments and issues that they wanted to include. But I knew it had to be kept simple. Being confronted with this shopping list of issues, plus trying to deal with the emotional aspects of it, were the biggest areas of tussle and tension.

In some ways the film represents a hybrid between my desire to focus on one or two issues and their desire to put everything in. It was a huge leap for them from the $500 videos they had done previously. I worked closely with Glen, who edited the film. We knew we didn't want to burden viewers. We wanted to find other ways of communicating information that weren't didactic or dull.

Did you have your own list of conventions you wanted to avoid? Are there conventions in mainstream documentary that particularly bother you?
Brenda. Why sure! Which one do you want to start with? Often the experiences of production feed you different strategies, and then after the fact you can rationalize them theoretically. Certainly, with my background in writing criticism and seeing innovative work I was inclined to experiment. To me the question of experimenting means being open.

The whole process of making this film was important. And that meant different kinds of decision-making with all kinds of logistical difficulties. We had an all-woman crew. We knew that for political reasons we didn't want a narrated voice-over. The women should speak for themselves, but through this dramatic mode, which could condense their experiences and highlight them emotionally. We didn't want everything broken up with a variety of women all addressing the same issue. Instead, we wanted a dramatic pull to explore the whole emotional and psychological experience, such as being left alone with children, and how it felt. We didn't want just the dry political economy of the situation.

It's interesting that you say you were trying to keep it simple, because I can imagine activists and other filmmakers looking at that situation and thinking that the simple way to do it would be the conventional way. What you've come up with is not at all simple in its structure. And it's scripted. You present information in an unusual way. There's no guarantee that audiences will accept that.
Brenda. I remember the first time we screened it for a funding agency. The whole board of directors was absolutely split, because some thought it was man-hating and it was presenting men as absolute ogres. They never addressed its form.

*I think I told you that when we were distributing it in DEC Films, one
Ontario government ministry rejected the film because it implied that
the government was lax in providing enough shelters.*
Brenda. Ha! Well, that was the point. There aren't enough shelters and
many that do exist are substandard.

*Why did you include the staged scenes of domestic violence? What
specifically do you feel they add?*
Brenda. It was to deliver the issues in narrative terms. Originally we
weren't going to focus on violence as the chief cause of problems for
single women, but because we wanted a dramatic element to instigate
the whole process of leaving we wrote those scenes. Abuse is not the
only reason for being single, of course, but being abused was a prominent
reason why these women were now single. Because abuse showed up
consistently in the interviews and because it worked dramatically, we
went that way.

   We wanted to be careful representing the violence and do it in a distanced way – to show only an edge of the violence. So we shot from outside the house. You get a tension between a suburban exterior and what
goes on inside these lovely domestic universes. The dialogue is fairly
banal, but the sequence points to a kind of escalation.

*Did the editing suggest any new formal strategies or turn up different
meanings from your original plan?*
Brenda. The film certainly went through several cuts, and I learned a lot
from Glen's work. We weren't sure how to work in Arlene Mantel's
music, and we only decided on using intertitles at the editing stage.
They were a nightmare to shoot. We wanted some kind of Brechtian
break that would provide another level of information: something that
would move from personal drama to the larger socio-economic realities.
Sometimes the intertitles also comment on the dramatic action. I
remember seeing JoAnn Elam's film *Rape* and liking her approach.

Who came first in your idea for Our Marilyn, *Marilyn Bell or Marilyn
Monroe?*
Brenda. Again, that was a coincidence. Bell was first. Monroe came
when I was doing stock-footage research and I discovered a newsreel
from 1954 that had both of them – Monroe in Korea and Bell in Lake
Ontario. That was very early in my research.

At times the narrator refers to Monroe as "their" Marilyn, but at other times she speaks about "living between the two Marilyns." Is that a contradiction?

Brenda. I wanted to play with this whole notion of property and whose Marilyn was what. It gets mixed up all the way through. It's also in the song playing over Monroe's image and talking about Canada. Both were vibrant public figures of femininity in Canada at that time. I was trying to think through their differences in relation to national difference: the way in which U.S. icons permeate Canada. In some ways Monroe is as much Canada's as Bell is. Monroe became an object for the world. I didn't want this to seem natural. I wanted to question ownership and national difference, and the way our fantasies of femininity get constructed. I questioned how nationalism was used in that period in Canada.

Who is "their" Marilyn?

Brenda. Mainly the Americans'. It could also refer to a certain historical period as well. To the fifties' audience, for example, who really appropriated Bell as an icon.

I thought it was going to be funny – an ironic joke about the fifties – growing up in this generation with Bell being pointed to as a perfect example of young Canadian womanhood. I heard many stories from my mother about Marilyn Bell. Once I started doing the research I realized the kind of national investment there was in this poor kid. The hoopla in the press was extraordinary. When we interviewed Marilyn Bell she talked about the ordeal in coping with this media adulation. There was a tremendous outpouring of support and fascination on the part of the Canadian public.

My admiration for Our Marilyn *stems from the rich blend of analysis and emotion that work side by side. I suspect that the original idea was fairly academic and planned, but that the emotion and power of the swim asserted themselves as you were working on it? Is that a fair guess?*

Brenda. I wouldn't call it academic. There was a theoretical start in thinking about popular images of women, how historical periods construct images of women, and how people responded to that image. The film also started out as a campy joke – you know, "The Fifties," nostalgia, a conservative period. There was no structural plan from the begin-ing other than knowing I wanted to do a lot of optical printing.

So much of the research and planning in these sorts of films speak to you in surprising ways – this happened in doing the optical printing. Then there was the limitations of the archival stock footage, which only covered Bell jumping in the lake and arriving on the other side. That's the way ideology functions, to eliminate the process of work – the per-fect shining images. I wanted to return to her experience of the physical ordeal of swimming and make it a focus.

The other way that I got fascinated was interviewing marathon swimmers, one of whom had kept a diary. Marilyn Bell could not remember the swim itself (after thirty years), but others were able to talk about the actual physical experience. I was fascinated with that pushing towards the edge of consciousness, the hallucinations – an incredibly visceral experience. Swimmer Vicky Keith had the best hal-lucinations, and I used some of those on the soundtrack.

I was surprised by the way that audiences got emotionally involved in the swim. I hadn't thought I was making a narrative, but it has a pro-gression, even though the time gets doubled back, folded over, and all the rest of it. There was a power and an identification with her, which was surprising. Audiences cheer when the U.S. swimmer is pulled from the water.

We're a little jaded now by all these sports spectacles, which I find pretty grotesque, compared to those days when Marilyn Bell did it. Bell did it because the CNE had hired an American to make the swim. She was incensed and set out to prove that Canadian swimmers were just as capable. Bell was eminently packageable for the fifties. She was this young, sweet, small, blonde from Loretto College. She was the little girl who made it across the big lake. She generated a wave of maternal feel-ing. Yet it's incredible that little else exists about her.

Have viewers commented on the allusions to birth in Our Marilyn? *There's an especially strong sense of a birth taking place that you hear on the sound track at the beginning.*
Brenda. That was intentional; a body moving through water, related to all that amniotic fluid. There is also the parallel of the woman giving birth to the third Marilyn, and the way in which the birth experience is repressed in society. There's the visceral hard work of labour, which I've spent a lot of time talking about these days. It's only recently that people

have started documenting the reality of birth. Woman's work in general provides the analogy. One woman viewer remarked to me that a lot of feminist art uses water imagery. Perhaps it taps some sort of primal memory of a physical experience.

Do you feel comfortable with critics or users applying labels such as experimental or avant-garde to the film?
Brenda. I think it's experimental. It crosses certain boundaries. Although it uses optical printing, I think of it as distinguished from Canada's mainstream experimental works. It's an experimental documentary, since it refers to actual historical events. In that sense it's different from the purely experimental work. The motivation is different. It uses archival sources in different ways – to question the way we write history, and to use those sources to tell a narrative. It uses experimental techniques to rethink and rework a national historical event. I think people find it interesting because it crosses those genres. It uses those techniques to different ends. It's not simply self-reflected. It's talking about history, and actuality.

I think the sound track adds considerably to the film. Did you have specific ideas in mind that you wanted to convey? How did you work with the musicians?
Brenda. I found a wonderful young woman to do the music. I was editing the film at Queen's University when I was teaching there. At first we had a synthesized track, which was too cool. And since the film was getting so much into the emotional I wanted something else. It has its own hypnotic pull, without the music. So I called up the journal *Music Works* and asked if they knew someone who could do film music and the woman answered, "Yes, me." And that was Gail Young. She's brilliant and makes instruments as well. Her music had an organic feel, an "other" visceral sound. We tried various things, looking for different components for different sequences. She foregrounded various instruments.

I see both Breaking Out *and* Our Marilyn *as representative of a convergence between social-issue documentary and avant-garde/experimental strategies in Canada. Do you agree?*
Brenda. I think there's a lot of other people doing documentary who are exploring the boundaries of documentary and drama. It's a question of more heterogenous practices within one film. This allows you to think on different levels, and in relation to other sets of issues, and certainly in

relation to representation about social issues. It allows you to think of how we arrive at social knowledge, and how we write history. It's such a media-saturated world that we have to think about our methods of representing that world. But experimenting and putting ideas together is fun.

You've had some critical attention and you've been able to pull down funding for your projects. Do you work at building an image or reputation for yourself? Are you ambitious?
Brenda. [laughs] That's a good question. I don't think I purposefully set out to build an image for myself. I'm often embarrassed, and I'm surprised *Our Marilyn* has done as well as it has. If you travel with the film there's an image that gets built against or with your will, and you're not really aware of it. It's a Canadian film dealing with issues that have been discussed internationally. One essay on it makes the comparison to Chris Marker's *Sans Soleil*, with its fictionalized narrator. Those kinds of things were fed to me by watching all sorts of international films. It borrows, steals, reworks, and presents a different angle.

I find it difficult to think of myself as a filmmaker. I make a film once every five years. It's a laborious, long process, and in between films I teach. I'm having a baby soon, so if I was ambitious . . . I don't know.

Our Marilyn got turned down for funding several times, and we never got money from the Canada Council. So *Breaking Out* provided no help in securing funds. Now with our new feature, *Gerda*, we came up against institutions saying "Who are you? What makes you think you can direct a $500,000 drama?"

For *Gerda* we had development funding from the Ontario Film Development Corporation and Telefilm Canada, but we couldn't find a Canadian broadcaster, which would have allowed us to tap into OFDC and Telefilm for production funds. No one wanted to touch the film – not because of its politics, but because it combined drama and documentary. "Why don't you make a seamless drama like *Scandal*?"[6] That was the general tone of the response. But the whole point of the film for me was to tell the story through heterogenous means. We eventually produced the film for $250,000 with financial support from the Canada Council, the Ontario Arts Council, and ZDF German television, which is designed to support innovative and political work. What a wonderful idea – producing *cinema* for television. In Canada we have the opposite idea – made-for-TV mush.

So you see, with every film we're always starting from zero. It certainly doesn't get any easier.

"It was painful
to make, I can
tell you that."

Alanis Obomsawin was born in 1932 in Lebanon, New York, but grew up some 110 kilometres northeast of Montreal on the Odanak reserve of the Abenaki nation. While she was still a young woman she had become famous as a performer and storyteller, and now, though known best for her filmmaking at the NFB, she remains a powerful singer and poet. But Obomsawin's first love centres on aboriginal youth. It's a love that has taken her all over Canada, the United States, and Europe, visiting schools, jails, and all manner of community settings, recounting First Nations history and inspiring Native pride.

Obomsawin's work expresses some of the best characteristics of the NFB as a large institution. The NFB allows its directors to shoot great quantities of film, provides strong technical back-up, and encourages people with talent to take up filmmaking. Obomsawin gets support from veteran producers such as Wolf Koenig and Adam Symansky. Yet in talking about her position at the Film Board she is quick to point out, "I have my own way."

The personal voice, the partisanship, and the close relations she develops with her documentary subjects make her work distinctive. The work has a kind of interaction that is oceans apart from the icy detachment of films like *Who Gets In*. She has a fondness for using storytelling as a device for shaping the actuality material: both *Incident at Restigouche* and *Richard Cardinal: Cry from a Diary of a Métis Child* use her investigation of still photographs taken by witnesses to a tragedy as a key building block, and *No Address* focuses on two young people as a way of telling a larger story about homelessness among Native youth.

Obomsawin makes no apologies for her socially driven art. "This is why I make these films," she states. "To go for changes." Yet the films continue to live beyond their original context, partly because of the craft that stems from the NFB tradition and largely because of the strong emotions she generates on the screen. The Alberta welfare laws may have changed since Richard Cardinal killed himself, but his tragedy still presents a challenge and carries enormous power.

I had met Alanis only briefly before arranging our first conversation. She was in the middle of editing her latest film, *Kanehsatake: 270 Years of Resistance*, and asked if we could do the interview at her apartment in Montreal starting around 9:00 p.m. I said, "Sure," but the late hour made me nervous that she would be too tired to carry on a lengthy conversation. As it turned out, I had no need to worry. Obomsawin talked softly, but with verve and incredible enthusiasm, so much so that by 12:30 a.m. I was fading and she was still going strong – with enough energy to dash upstairs at one point to search for a book by a U.S. psychiatrist who had written about the Richard Cardinal film.

I know you are editing right now, working on a film about the 1990 events at Oka, Quebec. I'm curious about how you work with an editor.
Alanis. Each project is different. There were times when I've done the first assembly myself, but I certainly wasn't prepared to do that with this film. There's so much material. I shot from July 12 well into October. It has taken six months just to log in the materials and look at them twice – a mountain of work. I work with a very fine editor, Yurig Luhovy, and we're now down to about five hours. It's exciting seeing the film take shape. You go through all sorts of emotions with this material. It's hard to get used to what happened at Oka. It's an historic event that changed lives.

Has it been that way with your other films as well, that the structure has come to you in the editing stage?
Alanis. Not necessarily in the editing stage. As I go along in the shoot I feel things taking shape. I'm a storyteller, so automatically a film becomes a story that I feel and live and see. When I start working with

the material it often takes on another shape than what I had in mind. But the story's the same.

I'm sure you find it hard to discard footage.
Alanis. Yes. But I will be making more than one film from all this. There's lots of interview material, and I'll be producing short films for schools too. The events at Oka happened to individuals, but these were historical events which also repeat from the past.

How much did you foresee that you would be able to make a series of films? Did that occur to you during the shooting or later, when you started editing?
Alanis. I was not thinking like that during the shooting. I was so much into it I just knew it had to be recorded. Not only for immediately after, but so students or others will be able to work with the material also. The Film Board is really the film archives of Canada.

I'm careful and very responsible to those I interview, because this material is going to have a long life.

Perhaps there's a need to do several versions then? There's many possible ways to structure it.
Alanis. The material is so moving, that's what makes it exciting to see the film coming together. I work long hours every day and I don't get bored. I'm continually so involved that I think about it all the time.

Do you feel a pressure to complete this film quickly?
Alanis. No. I just think of making the best document I can. I don't want the film released now and not be as good as it should be.

Since you travel and talk to so many students and teachers, is that experience a basis for knowing the audience for your films? When you're editing do you consciously think about those students and wonder how a scene will be perceived at a particular school?
Alanis. Yes and no. I don't think about it that way. I always thought it was important to talk to students and show my work. But when I'm working on a film I first want it to be honest and true to what happened. Then it can go anywhere. Of course, it's going to touch people in different ways and upset some people. But as long as it's strong and stands on its own it will be understood.

When I talked to John Walker he said that when he's filming it's as if he has the audience in the back of his head.

Alanis. Not me. I don't feel that. When I'm working all I think about is people in my past – old people that are gone now, or generations in the past. I felt that especially when I was starting to make films. I had lots of difficulties in all aspects, but there was one thing for sure. I felt I was pleasing my ancestors, and I don't mean just my village but where I came from as an aboriginal woman. I felt they were happy because this work is so important. I was running around like crazy from one school to another but in the back of my mind I felt it wasn't me speaking, it was someone else through me. I just had to do it and it made me feel good. I feel that now too, especially knowing these documents are going to be here for a long time. The film must be valid all around. It must speak for and to the young.

Do you see your work in any particular filmmaking tradition?

Alanis. I've certainly learned much from the Film Board, but I have my own way. I guess it has to do with expressing yourself, and knowing who you are, and that brings many people with you. I'm never tired of Native subjects. Every day I meet Indian people on the street and I find so much poetry in them: the way they express themselves, the way they tell me what's happening to them. I'm always so amazed by my own people, by their language, and the way they think. Beautiful people. There's only so much time and there's so much more I've got to do.

Can you talk about how you work with your cinematographer? To what extent do you direct in your documentaries?

Alanis. It depends. The Oka situation was different from anything I've ever done. There was one point when I was completely alone in the treatment centre – the main building used by the Mohawks during the siege – and I could only communicate with the crew by phone, telling them which way to go. It was an odd situation because I wasn't there with them.

   With every crew, before we go on location I spend many hours just talking to the camera-person, and then to the rest all together about why I am going to a particular place, why I want to do something. I want them to come inside the situation with me, so they don't contradict what I'm trying to achieve. Then they don't feel simply as technicians. They feel part of the creation and part of the story. Most of the time I have people who will work long hours and will do anything for me, even during the Oka situation.

So you feel free to give instructions to the cinematographer while the camera is rolling?
Alanis. Oh yeah. I do that all the time – without pushing. I'm always talking right at his side. Saying, "Take your time, don't make a rough move," etc. At Oka it was crazy. Something would be happening and I would be running over, calling the crew to catch up. There was a lot of danger and I was not about to send the crew into places without going there first. But that is an incredible kind of situation.

Did you have a sound person at Oka?
Alanis. Yes, but sometimes I recorded sound too. I'm very fussy about sound. I come from a place where hearing and listening to people is important.

The Oka situation recalls the events in your earlier film Incident at Restigouche. *There's a strong sense of community in* Incident *even though they're having a difficult time, and in the events covered by the film, they're losing a battle. What do you think was learned by the community through the filming process?*
Alanis. They were given time to express themselves. A lot of time. Some came to see me editing in Montreal. I had the première in the Restigouche church hall. We showed it twice through in a row.

I'm not sure if you know, but children take part in everything in Native communities, and even for something like our film première they're running around, noisy and screaming. Usually they can stay tranquil for only a short time. But for the première the minute the film started – with the noisy opening scenes of the police troop entering the village – all the children were quiet, because most of them had been there when the incidents happened. They sat still the whole time.

The film gave people dignity. There's one man who was badly beaten, and pulled by the hair, and paraded through the reserve – we see him on screen. And he told me that his son had seen him being arrested and had heard what people were saying. I guess the young boy was humiliated and embarrassed about his father. The man said, "After the film, my son kept hanging around and then told me he finally understood what had happened." It brought dignity to his father, and so from feeling ashamed the boy's feelings switched. So if the film gives a person a chance to speak and say what he or she is going through, the events take on a whole different tone.

It seems as if the community would be stronger after viewing the film, seeing the fight they put up. Not just as individuals. At what point in making Incident at Restigouche *did you settle on the structure?*
Alanis. I went there several times. It's like a puzzle when you make a film. You're telling a story, and you must have a beginning and an end, but in the middle the people make the story. For me, as I am working along, someone will say something and I'll know, that's the end of the film. I don't worry so much about the middle. I know it will come together. When I'm editing and working with the material and something is missing, I usually know which person is going to fill that gap. I go and explain what's missing and I ask about a specific aspect of the story.

Do you feel tension between your accountability to those you are filming and your position as an independent filmmaker? For instance, have there been any cases when people in the community insist that you include certain elements, or tell their story, or talk to so and so?
Alanis. No. I can't have that. But I work with a lot of people, especially during the research. I knew with Restigouche and now with Oka that many people worry that the story will be told right.

I feel very responsible for all the people involved. Even at Restigouche the situation was dangerous. I remember, when we were shooting there was a young woman involved with the film who came back from lunch one day and said that her boyfriend from Campbellton had warned her that a large group of whites were coming to kill people on the reserve that night. You could almost feel the tension in the air. It was awful. Nothing happened, they never came. But it was a threat.

Your film Richard Cardinal: Cry from a Diary of a Métis Child *makes a strong impression on young people. One reason, of course, is the story itself – how shocking it is. The other element that makes it work is your use of the actor. How did you prepare Cory Swan, the young boy who plays Richard?*
Alanis. I spent a long time with him, on every sequence, every shot. He's a boy who's had some similar experiences himself and could really relate to Richard. He knew Richard's story. He could feel it but I didn't want to damage him. I would read him portions from Richard's diary for the

particular section we were going to film and he understood that. He was wonderful. I just adored him. That's why the film does what it does for people.

The diary finally allowed Richard some time to be heard. But he speaks for thousands of children. I've done workshops with young children in group homes and lock-up facilities, and afterwards I can't get out of there, because children have so much need to be heard. You just stand there and spend hours talking to them. I say, "Write it down, write about yourself and about what you feel." It's a wonderful exercise, to try and encourage them. Each one of them needs so much attention, and they don't get it. The film is powerful because I guess a lot of Indian people identify with Richard. A lot of them say, "That's me."

They want the chance to say "I know that feeling too."
Alanis. Yes. Many people tell me that they tried to commit suicide: "I'm so glad you made this film," they say, "because that's me." I tell the kids to look at the loss that we have, what a poet he was. He's gone. It's too bad nobody realized, what happened, how he got there. The kids must gain esteem. They must look in themselves and see what they can do.

I was very pleased when the Alberta government bought the rights to the film. Many social workers in different departments see it now. One time I was in Edmonton for the première of *No Address* and a man who had been the provincial Ombudsman presented me with two new reports, saying that the Richard Cardinal film had helped force new policies and laws in Alberta. Young people in the audience said to him, "Why do you need a film to be made before you change the law?" He quickly replied, "Well, sometimes the government waits for the public to make a move, to push, otherwise they don't know." It was incredible. I was shocked, but happy that the film was able to do that. But primarily I made it for Richard.

Most films don't have that immediate impact.
Alanis. It was very painful to make it, I can tell you that. Ooh-lah-lah, so difficult. When we went to Richard's home town, Fort Chipewyan, I went to the cemetery. I remember it was a sunny day in the afternoon, so beautiful, yet such a sad time. It might sound funny, but I just had this feeling that Richard was there saying, "Well, finally you got here." His brother Charlie was so wonderful too: an intelligent and sensitive person who had gone through a lot himself. He went to all those places with me and introduced me to the foster parents. It was Charlie that I first

discussed the film with. I wanted to know how he felt about it, if it would be alright. He said yes. And imagine, for Richard, Charlie was his idol. Everybody loves Charlie in the film and wherever I go people ask, "How's Charlie?" They want to know what he's doing.

Did you ever consider making a more confrontational film? I imagine that would have been the conventional CBC approach.

Alanis. I didn't want to do that. I went to see the worst place Richard had been and I met the foster father there. The man was very upset and angry, and wouldn't co-operate. I told him that I was going to make the film anyway. Richard's diary had already been seen publicly. He said that it's all lies. But I also saw that man as human, for who was to know back then when he had Richard what would happen? Many Native children and white children were in bad situations. Then you expose that situation twenty years later. Some of these people just didn't think. So much has gone on unknown to the public. I wanted everybody to look at it, especially social workers.

Many people said I should interview social workers. It seemed the social workers didn't care. Many young people in university decide to be social workers and don't have a clue what they're getting into. Yet I attended the inquiry into Richard's death and by the time the last social worker came into the box, I began to feel for him too. He told the judge he had a hundred cases and had to travel two hundred miles. The rule was that they had to see each placement once a month. Now, nobody can do a good job with that – with all those teenagers, each one with problems, who need help and friends.

The government's whole system was so bad. But when you look at the immediate situation you blame the first person you can. I didn't want to do that.

Are you saying that a confrontational approach would have weakened the film and your general point?

Alanis. My aim was for Richard to be heard, and to focus on what he wrote. The first time the film showed in Edmonton, at the Film Board, I saw many people I assumed were social workers. Their faces were severe and some took notes. They looked very unfriendly. I understood. I knew how they felt. After the film, I'll tell you, it was dead silence. But when I started to talk the atmosphere changed totally. I said to them, "I know some of you think I've made this film to point the finger at you. I didn't do that. I want all of us to look at what has happened to this child. I want to force the government to change the rules – to find better foster places for these children." Everybody was very sad, to be sure. But I wanted the feeling that this must not happen again. That's what I felt the document had to do.

You briefly mention the Métis Association in the film. What was their role in all this?
Alanis. After the film came out the Métis Association in Alberta for the first time received money to administer their own programs and to hire their own social workers. This will help set up Indian foster homes too. Of course, not everything has turned around. There were so many terrible years for our young people. At least it's changing. Now the children are not going to lose their identity. They have a better chance to develop.

You have said that all audiences are important to you, even small ones. Were you thinking of Native communities specifically?
Alanis. Native and others too. Sometimes I'm asked to go somewhere, but the organizers apologize by saying there's only going to be twenty people. But to me if it's *two* people and they get something out of it, fine.

Some filmmakers think only in terms of TV and the largest possible audience. But it's often more important politically to reach a small group of people who are going to act.
Alanis. Oh yes, and it's also the chance to speak to a group of people and be close to them. You can't buy or put a value on that.

Your films use different structures and styles, but in all of them you are present at least in the narration, and you speak as an insider. For example, in Poundmaker's Lodge *you refer to "our people" and in* No Address *you say, "Many of our people come to Montreal." Why is this "inside voice" important to you?*
Alanis. I can't separate myself. Some people would say that's wrong. I've been told by a person at the Film Board that I'm losing my objectivity, especially with *Poundmaker's Lodge*. I got so close to the people in that film. But I don't want to be an outside eye looking in. All my life, wherever I go I feel the story of the people.

Would you say that your personal involvement with the people you film is a major difference between your work and that of others? Does it make your work unusual?

Alanis. I don't think of it as unusual. I just think I come from someplace else. There's so much emotion in these films between the people I work with and myself. It's for a lifetime. Certainly I do a lot of research, but then part of what I feel ends up in the writing. What I feel about the people comes out. There's so much love that develops as we work together.

How did you meet the young people in No Address?
Alanis. We met through the Montreal Native Friendship Centre, which by the way is only a drop-in centre, not a place to sleep. I also met people on the street. The Centre had recently completed a survey of people on the street and the need for places to sleep. I had also become a board member of the Centre. We were trying to get a shelter, and through that work I was able to spend long hours with these young people, explaining what I'd like to do with a film, why it would be important. I was searching for people who would participate. They had lots of time to think about it. I got closer and closer to those you see in the film.

And now we have a shelter. The film played a part in changing some of the rules, for instance when you see the young guy at the welfare office unable to get assistance because he doesn't have an address. Now the Friendship Centre can be used as an address for those people. This is why I make these films. To go for changes.

A lot of workers in the federal Department of Indian Affairs just process people like they're a number. So I arranged to go to Ottawa with women on the Friendship Centre Board to show my films. Forty-five people came to our screening and by the time it was over they thought differently.

When I see *No Address* today I see so much poetry, just in the way people talk about themselves. It's awful, it's terrible, and you feel sad, but it's poetry the way they express themselves. When they're talking they say what they feel. There's nothing in the film that the young people can be ashamed of, no laughing at or pointing. They're made to feel they are valuable human beings. They weren't born on the street.

Are there any drawbacks for you in working at the NFB?
Alanis. You know, I've been there for a long time – twenty-four years. For some time it was difficult, but now I get a lot of support. I feel I've earned their respect. I have things to say and I can say them there. And I think I've opened doors for others. I couldn't have made my films anywhere else, certainly not in the seventies. I've had time. The Film Board is

there for the right reasons. Whenever I decided to make a film I always made it. But there were many fights and I had to work as the producer to raise some of the money elsewhere. I have a hard head and I'm a fighter.

You've talked about the importance of Native people gaining access to filmmaking facilities. Is that also a question of different strategies and styles normally pursued by Native filmmakers?
Alanis. People develop their own styles, of course, but Native filmmaking is important because there are so many communities, cultures, and traditions. Many traditions have been lost, some are coming back, and some have remained underground for a long time. There was survival of the people through everything. It's so important to document how the people feel and what they've experienced. Each family and tribe has its own history. So there will never be enough people making documents. We need to develop filmmakers in their own communities doing programs for themselves, which can be applied in their schools, about what went on before and what they would like for the future. That's a powerful place to speak from in a document – to tell a story from the inside. The more people that gain this knowledge the better. I see a richness across the country, and ten years from now there will be many documents for the children to look at, to feel good about themselves.

The educational system has been turned around, through the efforts of our people right across the country: closing the residential schools, people sitting in and going to jail to get better schools, taking their kids out of the public system in order to transfer funds to Native schools. I feel grateful that in my lifetime I saw the changes.

"It was necessary for the film to scream."

Yvan Patry, born in 1948 in the mining town of Iroquois Falls in northern Ontario, and **Danièle Lacourse**, born in Montreal in 1949, have managed an astonishing output of documentaries from a great variety of locations. Since 1980 they have filmed in Central America (particularly Guatemala), South Africa, Mozambique, and a number of times in Ethiopia/Eritrea. The films and tapes on Eritrea have received the most attention, including television broadcasts in Canada, the United States, and Britain. One reason for this success is the superb technical quality of their work, immediately evident in the rich music and sound-effect tracks worked out by the composer René Lussier and the sound technician Claude Beaugrand.

Night and Silence was shot in the spring of 1990 during the last and most brutal stage in the war between Ethiopia and Eritrea: the massive bombing of Massawa, Eritrea's Red Sea port. Lacourse and Patry were the only foreign filmmakers in the country during those months, making the pressure to communicate what they saw even stronger than normal. *Night and Silence* won the Canadian Association of Journalists' Award for Best TV Program on a National Network in 1991.

Winning the Peace (1991) shows the incredible change brought on by Eritrea's May 1991 independence from Ethiopia and its people's attempts to build a new country. The victory celebrations produce a different feel from the horrific mood of *Night and Silence*, yet like the earlier documentary this film walks a fine line between hope and despair. We see, for instance, the grim reality of reconstruction and very basic health care. Prison survivors of the Ethiopian garrison in Asmara tour their former torture cells and mourn their dead comrades.

All the films on Ethiopia and Eritrea, which include a 1987 trilogy made for the NFB – *The Forgotten War, A Time to Heal*, and *Songs of the Next Harvest* – followed by *Harvest of War* (1988), *Food under Seige* (1989), and *The Forbidden Land* (1989), differ from mainstream journalism in subtle but significant ways. They focus not on political spokesmen but on extraordinary civilians – doctors and teachers – who develop as complex human beings with past histories and a range of emotions. And although the filmmakers' strong sympathies and commitment clearly emerge, the two partners remain journalists in the background, in a manner quite different from the style of field correspondence seen on CBC's *Prime Time News*, for instance.

You do so much travelling, do you still experience culture shock?
Yvan. There is an element of schizophrenia travelling between two worlds. The more we work in Third World countries the more we feel the gap between the North and South. We spend more than six months a year outside Canada, researching, investigating, and shooting. What we see in the South gives us a way of understanding the different systems and the outstanding problems. It gives us a new understanding of what's going on here.
Danièle. The culture shock is always there, but it's more obvious the first time we go to a country because of the images we carry: TV coverage of the famine in Ethiopia, for instance. Our main images of the South include violent yet passive and lazy people – people unable to get organized, unable to take destiny into their own hands. When you get there you find something else.

Every trip you discover new things. The international agencies were very proud of their work in Ethiopia, yet the last time we went, our fifth trip, we visited the Ogaden refugee camps and found people living there for four months with next to no food. This was a big scandal, showing corruption in the bureaucracy. So that was another face.
Yvan. Now that the Cold War is finished, the bad guys by Northern stereotypical standards are the South. That puts more responsibility on us. Europe is closing borders, Texas is closing its borders. These events open a whole new set of problems. We have to question the way we work and the way we deliver messages.

Is it difficult and frustrating coming back to Canada and finding people who don't want to hear?

Danièle. It's hard coming back because you feel people are indifferent. The problems of the South are not part of their lives. When we returned, especially after experiencing the bombing of Massawa we felt such a responsibility and such a revolt that it gave us strength to get these images across and to tell people. The indifference really makes us consider the kind of documentary we produce. We can see an evolution in our work. Now we try to follow specific people and their struggle of daily life. I think that helps audiences overcome indifference. Audiences normally see people in the South only as objects, with a little journalistic commentary and that's it. You have to show human beings with their contradictions, their lives and aspirations, and their will to live. Then audiences will understand and get closer to the reality of the South, and feel more open to share.

When you are on location and attending one of those public meetings in Eritrea, are you thinking of your audience? Obviously you try to anticipate what the scene will look like on the screen, but do you consider at that point whether viewers will understand what you are showing?

Danièle. The first thing is *for us* to try and understand – the culture, what is at stake during the meetings, the interventions that people make. When you're there meanings are not always obvious. We try to emphasize the expression of the people themselves. That's the main point in all the shooting we do.

Yvan. If you look at Quebec documentary historically, when we started we were giving a name to a place, to people, literally naming our aunts and uncles. But you can't do that any more. It's too shallow. All the problems are so complex – economic, environmental, political, scientific – you have to find different angles, different ways of showing the subject. So our films always attempt this multiple focus. And because we make large documentaries as well as current affairs we have to keep that in mind. We have to be able to reach a miner in Quebec and a longshore worker in B.C. on economic issues and on this relationship we have to the same world. We have to find the angles, the characters, the situations that exemplify. But it's not a six-week job. It's two or three years in the making. It's a multiple time-and-space relationship with many elements.

Dr. Assefaw Tekeste, whom you see in *Night and Silence*, is not the same man you saw in the earlier films. This guy has changed by what he has seen, by the suffering, by the war, by the difficulty of healing himself, by his new analysis. He's an evolving character. He helps us to understand a pain-sharing situation. He was the key mediator.

How did you meet Assefaw Tekeste?
Yvan. We met him on our first shoot in Eritrea and used him in a couple of scenes. He became a central character because of his capacity of mediating different elements. We showed *Night and Silence* in Montreal again last week, and I don't know how many people I've met since, at the barbershop, wherever, who ask me, "How can that doctor smile in that hospital?" In a film that's so hard and so harsh, one of the key moments that people remember is this guy's smile when he goes back to his old hospital.
Danièle. You want the character to communicate and you want the situations to be expressive enough and representative enough that they say something to the audience. When we shot the napalmed children at the hospital we had discussed it in detail beforehand. Do we show the wound and the blood? No, we should show the support of the people around, the sharing of the pain.

What kinds of discussions have you had with the doctors in your Eritrean films, and what contributions have they made about what you should be shooting? How much background preparation occurs with them before filming?
Danièle. We tried to film the doctors in action. And in the hospital they felt such revulsion it wasn't hard to get them to speak. We don't do involved set-ups. I know this is a big discussion – that some filmmakers will do a lot of preparation and set-ups. I feel we didn't have to do that. People wanted to talk. Usually if you achieve good communication with someone, explaining why you're there, what you want to do, it's not a long preparation.
Yvan. You spend long days and nights together. We start shooting early in the morning because it's Africa and it's hot. We screen at night and go back to talk. The woman Fatna Ari, in *Night and Silence,* was at first reluctant after the bombing to go back to Massawa to show us where she had lived. She was too afraid since she had been taken hostage during the battle for the city. So we respected that. Then she heard an interview we had done on the radio saying how the outside world didn't know what was going on, so she came and said, "I want to speak." She was afraid during the whole day we shot but she was able to exorcise her fear. This had such an effect on the camera and sound people. And on us.

We do long investigations before and after. When we arrived at the Ogaden refugee camps our first instinct was to start filming immediately. All those kids dying. But after three or four hours you back off and say, "What the hell is going on here? Why haven't I understood the anger of these people?" We tried to find the anger and how they express it. Once we found it we tried to follow its moral itinerary. That was demanded. It was an entirely different story, not death by famine. We wanted to show the cultural reaction to death, and that needs investigation plus a level of complicity with people.

Danièle. You must want to hear people. Some journalists we saw came to this camp with their story already in mind. They were just coming to get pictures and the typical colour of the place. And the questions they were asking: "How many died?" "Do you have something to eat?" But nobody asked them why this had happened! Yet the people had a strong point of view. They told us that a guy in charge sells the food at the market to his friends. They were angry. So if you think they have no voice, that they are illiterate and they don't think, then you don't even ask. That reflects the point of view you have before going. If you think that people are hopeless and can't do anything for themselves, you will find that.

So it's not just a question of your preparation but your point of view?
Yvan. And your analysis of the context. Some of our friends working in these areas don't have the same analysis. In *Winning the Peace*, for instance, some people thought that our metaphor of the central jail in Asmara was a bad thing to show. But that place was the biggest garrison town in Africa. It had thousands of political prisoners. When we met the three ex-political prisoners and the one man had a list of his friends who had died, he said, "My responsibility is to keep and to tell this memory." That was an extraordinary element. But the aid organizations don't like that. They say it isn't "development."

Is there any tension for you between making work in solidarity and practising responsible journalism? Are those categories a contradiction for you?
Yvan. No. Some people who work with us from the CBC think we're hard-to-handle mavericks, others think we're easy nice guys. But we don't care. We try to do our job in the most fulfilling way, like Danièle said, trying to understand, giving a voice to people who don't have a voice. The rest is contingency; it's winning a battle with CBC or ABC.

Of course we get scratched, but we have a responsibility to get these images and voices on air. But ABC tells us it's not a journalistic point of view.

Danièle. There's no contradiction as long as we do a good investigation, for instance in the camps where we found corruption. We care about that. Although we go to be sympathetic to the people and to certain movements, we don't go with closed eyes. We try to see the reality.

Yvan. Others say we're not partisan enough. But our job is not to defend a political organization, our job is to tell the contradictions as they evolve, and obvious contradictions are not black and white, they're all grey. We try to give a voice to the different components. For the story we did on Guatemala about the massacres in Aguacate, one of the guerrilla organizations criticized us because we didn't use a loudspeaker to clobber the army. But the elements of proof that we had only created a reasonable doubt about the army's version of events. Still, the Organization of American States human rights group thought that was enough for an investigation. Afterwards we lobby and help organize the political work that's necessary so the issues don't stay in the video-cassette. Filmmaking provides tools that help generate public debate, help push a lobby, so that issues can be debated without having a monopoly of truth about them. That's part of our responsibility also, not only to film, but to generate the public debate, to participate, and to give people an ability to act on these issues.

When did you first get involved in making films?

Danièle. Ten years ago for me. Yvan started way back in the sixties. I did theatre, journalism, languages, politics, and everything combined.

Yvan. I started out in fiction, in 1969, but I didn't see much relevance to it. In the seventies I was more involved in trade union films, community organization films, Société nouvelle stuff, with video too. At one point I felt an international horizon was necessary and I wanted to see other parts of the world, so I went to Africa. I felt we couldn't keep addressing problems and arriving at solutions without an international horizon. Nobody else was doing it. We wanted to produce different forms of international coverage, combining documentary series with other forms of reporting. That was a choice right from the beginning.

I'm interested to know more about how you work with your cinematographer on location. How much direction do you give, how much instruction? What sort of back and forth goes on?

Yvan. We always let the crew know the results of our initial investigations, the threads we will follow, what the central elements of character and situation will be. They know up front. We do daily evaluations, going from very subjective to objective elements. If something happens, we'll follow it, but we also have an agenda.

Danièle. It depends also if you have camera people who are more independent and who have more interest in directing and editing. With these people you don't check every shot. The cinematographer must first understand the characters – where are they going, and where is the film going? Of course, sometimes when you arrive at a place the reality has totally changed, even with people you have worked with before. Massawa, for instance. When we went in January 1990 we thought that since the Eritrean Peoples Liberation Front had taken the city there would be feast days. Instead we were bombed. We certainly had to adjust, to see the impact of the bombings, the impact of hiding for fourteen hours a day. We finally found the thread in all that with Assefaw Tekeste, because it was his town, he could show us the destruction, the fear, the pain. That wasn't at all the scenario before we arrived. The whole crew had to adjust. So every night we looked at the footage, to ask what's the meaning of all that? What do we want to show and how do we show it? Before filming, the cinematographer must understand what we want the audience to feel – not just to know the people and situations, but what orientation we will take.

Yvan. I'll give you two examples from *Night and Silence*. First and foremost we had a problem in subduing the pain. We had to find a way of showing it. And we needed enough elements so that in the editing room we would have a way of subduing it. It was so horrific. Second, there was the skull scene. All those skulls. We knew from listening to the Assefaw interview that his reflections on the culture were what we wanted, so we decided to work on that scene in that spirit. All the camera movements and all the elements on the sound track reflect an interior feeling. This culture of death was the price they had to face. Freedom is the most expensive thing in that country. We knew that in those frames we had to show the movement of life and death, of life and drought, pain and freedom, the sounds of the leaves on the surrounding trees. We worked like hell to get that.

Danièle. Our cinematographer for *Winning the Peace* knows a lot about filming. So in Asmara he suggested that because the jail was empty and that now the idea of torture there seems totally strange, he should compose an unbalanced frame with no movement in the shots. It was a great idea. It's an abandoned place that reminds you of the past.

Yvan. Sometimes things don't work. For the opening of *Night and*

Silence we wanted shots as if Assefaw was coming into the city. But it didn't work well, so we made those long shots of the palace, the sea, and the boats, which create an impression that we're going there. That film was really hard shooting, over seventeen days. Everybody lost weight, and we were struggling with parasites and the lack of water.

Danièle. Mood is very important for the cinematographer. With the mood you know which kind of light, which rhythm, camera movements, which length of shots. The rest is sensitivity. Some cameramen you get along with very well and others . . . it's the last time you shoot with them.

Yvan. The crew come to meetings with us, to see. There is no division between us and the "technical" people. When they start shooting they are not meeting the people for the first time. Like Assefaw's smile. They knew that. They knew that sixteen years ago he used to be a dandy in Massawa. His whole personal history in this town was coming out. We had to gather that. These are psychological relationships which have an emotional roller coaster, particularly in war.

Danièle, do you direct differently from Yvan?
Danièle. I intervene less than Yvan. I have a tendency to let the people go and to film more. Maybe it's a lack of confidence, maybe it's because I want to see what will come out in a situation. I don't want to interrupt. Maybe Yvan knows more about when a scene is finished. I have a tendency to do more shots, and to let the situation develop by itself.

Yvan. Danièle has a very good relationship with people. She can get people to deliver without being obsessed. One day we were shooting with Mama Zeinab, who was very angry and tired but Danièle was able to get her to express her anger and still come across as this wonderful poet.

I know I edit while I shoot. So if the cinematographer asks if we need more covering shots I can say yes or no right away because it's already edited in my head.

Danièle. For me it's not edited then. It's edited in the editing room. And I like to have many choices in the editing room because I don't know exactly what the length of a sequence will be – the different angles, the rhythm, if I will need fifty shots or two. In Massawa we couldn't have edited the film in our heads beforehand. The characters will lead the story but then things come up.

Yvan. The editing process is crucial. For the past five films we have had the same editor, Nick Hector – a big plus. He has an incredible register he can work in. So we literally feed him shots. We know his creative capacity to orchestrate. Nick reads a lot before starting. On this new tape about Guatemala we are editing now, he has done his own research, including reading novels. He will bring a fresh look at the Native culture, for instance, and he'll say, "In this shot maybe the corn should go in this way."

Filmmaking is teamwork. It's not all this bullshit about the artistic, one-person point of view. Documentary is giving a voice to people who don't have a voice, understanding complex issues, finding the thin rope for the ethical perspective.

Do you see your work and your perspective on events in any particular tradition? Does Quebec history play a part?
Yvan. I think our work is closest to Italian neorealism. We go to stories, we stay there a long time, we try to follow processes. We get into a special social dynamic.

Quebec documentary rapidly lost its roots from its social culture. The good guys in the beginning, like Groulx and Lamothe, lost it after the seventies. They left the social-comment documentary. There's no strong tradition since 1980. Groulx had the last candle on the cake.

Doesn't someone like Maurice Bulbulian represent that tradition of continuity?
Yvan. Maurice has always had the capacity of going to the margins and bringing what he finds to the centre – in his Mexican film, *Land and Liberty*, for instance. He always finds marginal characters and builds around them. But it's not the same as the social commentary on *this* society, such as Lamothe's *Les Bûcherons* and all the first Quebec documentaries. This necessity has left Quebec filmmakers, and there's no thread to the social movements: to the feminist movement, to the trade union and environmental movements. There's a real dislocation compared to the seventies between artistic expression and social movements – a failure to connect. That's the filmmakers' responsibility.

What's the difference between your work and that of other journalists? For example, Brian Stewart at the CBC and Michael Burke of the BBC have also filmed in the Horn of Africa.
Danièle. In the mainstream the journalist-reporter is the main character, the one who thinks, and analyses. He listens and sees. He is the star. Then there's the whole concept of objective neutrality. But no journalist

is objective, anywhere. You always go with a point of view. You react with who you are and with your knowledge. These mainstream conceptions often create a need to have the leaders of one organization facing the leaders of another organization – politicians confronting politicians. They start the film and they have the last word. We do not concentrate on the leaders because [laughing] they're all liars anyway. We focus on characters among the people and try to give them the voice. We try to develop commentary that is more like our impressions, our feelings for the feelings expressed. It's not this cold third-person narration. But the main point is to have ordinary people talking.

Yvan. Current affairs in general has preformatted sizes to deal with issues. CBC has very good journalists. Brian Stewart is one, Linden MacIntyre another, but style and format are so rigid that you must tell the story in a certain way. The world isn't like that. I have nothing against those journalists, but it bothers me that the preformatted styles have become the only format for TV. There's no place for other types of documentary. Maybe it's good journalism, but when it's the only format it takes other dimensions of public debate from the Canadian fabric. That also breaks with our cultural traditions.

We're at the crossroads now. We must choose to open up the valves of public debate and have multiple choices. If we try to put everything into *The Journal* format, the debate is reduced.

Danièle. The formats are very strong. If it's a story about another country they say you must have a Canadian angle. Also, you cannot let the image speak for itself. If there are three seconds without commentary, you have to cut. You cannot let the public discover the story by itself. It's all anti-documentary and based on a conception that the public is not very bright.

Many documentary makers now question the device of voice-of-God narration. Does that debate interest you? Isn't there a danger in using Augusta LaPaix, someone closely associated with the mainstream CBC, as a narrator in Winning the Peace?

Yvan. That's a very closed-circle intellectual debate. When we go into schools and into different communities, nobody gives a damn about that. The proper question should centre on *the function* of voice-over. It's a relation between the particular and the general. It's a communication process, a writing device, valuable in certain cases, not others. But when you have to do a story about Eritrea and nobody knows where it is, you have an outstanding challenge. You have to use all these things together. Sure, we've done films with no narration. That's the way to convey direct emotion, but more and more because we're dealing with complex issues, we need narration to synthesize. That doesn't mean that you can't convey emotions with narration.

Danièle. It depends on which kind of commentary you're talking about. I don't like the cold journalistic third person that knows everything. People tell us that our commentary is more subjective than that. Take Chris Marker: who the hell speaks more than him? His *Sans Soleil* is commentary from beginning to end. Beautiful. I would like to write commentary like that. [7]

Yvan. It's also a question of what to expose from what you're seeing and feeling. What do you want to explain? People give us public funds to do these films so they can understand something. Our obligation is to try and explain, not in a pedantic way, but so that people can see all these zones of grey.

Danièle. Some things are simply not carried by interviews. If you want a deeper reflection sometimes you need commentary. But it's hard to write good commentary.

Yvan. More and more we write commentary as counterpoint to the action as its unfolds. The action is going one way, the commentary the other. It's a component of a sound track. We witness and we express what we witness. Why should we hide behind an aesthetic, saying commentary is the voice-of-God? Well, God is a point of view. If you believe in God then you'll believe that there's a voice-of-God. But I don't believe there's a God. [laughter]

Some viewers have complained that Night and Silence *is too shocking. It's debilitating and numbing. It's not an easy film to watch. How would you respond?*

Danièle. Massawa was hell. It's normal and painful that audiences react that way, because we did when we were there. For the scene of the seven-year-old having his napalm-burn dressing changed, it's normal that you react with pain. We had tremendous discussions and I can tell you that the worst images are not in the film.

There are different aspects to this problem. We were the only media present during those weeks, and the Ethiopian government was denying that they had bombed. Israeli cluster bombs were being used and everything was hidden and denied. We had to denounce that. And if you want to denounce and prove that there is bombing, you have to show it.

Yvan. Israel was saying all over the world that they never sold cluster bombs, but we had shots of the Israeli device on the planes. We had to show it.

Danièle. That's the first thing. But *how to show it*? We talked about this with the editor. We avoided everything that would present people as objects, as flesh. We could have done terrible things, and I won't tell you some of those images. What you see is reality, but it's chosen. With the child in the hospital you never see the wound. You see the mother, the brother, you see people thinking. Those were intentional choices.

Yvan. It's sanitized. The bodies split up, the gathering of the bodies by the mothers, stuff like that we never put on screen, out of respect. Showing that would not be giving justice to pain.

Danièle. We also wanted to present characters. When Fatna says that these wounds are the price of freedom, I hope people understand that too. We show pain but also the hope. Fatna also accuses us of being indifferent.

Yvan. She was angry. "Why are the powerful white states of the world sending all these troops to Saudi Arabia and they're not saying anything about us?" she said. That's a strong statement. We tried to put the stress on the victims. Compare that to the media on the Gulf War. That was a Nintendo war. You didn't see any victims. When was the last time we saw cluster-bomb effects on people in real war? The last napalm pictures were from Vietnam. So it's important to show the scars, but also to hear the war from the victims' point of view. We were in a privileged situation to record that. We tried to hear the voice, the anger, and the challenge. It was not sensationalist.

I understand what you're saying. We had a friend who couldn't look at the film. But our job was to get the U.S. Congress to move and get the U.S. Jewish Congress to clobber the Israeli government. We made choices to subdue the pain, but we knew it was necessary for the film to . . .

Danièle. To scream.

Yvan. Yes, to scream. To wake up the indifference, and show what the powerful white states are doing.

There are levels by which you can submit yourself to pain. That's very subjective. Yet every time we've shown *Night and Silence*, people who put their heads down during the bombing scenes stay for the debate. That says something about what you can bear and what you feel challenged to do afterward.

The doctors play an important role in these films. Dr. Tekeste says angrily, "For you guys we're only statistics." Another man said, "I don't know whether to laugh or cry when I know that the world doesn't say anything." He had lost his cousin. Viewers are shocked that things like this war can happen and that they are powerless. They ask angrily, "Why did you bring this to my living room?" That I can understand. Our job is to help them channel that anger and frustration. We've had phone calls from all over. A doctor from Tucson, Arizona, called us and said, "I saw your film, what can I do?" He started a whole campaign to get antiseptics to Massawa. He sent truckloads with other retired doctors. Another guy in California saw the film, then phoned Senator Alan Cranston and said, "If you don't go to that hearing [on Eritrea] I'll get my whole Long Beach village to vote against you." It's a traumatic experience being there *and* it's traumatic from a spectator's experience. But we didn't overemphasize.

Still, in my experience many people simply will not watch such dread-ful images, either because they have no stomach for them or because they feel they've seen too much bad news already. It becomes a question of filmmaking strategy.
Yvan. *Night and Silence* showed on TV in Quebec on a Tuesday night, and at 9:05 there were 830,000 people tuned in. That's a popular audience – thirty per cent of the audience in Quebec. And they stayed with it.

I have one more question that I ask everybody.
Yvan. We'll give you the wrong answer, I'm sure. [laughter]

You've achieved a fair amount of success in getting your work broad-cast and discussed. To what extent must you create a name for your-selves as responsible, intelligent, ambitious filmmakers?
Yvan. We receive public funds. We have to be responsible. The other level of responsibility, which is much more important to us, is to the people we are filming. The result of all our Horn of Africa experience is that we are now back there helping to create the Eritrean Television Network. That's better than anything for me. Better than ABC, CBC. The memory of our work is first and foremost taken by these people, and they'll pursue it. That's the best follow-up you can have.
Danièle. Some directors are completely separated from the distribution and diffusion work. The film can stay on the shelf. At the NFB there are many of those – some good films. We work to get shown here in Quebec, in English Canada, the States, England, Europe. We try to create an event when the film comes out.

Yvan. We release films in different formats, we produce study guides, set up discussion panels with groups. To get people discussing: that's a big part of our work, every year.

Danièle. I think we're better known because of the issues we deal with. Since we witnessed the bombing of Massawa, Yvan was able to get on *Nightline* with *Night and Silence* and I went on Channel 4 in England. We try our best to get on air, get interviews, etc.

Yvan. Not many filmmakers in Canada work on international issues. We're the happy few. We get calls from the networks to produce current affairs, but we combine investigative journalism and documentary, which is rare. That combination created a bit of room for other work on international issues, unfortunately, most of it is superficial and shallow. Our relationship to institutions is to those people in them who share our preoccupations. Telefilm supports most of our films because we developed a good relationship with many people there. When we started our Central America series we had only $50,000 for eight half hours. We got people to understand that these were important issues to address. But for every broadcast you've got to make fifty phone calls. If you don't want to do that, then switch to sports series and figure skating. It's not a one-shot, one voice-of-God visit. It's not, "Drop by and have a coffee when you're in Montreal."

"You have to take the long view."

Claire Prieto (born 1945) and **Roger McTair** (born 1943) have been collaborating on film projects since the late 1960s, after immigrating to Canada from Trinidad, and might now be considered Canada's senior Black filmmakers. Along with their young son they live and work out of a downtown Toronto housing co-op. In a series of modest but effective and widely seen films, McTair and Prieto focus on activists within African-Canadian communities. Yet, perhaps surprisingly, their best films deal not with Caribbean-born newcomers but with the much older Black communities. The similarities and differences between the old and new African Canadian communities provide for a complex relationship between the filmmakers and their subjects.

Home To Buxton (1987), the couple's best-known work, is a portrait of a small southwestern Ontario town that was a key Black settlement during and after the period of the Underground Railroad. The town continues as a spiritual and historical centre for African Canadians and African Americans who trace their ancestors back to the earliest Black people on the continent. Black Mother, Black Daughter (1989) was co-directed by Prieto and Sylvia Hamilton for the NFB Atlantic studio. The film sketches a history of Black settlement in Nova Scotia as told through the eyes of women activists. Hamilton occupies the emotional centre of the film, acting both as narrator and on-screen facilitator. The scenes with her mother are particularly effective. As in their earlier works, *Some Black Women* (1976) and *Home To Buxton*, and Prieto's *Older, Stronger, Wiser* (1989), *Black Mother, Black Daughter* derives its strength from strong interviews with passionate, politically motivated women. There's a rapport between the filmmakers and the women on camera that can only be gained through a shared outlook and long conversations prior to shooting.

These works are clearly and proudly educational. Their *Children Are Not the Problem* (1992, sponsored by the Congress of Black Women, Toronto Chapter) for example, starts from the need to generate a useful resource and is unique in its argument for anti-racist schooling among young children. Parents, teachers, and educational consultants discuss how children develop prejudicial and racist attitudes at a very young age and consider how Canadians must start dealing with racial difference honestly and directly.

Prieto and McTair's films rarely play in festivals, and they certainly present themselves in the guise of conventional documentary. Yet no one else in Canada has developed the interest or the drive to focus so clearly on African Canadians, especially the historical strengths of the various communities. Their deep rapport with these communities and their dedication to serve Black audiences are far removed from the conventional relationship between documentary producer and subject. The commitment to a specific audience carries its difficulties, because Canadian television executives apparently feel little confidence that others will be interested in "Black subject matter." The prevailing TV assumption of minority subject matter for a minority audience only infuriates Prieto and McTair, and they show no signs of changing their ways. When I interviewed them they were busy making a new film on Black communities and politics in Nova Scotia.

Although much of our conversation dealt with the frustrations in their work, there was also a great deal of laughter. Like many long-time couples and collaborators, Prieto and McTair have the amazing ability to finish each other's sentences. When they disagreed they said so, but most often the conversation weaved back and forth, and they took on my questions like a tag team in wrestling. So, although I have strained to transcribe accurately from the tape recording, I can't be totally sure that Roger said this and Claire said that.

How did Home To Buxton *come about? Was it a project you had wanted to do for a while?*
Claire. It was always there as a project, maybe in an unconscious way. For me it was a kind of focus. It was really important to say that Buxton is a physical place where Blacks have lived for a long time. It was a locating of myself in this country. People in Buxton had a long tradition in a specific place. That's lacking for people who move from one place to the next. As a Black West Indian, I didn't know much about Canada, so this project involved recovering that history.
Roger. We saw Terence Macartney-Filgate's NFB film *Fields of Endless Day* way back in 1978, and thought of Buxton as a subject we would like to do. We went to various funding bodies and never got any support, so finally we decided to do it ourselves.

What sorts of research did you do in preparation for Home To Buxton?
Claire. We always work from the general to the specific, focusing as we go forward. We start with general books and articles, for example with the Buxton film, on that Southern Ontario area and material on the Underground Railroad, always looking for different points of view. Next we research more specific aspects such as the key people, times, and dates. Then we go to the primary research in the location itself, getting in touch with people: who's doing what in the community, who were the old families, which are the key institutions in the community. As well, we research the visual elements and begin to put everything together as a story. And right through to the point where the narration is written at the end – perhaps two years later – we are asking, what is it we're trying to say? Are we saying what we want to say? Does it feel good? Does it feel like the people there feel? Is this how the community would want to be represented? Is there a sense of what their community looks like, what's in their homes, what they laugh about?
Roger. Fred Landon at the University of Western Ontario had done a lot of research and writing on the Black community in Western Ontario, and Robin Winks's history was helpful for background. [8] Also, people had written specific local histories, family histories, etc. And there's James Walker at the University of Western Ontario, who has written extensively on Black Canadian history.

How did you decide which people to focus on? Was that your choice or did people in the community have strong ideas on who to talk with?

Roger. First you have to pay respect to the elders.

Claire. Unfortunately, people die on you. For instance, Allie Robbins, who had written *Look to the North Star* and had also been a founder of the Raleigh Township Centennial Museum, died before we could begin shooting. But everyone has ideas about who to talk to. Some people would say, "Ah, you're talking to all the wrong people."

Roger. Small communities have more politics than the Senate. So you have to find the really pivotal people.

Claire. They ask, "Who are you?" and they ask why you'd be interested in old buildings, and why you want to do this. You have to leave yourself open and try to anticipate what they'd want to know. Otherwise people fade away and they're just not available.

Roger. One national CBC news story had focused on what the community considered the negative aspects of Buxton. The community is very mixed. There are nice houses and some more run-down properties. The CBC producers took a kind of First World-Third World approach, and the community was angry because they have great pride in the place. They are a minority but they are also incredibly Canadian.

Claire. It's their life and they don't want to be shown as some poor rural community of Black people. Buxton is theirs. They own it. They have history and a tradition. It's not isolated, it's a centre of activity. The mainstream Canada may see them as a minority, but in their own community it's quite different. We should realize that the idea of a "minority experience" often comes from the outside. So if you look in and say, "This is a minority," they'll respond, "Hey, this is my space. It's living and thriving."

How did you see yourselves in relation to the community? Was there any tension between your work as independent artists and your accountability to the community?

Claire. They asked why a West Indian would be interested. I originally thought, "I'm Black, they're Black," but that's not really enough. They need to know your credentials, and they wanted to know *specifically* how we were going to do it. A lot of difficult questions. But mainly they wanted to know how the community would be represented and with whose voice the film would speak. That's good because you know they're going to keep you on track. You have to think it out. It's not going to be a big love-in where you come out with nothing.

To me one of the most important elements of the film is the depiction of an African-Canadian community stretching so far back. There's also the unique rural nature of the community.

Roger. It's an irony that most Canadians think of Blacks in the big cities, but most Black people in Canada grew up in rural areas. For instance, most Jamaican-Canadians grew up in the Jamaican countryside, outside the capital city of Kingston. And in Canada, while there were important Black communities in urban areas, Black Canadians also had a strong agricultural and rural background.

Claire. The people of Buxton resented very much being thought of as immigrants. Blacks lived here from the time before Champlain. The Black loyalists in Nova Scotia even served as translators for the Mik'maq. There were Black regiments in the war of 1812; Saltspring Island in B.C. has a very old community; many Black units served in World War I, etc. So historically, both urban and rural Black people have been integral to the Canadian landscape.

In preparing the interviews with people in Buxton, how did you go about putting them at ease? For instance, the older couple who sit in their kitchen peeling pears? Did you tell them what you were going to ask?

Roger. That was two years of work to get to that point.

Claire. Mr. and Mrs. Johnston knew what we were doing. They were among the first people we talked to during the research phase. We had said, "We want to use you for these reasons." But they didn't know the exact questions. At the point of the filming it becomes a matter of trust. You say, "I know it's a pain in the butt but let's try." It's basically an interview. Now, they were going to be peeling pears that day anyway, but not for us; for us they were going to be all proper. Joan Hutton, our cinematographer, suggested we film the pear-peeling as a way of easing the initial tension.

Roger. I had my doubts at first about shooting while they were peeling the pears, but the activity was not strange to them so it seemed a good thing to try. Of course I was also thinking how the activity would affect the sound. But making people relax is more important.

Claire. We always say to people, "You can stop this if you feel uncomfortable." It's just a matter of taking it really slowly.

Roger. It's important to stress that I'd talked with the Johnstons many times before the shooting. By the time we got there with the cameras

and the crew, they knew us very well, almost like family. And since the
film came out we've kept in touch.

*Did you feel any tension between generations in the community? For
example, the older people stress family and church, but a younger
woman gently stresses the Buxton annual reunion as a gathering of
Black Canadians. She says, "It's not just family but heritage."*
Claire. People have different reasons for coming to the reunion. Some
for family. There's a great sense of tradition; you go and say thanks to the
land. You meet old friends. You look at your father's house, you walk on
your parents' land, you go to church. You visit the cemetery. Really, it's
about coming home.
Roger. One old man drives every year from New York, and the year we
were shooting he got lost. He's becoming senile but he still comes. Some
younger people have a sense of politics in the Black nationalist sense,
but there's no tension. Overall there's a strong influence of the U.S. civil
rights movement in Canada. They respect their elders, and the elders
respect that the younger ones might be taking it a step further.

When did you know that you wanted to be filmmakers?
Roger. I wrote since I was pretty young. I started my first novel when I
was twelve. As a kid I read Western novels, especially Zane Grey and
Louis L'Amour. My novel was a western set in Texas. My father wrote
and my uncle was in theatre. Later I got interested in art and at seventeen I first saw movies that weren't from Hollywood. It was an incredible discovery – at the Roxy theatre in Port-of-Spain. I saw Bergman, lots
of English stuff, and Fellini – none of it narrative driven. The different
pace fascinated me. I thought, "Wow, I can do this." [laughs] Some crucial movies I still remember: Bergman's *Smiles of a Summer Night*, Fellini's *La Strada*, and Godard's *Masculin-Féminin*.

I did some theatre in high school, then advertising work, then I had
plans for the New York School of Visual Arts, but by a strange coincidence I ended here.
Claire. I wanted to be a teacher. I always liked school. Television came
to Trinidad in 1958 when I was a teenager, but since we were poor we
didn't have one. I remember a woman down the street used to put a TV
out in her yard, with benches for kids. Years later I realized that TV
would be a good way to teach people, in any Third World country. That
was my first conscious thought about doing anything like that.

As a teenager I went to the movies with my friends every weekend:

westerns, *Where the Boys Are*, all that stuff. You just went to the movies. When I was seventeen or so I also started going to the Roxy to see
those other movies. I remember *The Victim* and *The Pumpkin Eater*.
There were no Black faces on screen, though. The first Black person on
film I remember was James Brown in the *TNT* show, which was in the
early sixties. There's a whole history to how you become what you are,
and it's important for me to say that as a female in Trinidad there were
not a lot of possibilities. I remember being completely dissatisfied and
discontented all the time.

Like most women I did commercial work, typing, etc. I was very
dissatisfied but didn't know why. Unlike Roger, there was no one to say
there were other possibilities for me. Later, I got into advertising, working as a production co-ordinator, which gave me confidence. There was
some freedom, you met people; it wasn't predictable all the time. As
well, from about 1968 there was a ferment and a move towards Black-
ness. By the time I left Trinidad for New York, then Canada, I had started
thinking about educational TV. Then I came to Ryerson, in Toronto, for
the Radio/TV program. In Toronto it seemed all the people I knew were
going to school, thinking about politics and about themselves as Black
people.

*You've described your films with each other as teamwork. How does
that work in practice? Is it easier or harder when you're so close in other
aspects of your lives?*
Roger. [laughter] We go back a long way and we know our personalities
and what upsets each other. [Claire laughs in the background] Let me
start with the advantages first. I trust her responses and know her
strengths. It's easy to ask, "What do you think?" We don't always agree,
but there's respect. And that makes it work.
Claire. In my case it works most of the time. There's a lot of stress in this
work, since you don't know by what means you're going to do it, and you
blame the other. We have two completely different personalities. We
operate in a different fashion. I want to have things done quickly. Roger
is a lot more reflective. It frustrates me when I feel we're not going anywhere. I also want to be more involved in the creative end of things,
since up to now I've been doing the producing, the money stuff. That
was a frustration in working with Roger at the beginning. Now I can say
in the midst of a situation or conversation, "That's *not* how I think." I
respect how he thinks. As simple as that. We want to work on Black projects. We want to do serious work. We have the same premises. Working

with other people in the past has been difficult since the premise was not the same, both in terms of style and also politically. For instance, in the way that you go and talk with people in researching or preparing interviews, personal style is crucial. Often, people don't make time to talk with people when they're researching, but I find it very pleasant and fun. It's good for the head. So Roger and I think in the same way in crucial aspects of work.

I started doing documentary film around 1969 by producing for Roger. It was exciting getting on the phone and making things happen. That worked very well. It was fun and it included research. Since then there's been ups and downs.

At what point in making Black Mother *did you decide to use Sylvia Hamilton as both the narrator and the on-screen facilitator? She plays the role of a guide, instructor, and researcher. I felt that Sylvia's relationship with her mother added another level to the film, making it more personal, less expository. This is quite different from the polished professional voice of Noelle Richardson in* Home To Buxton *and even from the more informal narration of Marva Jackson in* Older, Stronger. **Claire.** We wanted a more relaxed voice, not somebody identified as *the narrator.* I think it worked out fine. I would like to have heard even less voice-over – because all of the things that need to be said get said, in the interviews, or in the overall feeling, or in discussions afterward, and even later with members of the audience going to get books on the subject – in all kinds of ways. With Sylvia, though she's not an external narrator, we didn't need as much narration: things were shown. Like during the baptism in the river scene, where the damn narration breaks in, "This is a whatever . . . how many years of history . . ." I think, looking back at it, "You don't have to be that specific. You can show it, let the film breathe."

I'd like to experiment more. I need to have my own vision. I remember trying a more visual approach with *Black Mother* and somebody saying to me, "What's the point of all that water and rock, shouldn't somebody be saying something?" But the song was saying it – the Lydia Jackson song. I wanted to get a feel for the landscape where people existed, also their personal landscape. I wasn't concerned with all the details, since I'm not a historian in that sense. For me it's the pictures, and the sound, and the feeling. I like films that combine information with the feeling of the people or the communities – that's what documentary is all about. I want people to look at the film and see

Claire in there. You don't have to tell the audience everything, though you want them to feel everything. You have to trust their intelligence, that they will continue on the road you have set them on.

I remember a big discussion about the ending of *Older, Stronger*, where we don't wrap everything up with the narration. For me Eva Smith said it all, why add anything? All that narration aggravates me. I want to say, "Just shut up and let me listen," because I feel that more stays with you than hard information after seeing a film. A film is stronger when you can get people to come out of themselves. The new Nova Scotia film Roger and I are researching comes partly out of all that. We are traditional documentary filmmakers. We want our work to unfold in front of the camera. We want to foreground the profilmic event (what occurs in front of the camera) – both sight and sound. Natural events, natural sound, and as little intervention as possible.

Are Black Nova Scotians more knowledgeable about their history than Black Ontarians?
Roger. Black Canadians with a long past here are very aware. They know their history here and they are incredibly Canadian. When we West Indians came up in the sixties they first saw us as allies, but in fact the alliance didn't happen – we're loud, you know. We didn't recognize the difficulties they had, and the overt/covert ways of this system. We had come from majority cultures where we could be doctors, lawyers, etc. So they had suffered a very overt kind of racism. Ten years ago a friend of mine tried to raise money for the Black Cultural Centre in Nova Scotia, but she needed an RCMP guard for months because of threats from some people calling themselves the KKK! In the Caribbean there were ways to fight that weren't possible here. In Canada, Blacks didn't have the large numbers, so their struggle was different. With the wave of West Indian immigration, first students, then general immigration, there was an attitude that the new Blacks knew it all. Well, it just wasn't so.
Claire. We tried to change everything and didn't look at what was here – the long history of Black Canadians – and this caused great frustration. The original Blacks couldn't say, "This isn't my country anyway, I'm going home." West Indians could. So these are the things you have to deal with when you go into Buxton and the Nova Scotia Black communities. We are newcomers. We shouldn't barge in. You are looked on as an outsider initially. You have to prove yourself. I don't think of myself as a West Indian, but people ask where you're from, and well, I am from the West Indies. But I am also a Black Canadian by choice.

You're asking people in the film to be open to you, after all.
Claire. Yes, and people are very sophisticated, they want to know why you're poking around, why you're interested in them – what you're going to do with it.

Aren't people enamoured with the media?
Roger. At first they don't like you because you are the media. They think any camera crew is from the CBC. Then if you say, "Well, I have a camera but I'm not the media, I'm a Black person trying to do a film about our history," they ask, "*Our* history?" [great laughter] So I try saying, "Well, I'm from Trinidad originally but I've lived here half my life, and I've got a kid who's Canadian," etc. It takes a while, then it's fine.
Claire. That's the work of any documentary filmmaker. If you're going to go into somebody's home and say, "Move this furniture around, and tell me about your life for the past fifteen years and all the details," there's something that they should be asking you. When we're working on a film there's a long period where you make people comfortable by explaining who you are, where your politics are, the connections that you see. I think it's important that people demand these answers.
Roger. Just knowing someone doesn't mean they'll really talk to you. It's at the point where they say, "Well, go and see what so and so says, and tell them I sent you," that you know you're okay. That happens a lot in Nova Scotia. I don't rush them. I want to see people in their setting.

Some people are saying that documentary is a dying art, that audiences, particularly younger ones, are bored by it. What do you think about the prospects for documentary?
Claire. It dies when the money dies. Many are moving away from the documentary because you can't make a living at it. CBC emphasizes drama. *The Journal* stuff is not documentary, in any way, shape, or form. But feature-length documentaries are being made. For instance, the CBC series *Witness* showed some interesting films. These were all point-of-view films by people who believed what they said, and when you see how it can be done, it's exciting.
Roger. Most of the people I went to film school with at Ryerson no longer make films. And sometimes I think they were bloody smart. They probably have a pension. There's no money in documentary film. You have to take a long view and be incredibly confident in what you're doing, otherwise the films won't even get done.
    We went with the Buxton film to the NFB, the CBC, and TVO for

production funding. Now, this film is sweet, not controversial: I thought they'd love it. They weren't interested. One media bureaucrat said, "Where's the story in the film?" In the end we got the money and it showed to really good response. PBS Buffalo even screened it right after *The Civil War* series, and it has been shown in at least twenty-five states, but we hadn't been able to get any money up front from television; we raised money from friends and doctors and lawyers, with the help of the Jamaican-Canadian Association. The Nova Scotia film is facing the same problems, but we're going to do it.

Claire. They say the golden age of the NFB is over, and we understand that, okay. But we were never part of the golden age.

Roger. I *like* documentary film, but we can't do classic works, with our resources, we have only a few weeks to shoot. We've never made a film where we had real money to shoot it. We have never had resources to thoroughly explore an idea. We have to be very careful and not explode the budget. It's a pressure so we can't take chances. We've never had a chance to mess up. With Buxton we could only capture the highlights. I'd like to go into Nova Scotia and spend as long as we need to shoot a true cinéma vérité film. Ain't gonna happen.

Claire. One bureaucrat told me, "We like you because you get things done on a shoestring and your work doesn't sit on the shelf" – even *Some Black Women* still gets used. It's so frightening and destructive when you don't know how things will end up with a project. We have to keep proving ourselves all over again, and I'm not interested in doing that. The main thing is you have to work. I feel the financial pressure all the time. You need time to talk to people. People need to see you and feel you. We need to see what other people are working on that we might be involved in. That's all part of the work that you do.

Roger. We've been thinking seriously about moving to the States. Sometimes you've got to cut your losses. [laughs] I've got a drama agent there. Unfortunately, you have to write those commercially paced quick scripts. But I like Toronto, I saw it grow up from being a little grey city to what it is now. I like this country, it grows on you.

When you're working on a film, do you think of a specific Black audience, or is the audience a more abstract entity for you?
Claire. To me, my first audience is Black. It's the reason to make the work, because we as Black people need to know and discuss what's going on out there, what our history is. Yet there's no reason why others wouldn't want to see our work. I received a letter from a white woman

after the showing of *Home to Buxton* on TVO, saying that she was frustrated and upset because no one had ever told her this history in school. The impression you get from the TV bureaucrats is that we're a really small audience, so why would others want to know? The mind-set is, "This is a Black film, they're a minority, so let's show it on a Monday afternoon." That's so stupid. They're telling us white people won't look at our films. I don't accept that at all. And in fact we think we reach a reasonably wide audience. *Home to Buxton* was seen by millions in the United States and Canada.

Roger. That's what they told us with the Buxton film. "We need a million viewers." As if everybody who isn't Black will turn the film off. If the film is well made, people beyond its "natural" audience will look at it.

Claire. We're often asked, "Why the focus on only Black films?" Number one, it's a silly question. I'm a Black person, what else can I do? Most filmmakers make films on what they are interested in, what they do, their lives. This is my life. What else would give me that connection, which is what you want?

Roger. It's an incongruous question. Because if you make personal films you work on what you know. But the fact that I choose to make Black documentaries on Black life doesn't limit me. I don't see why I have to explain that. Black history isn't only my history, it's the history of the world. If I wanted to I could make "universal" films.

Claire. It comes back to the "minority" issue. What they are really saying is, "Why would you want to remain a powerless minority?" I don't see it that way. I don't feel powerless. I feel angry and frustrated sometimes, but when there's movement in your life you feel fine – completing and making things whole.

Roger. There's no contradiction between making films about my community and making other films. This whole "political correctness" movement where you are not supposed to write films about others is nonsense. I have no problem in other people making films about Blacks – if they do it right. I'd rather we did it, but . . .

Claire. If Peter Steven makes a film about Buxton, then that's Peter Steven's film. No problem. Still, I'd like more Black people to have the power to do it. Another Black person could go into Buxton and make a completely different film than we did. Some of that [cultural appropriation] movement of "You shall not make films about us" is really only saying, "We want to do it ourselves."

I've begun to tell people, I'm not a minority, I can't live like a minority. I have to feel ownership of Canada and the institutions or I can't keep going. So, as far as filmmaking and my life is concerned, I'll simply continue to demand my rightful place in the world. We will keep pushing because we have the skills to do the job. Regardless of attitudes, we will continue to make films. We have learned to create openings and to be more pro-active. It's a tough job, but we have done it and we will continue to do it.

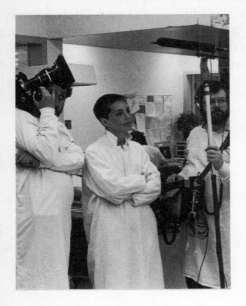

"I want to make beautiful and useful movies. But I'm not a saint."

Laura Sky (born 1946 in Montreal) brings to her documentaries a long affiliation with the women's movement, which has both encouraged the exploration of themes about women and work and stimulated a personal commitment to the women in her films.

At first Sky's work in film and video, starting at the NFB's Challenge For Change Toronto office in the 1970s and followed by her first independent work in the 1980s, bore the rather conventional stamp of expository documentary. In the mid-1980s her films shifted considerably to encompass experiments in cinéma vérité and a more staged and constructed approach. That shift away from the conventions of mainstream documentary combined with her deep commitment to the people she is filming makes her later work fresh and emotionally powerful.

Moving Mountains (1981) on women miners, *Houdaille* (1981) on the effects of a U.S. factory closing in Oshawa, and *Good Monday Morning* (1984) on the impact of computers on women's office work marked Sky's first efforts away from the NFB. These films earned a solid reputation as serious and well-researched essays on the lives of working people in Canada. Produced respectively for the United Steelworkers, the United Auto Workers, and the Canadian Union of Public Employees, the films were used both within the unions and by a much wider audi-

ence. Although Sky now feels dissatisfied with the conven͗
and pace of these films, *Good Monday Morning* in particular sᴛ͙
valuable role in education, stirring up considerable discussion and doiᴨ͙
valuable consciousness-raising.

All of these films were successful for one main reason – Sky knew
her audience. She felt committed to their struggles, researched their
needs and concerns, and drew the people in her films from their ranks.
Indeed, accountability, especially to working women, is the main principle that guides her documentary practice.

To Hurt and to Heal (Part 1, 1986, and Part 2, 1987) illustrates
another facet of accountability – to the people who appear on screen.
The films, which deal with babies who are either critically sick or die in
infancy, are structured by a series of extended interviews with parents,
nurses, and doctors. They frequently delve into the most painful areas of
parental and medical ethics. To reach this level of depth in interviews
requires lengthy, painstaking preparation with the subjects. Then to run
the interviews uninterrupted, nearly unedited, without resorting to
conventional cut-aways or the intervention of outside experts demonstrates a commitment to the subjects. The work is based on a form of
cinéma vérité interview where the director and the presence of the camera serve as a catalyst. It was a daring move – a radical shift away from
conventional exposition – requiring a stronger faith in the attention of
the audience than typical in documentary. Would viewers find the interviews too long and rambling, too emotional and self-centred?

This shift towards a more demanding style (for the director and the
audience) coincided with Sky's fundraising work for Peter Watkins's
The Journey (1989), a monumental fourteen-hour film about nuclear
weapons and the international peace movement. Sky and others, such as
Richard Fung and Montreal director Peter Wintonick, express admiration for Watkins's critique of standard documentary pacing – especially
the rapid-fire TV style based on the belief that viewers' short attention
spans need a jolt every few seconds. Although seen by few Canadians
(*The Journey* has been ignored by Canadian TV), Watkins's film will continue to challenge and inspire documentary filmmakers for years to
come. Sky later went on to co-teach with Watkins in Sweden.

Crying for Happiness (1990) takes the principles of accountability
even further than her earlier work. In this film on elderly patients suffering from depression, Sky's role as a filmmaker parallels and questions
the role of the doctors and nurses. Each must find methods of collaboration. Each wants the patients to be involved – in the film and in the institutional treatment. Around this time Sky began to develop the idea of

"informed consent," a term used in medical ethics, as a guide to film-maker/subject relations. Informed consent, as she defines it, is based on the belief that a patient "has the right to expect information from care-givers" and "on the basis of that information . . . may decide to give or withhold consent for medical treatment." Sky is convinced that informed consent should operate as a central principle for the film-maker as well, parallel to issues of medical consent between doctors and patients.

Sky also expanded the notion of informed consent to become a metaphor for the rights of film audiences to be informed about their society. In an open letter to the B.C. filmmaker Moira Simpson, she spoke about the role of independent documentary in providing information "so that the members of our communities can make informed decisions on the strategies that are vital for dealing with very crucial issues in our society." [9]

Crying for Happiness is designed primarily for a specialist medical audience, since it delves in great detail into the case histories of patients and includes intensive discussions among the doctors and nurses about their methods of treatment. Yet the obvious parallels between medical and documentary ethics set out a clear challenge to all documentary makers to examine their relations with those they want to put on screen.

The Right to Care (1991) bridges Sky's two interests – the practice of Canadian health care and the concerns of working women. With her lengthy portraits of five front-line nurses, Sky returns to communication with a general audience, but she assumes nevertheless that viewers will want to grapple with the complexities of the health-care system. The film assumes that viewers want to be better informed, and that providing detailed information is the role of the documentary filmmaker.

How did you become interested in film and video?
Laura. I've loved photography since I was very young. And I used to go with my mother to the art cinemas in Montreal. It was very special and we always dressed up to go to the cinema like on a date. I felt a strong relationship between imagination and the image.

I made my first film in Super 8 about my son's experimental day-care centre and then I did a film with people active in the Toronto school's movement about high-school streaming. I had been streamed in high school into a class for slow learners. I didn't think many parents really knew what was happening to their kids. I didn't know how to make movies and I was really scared about learning. Even then I still believed that I was a slow learner. But I became quite driven in an effort to make things better for students who were labelled and stuck in the slow stream.

Then you joined the NFB in Toronto. What were your goals at the Board in the seventies?
Laura. When I was first offered a job at the Film Board I refused it. I was worried about being co-opted by a government institution. Then a year later when the job came up again, being a single mother, I said yes. In fact, I was able to use the time at the Board as my apprenticeship.

The mandate was to make useful work that was part of community-based movements, so I started working with labour unions. At that time labour had a very broad sense of social and political member education.

We worked in video Portapak, then later in film. I was part of the Challenge For Change program, which we saw as a kind of political caucus within the Board. We were both renegades and participants at the same time. Working in video allowed us more freedom from the institution since it was so much cheaper. Perhaps the best tape we did was the one on the Artistic Woodworking Company strike, in 1974. We tried to use the apparatus as best we could, but we didn't trust it either. For example, my last film at the Board, *Shut Down*, was held up by the Board for being too anti-government.

Why did you then switch to producing on film? Have you thought of doing video again – perhaps for a smaller-budget project?
Laura. It's not a question of big scale/small scale. I could do film in a smaller way if I wanted. I've always hated video. I think it's flat and untextured, and I find the electronic process really remote to work with. The economics of the video process is transforming and deforming film language. When you're in a video-editing suite that costs hundreds of dollars an hour you're making choices based on a different time relationship to the creative process. It's no accident that information on TV is presented to us in a kind of confetti-like way since the economic pressures make us work too quickly. Our language is shortened, the process is shortened, and the image becomes a commodity. So video has changed our language and our perception as audiences, craftspersons, and artists.

I have recently been working with video in new ways, and in *Crying for Happiness* I used video extensively. I tried to experiment and bring the strengths of film language to video, in the dramatic re-creations, for example.
The production of the film was very complicated. I used video for its

instant playback since with that film in particular I wanted to build in real consent with the subjects. I wanted to democratize the document-ing process, and the new video technology did open up creative possibili-ties in this case. All the interview material was documented on tape, then transferred to reversal film for my editing. I love editing on film, I really love it. All the illustrative material in *Crying* was shot on film. Then I did an on-line video edit [computerized]. We did many tests to get the best sound and picture quality. Some of the technical people had a difficult time with this process. They thought I was nuts and could be more cost effective if I edited entirely on video. In choosing to do all the interviews on video, I found the freedom from the economic pressures of film interviews. We usually have to be very selective about how much of a conversation we put on film. So we went ahead and shot everything, which caused me to miss the discipline of being more selective. This, I think, was a weakness in the final film.

I see your three medical films, To Hurt and to Heal, Crying for Happi-ness, *and* The Right to Care, *as departures from your earlier work. Were you conscious of wanting something different when you started* To Hurt?
Laura. It was a very deliberate departure on two levels, both politically and formally. All my films till then had been related to issues of work, or the labour movement. But my analysis in the mid-eighties led me to believe that labour was now less interested in doing broadly based edu-cational material. Because they are under attack they are now more interested in producing material modelled on PR and advertising. In 1984 they were willing to spend $130,000 on *Good Monday Morning* – now they want to spend $50,000 basically to say how terrific they are to their members. The commercial mass media are now their model. Those films I can't do.

Previously my political and documentary models had come from Latin America. I had spent most of my time filming working-class people. I thought that perhaps it was time to try and work effectively with the middle class. I decided that I could focus on the ways middle-class people become politicized. Generally that happens when they per-ceive that what is being expected of them, in their workplace for example, is morally or ethically wrong. This doesn't necessarily mean they develop a political perspective related to public policy, for example, but rather, their first turning point comes when a real separation arises between what they experience in their gut and what the corporation or institution expects them to do.

In medicine this conflict was particularly clear. Also, I saw medicine as a microcosm for the relations between economic agendas and human need in our society.

In 1984 I started sitting in on medical-school classes and found that the most connected students were the ones who would stay after class and say that some of the issues were really bothering them. I spent a lot of time in hospitals trying to go beyond being an observer, to understand the experience of the issues from those people directly participating in hospital life. I immersed myself in it. For example, nurses were beginning to identify as a group and so I thought it was an area where I could contribute something.

In retrospect I made a mistake with *Crying* because I didn't work with groups that were mobilizing around ethical or political issues in psychiatry. I didn't make all those connections. The people seen in *Crying* are relatively unorganized and disenfranchised so the film has real political limitations. Some of these limitations are not only filmic but political. There are some politicized organizations that are working on health-care issues, but at the time I had become enclosed by the hospital experience.

In the future the only way I'll continue to make films on health care is to work with groups who are mobilizing. That's why *The Right to Care* looks at nurses.

In To Hurt and to Heal, *did you know before the interview with the Lévesques that you wanted to do the interview with minimal editing? Did you tell the Lévesques your stylistic plans?*
Laura. No. My plans changed completely. It was only after we got rolling that I thought "holy shit," we're not stopping this for anything. The Lévesques didn't think about it, which is normal in interviews. People are never prepared for all the stops and starts and the cutting, which they hate. It's part of the director's job to minimize the effect of the technical interruptions – to focus on the momentum of the conversation and keep the feeling that there's something real happening.

We had anticipated working in our normal way with continuous sound from the beginning to end and shooting a maximum of three rolls of film [thirty minutes]. Ordinarily we would record thirty to ninety minutes of audio and thirty minutes of film. There was no way I could shut off the conversation, which was a wild extravagance but it was so electric, what was happening.

And then the plan was to edit the interview into the overall film, and we tried working it in but it was just awful. Finally we left the interview intact and we only cut out a noisy airplane and the slates, which would have been silly to keep in.

During this time I was working with Peter Watkins as part of a support group in production of *The Journey*. We also taught together in Sweden. His way of working had a real effect on me at that time. He feels that audiences need to be free to wander away a bit, and then have their attention, imagination, and memory return to the screen. For me as a documentary filmmaker this was a very freeing concept. I became more comfortable with, and excited by, the longer interview. My earlier films are relentless – info, info, info. You're always stimulated. But I now see the value of the pause, and that losing the audience for a few seconds is not a failure. In fact the cameraman appreciated my leaving in the lingering moments, which he had valued during the shooting.

At the beginning of To Hurt and to Heal *you bring up a title that says, "The following conversation appears as it was filmed, unedited and in real time." Why were you concerned that the audience know that?*
Laura. [long pause] I wanted them to know that what they were seeing was in fact what had happened. There wasn't a filtering process through editing the material; they were getting everything – a process with no sleight of hand. We test-screened that long interview to see if people would lose concentration but in fact, in comparing the two versions – the unedited version and an edited one – people lost concentration in the second part of the film, which is a much more conventional style of documentary. People were riveted to the screen during the long interview and got more meaning from the conversation in that form.

How did you find the Lévesques?
Laura. There are witnesses and truth-tellers who always come forward. I met them the day their baby was born, which was also my first day in the neonatal unit. Because I didn't have a medical role or medical agenda I was the person there who Gaylene chose to lean on and talk to. Later, after the baby died, she called me again. I have a very profound ambivalence about privacy, and I only later thought of filming her.

Was there a sense that they would be read by an audience as role models or as representative?
Laura. The Lévesques did what they did for the same reason many people who I've filmed do. They feel something very hard has happened to them and the filming process is a way for them to deal with it, at the

same time as they make it better for others in the same situation. Helping others helps them too in the long run. The film has been effective for families, individuals, and also for self-help and support groups that deal with these realities.

If The Journal *or* Sixty Minutes *did this story they probably would have searched for a "bad" doctor or cases of "bad" decisions on the part of parents. Did you feel that approach would have been inflammatory?*
Laura. I thought it would have been stupid. Everybody doctor-bashes. One of the principles I've used is that it's not useful to make films that make people look like shits. I don't want everything rosy or everyone looking terrific, but I'm trying to support the audience to identify with people in the film, so that there's a real relationship between those on the screen and those watching. I'm trying to support that part of doctors and health-care professionals that in spite of all the problems shows a capacity for change individually and systemically.

Crying for Happiness *begins by stating that it was created with the consent of the participants. I know you mean consent as something more than the legal minimum release form. Could you talk about your notion of consent?*
Laura. Some of the interviews I've read with filmmakers about these questions make the hair on the back of my neck stand up. I saw Wiseman's *Titicut Follies* and a CBC film on a Hamilton psychiatric hospital, and these shaped my ideas about the need for proper consent. [10] This is my theory of the pinned butterfly documentary. "You may be a beautiful butterfly but I've got you pinned under this microscope and you're not moving." It's really problematic. In the CBC film a psychotic man is being filmed getting a haircut and he says, "Turn the camera off," but of course the camera doesn't go off.

We don't own a lot in this world, but we should own our privacy and the boundaries around us. People intrude on those boundaries all the time. But I believe that we only document with permission. It's more than consent, it's permission, and that has to have limits. I once had a paediatrician say to me, "You know we can get parents to agree to anything." Filmmakers can get film subjects to agree to almost anything too, they're flattered and enthusiastic, nervous, but it can be abusive in many different ways. It's not easy for my film crew, since they see it as double messages that I'm sending out; like I'm giving away my authority as a director, which can make it more difficult for them.

*Did you sense your participants felt the "obligation" to be a good inter-
view subject — sort of like a good patient?*
Laura. Oh yes. They feel obliged to open up their hearts and their lives.
At times in very surprising ways. And how do you deal with it? I guess by
acknowledging it as a gift. That sounds schmaltzy, but it is a gift. I tell
the subjects that if they feel unfairly represented I will alter the material. But it's always worth it.

In *To Hurt* the older doctor was very involved and I showed him portions of the film many times. But when he showed it to his wife and
other doctors they had real problems. So all of a sudden he saw how others were going to see him. I went back a year later and asked him how the
film had affected him. "The biggest problem," he said, "was that my
part went in *me* and came out *you.*" And he's not wrong. Hopefully it
comes out *we.* Now that's easier when you're working with political
people who have the same agendas. Consent has had a different meaning
in these medical films than in my earlier union films.

*This obviously parallels the model of medical collaboration and con-
sent between patients and doctors. In studying the medical model,
were you able to become more critical of normal procedures in filmmaking? Did you learn anything for your practice? To me it's this tension in the analogy between documentary practice and medical
practice that makes the film so rich.*
Laura. I learned how not to do it. I don't think you can ever say the word
"ethical" without saying "political." In the medical model you can certainly see paternalism. Doctors often pressure patients to accept what
the doctor thinks is best. By analogy to film it's like asking, "What's in
the best interests of the audience?" and then getting it wrong. In the
union films I felt we were working to the same purpose, but I was certainly coming from a different class situation. How do you compensate
for different daily experience?

The weirdest thing about being independent is that you cannot
function independently. The hardest thing about being political is that
you have to be responsible and accountable, and sometimes that tension
is unbearable.

Peter Morris says of you in his Canadian Film Companion *that your
films have "constantly challenged middle-class ideology and aimed at
radicalizing the audience." Could you talk about that notion of challenging the audience? First, who's the audience for the medical films?*

Laura. The strongest audience group is nurses. But what I want to say to them is, "You're right – the institutional powers are trying to tell you 'you're wrong,' but you're right." Film can play a role in a process of affirmation. That's often what I want to say to audiences. People are capable of understanding and have the capacity to act.

I'm trying to affirm what people might have only thought of in a private sense. I want to show models of people taking their thoughts to action, but without constructing simplistic heroes. I want to show people with fears and acknowledge situations that are scary. The image has incredible authority. I never want to say, "You assholes, all this terrible stuff is happening and you're not doing anything about it." That's destructive politically.

You've managed to become fairly well known and you've had success in making a living in documentary. Is it necessary to work at developing a profile? Do you see yourself as ambitious?
Laura. Well, us girls, we're not supposed to say we're ambitious. [long pause] In order to get money, lots of money, one risks becoming a commodity. Also, we don't often get recognition, and when we do it's a very ambivalent process. These awards that you see on the wall are very nice because they're from other filmmakers. For instance, I got this women's movement award that has been incredibly helpful for raising money. But the weirdest thing about raising money is that you have to look like you don't need it.

Two kinds of people give money to our projects: people who believe in them and people who give because they want others to think well of them for giving money – and for them you've really got to sell. They need good reasons from you. So I say to myself, "I'm going to have to wear pantyhose for this one hour, fine, I can handle that." I use the fundraising process as part of my research, the two are linked.

What I want to do more than anything else is make one movie per year till I'm sixty-five. So I'm wildly ambitious and ambivalently ambitious. There's no correct answer to your question. But it's disturbing that ambition and purpose have come to seem contradictory. I want to make beautiful and useful movies. But I'm not a saint. There's envy, jealousy, and competitiveness in our film community. We have to hustle constantly, and it's a strange process. Hustling is the centre of the film world, and the more you hustle the more you feel like you're selling a plastics product. You feel separated from the project, sailing off into the Pepsi world.

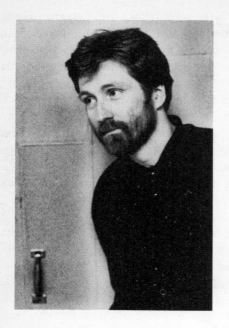

"I like to feel when I'm
shooting that
I have the whole
audience in my head."

In conversation **John Walker** uses the words "instinctual" and "emotional" to describe his artistic method and philosophy. Such terms can seem hopelessly naive and romantic, in these times of high theory within cinema studies, but in Walker's case they sit on a hard base of craft and technical training. Born in Montreal in 1952, Walker first became known as a cinematographer and has gone on to shoot more than fifty documentaries on all kinds of subjects for other directors. Since the early 1980s he has gradually moved into directing works of his own. His extensive technical experience lends a distinctive look to all his films and works to sharpen his ideas.

Chambers – Tracks and Gestures (1982) is a biography of the late Jack Chambers, a man who exerted considerable influence on his generation of Canadian painters through a series of works based partly on photography, in a style that Chambers called perceptual realism. But Walker is quick to point out that unlike the hyper-realists Ken Danby or Alex Colville, for example, Chambers's work was "painterly" and "emotional," based on classical training. The film won a number of international awards and immediately established Walker as a talented director. It also set the pattern for his subsequent films in its heightened discussion of history and art. *Chambers – Tracks and Gestures*

224

assumes that its audience knows something about Canadian art history, the history of Spain, and basic art technique.

Although he is not known as a political radical, Walker lives by a deep social conscience that leads him to complex political subjects. *Strand: Under the Dark Cloth* (1989) helped revive the reputation of Paul Strand, the brilliant U.S. photographer and master of the committed documentary. The film, which took eight years to complete, is a visual masterpiece and a moving labour of love, presenting in meticulous detail Strand's powerful photographs of Manhattan, rural New England, Mexico, Scotland, New Brunswick, Italy, and Ghana. *Strand* also delves into the photographer's fascinating and explicitly political film career and troubled emotional life. What emerges is a complex portrait told in Walker's partly autobiographical first-person narration.

To my ears, the personal voice within Walker's films is strong without lapsing into the standard journalistic tone of self-aggrandizement. Two films made in the Soviet Union for the BBC show that low-key journalism at work. *The Hand of Stalin: Leningrad* and *The Hand of Stalin: Leningradskaya* (both 1990) deal with some of the horrors of Stalinism only recently unearthed. *Leningrad* features intense testimonial interviews of victims and perpetrators of the old secret police. These interior conversations are punctuated with eerily quiet transition sequences of Leningrad streets and buildings, with camera work that hints of the secrets and menace behind closed doors and windows. The unpeopled outdoor transition sequences also provide a breather from the increasingly brutal stories being recounted – a cinematic pause that recalls the silent outdoor transition sequences in Yasujiro Ozu's Japanese family melodramas.

Leningradskaya reveals some of the same tragedies in a rural setting, following the trail of a young woman from the dissident Moscow Memorial research group. Walker's use of late-afternoon autumn light and landscape at harvest time provides a stark contrast to the conversations about the famines of the 1930s.

Distress Signals (1991) marked a departure from Walker's personal, emotionally charged Strand and Soviet experiences. An intricate co-production involving the NFB, the CBC, and Britain's Channel 4, *Distress Signals* examines in a current affairs form the business of global TV – the U.S. domination and the resistance of filmmakers and local broadcasters in France, Zimbabwe, and Newfoundland. Yet even with this essay film, which is not structured, Walker admits, in his favourite style, there is strong emotion, often anger, bubbling beneath the surface. He says, "The idea came from a very personal frustration about this industry that I'm in."

Both Chambers – Tracks and Gestures *and* Strand: Under the Dark Cloth *begin with shots of the materials of the art – close-ups of paint in one film, and of film chemicals in the other. Why are you concerned that the audience remembers the physical/material aspects of the two media?*
John. In the case of Chambers, his studio was left intact in all the details of the place. Nothing had been touched. His wife, Olga, had left it as a sanctuary. It was very strange to go in there with cameras, because she didn't want anything disturbed. It was almost as if his life had ended there in that room. The film was going to arc around to his death, so we started there. The choices made can't necessarily be intellectualized, and I tend to work instinctively.

In the case of *Strand* the darkroom is a place where you're alone, and there's an excitement dealing with the materials – a relation between person and image. I wanted a visual preface to the emotional themes. This is the material of the film, not just physical but spiritual and emotional that the film is about to explore. I wanted to establish myself as a storyteller. *I* work in a darkroom, *I* met this man, *I* have something to say about him. It was a way to establish me as a character. You try to get things working on different levels.

Tracks and Gestures *strikes me as a meticulously structured film that required a lot of planning for travel, location shoots, and writing. At what point did the structure come together?*
John. The producer Chris Lowry came to me with the idea about Chambers. I asked him to get slides and photos of all Chambers's work, then I took it all up to the country and started to look closely at it. I tried to respond to it in a linear fashion, and asked "What is this telling me? What is my emotional response?" Out of that I developed my first sketch of what I call the emotional structure. I don't work on a historical structure. I tend to see films in movements and I start off with movements. I see it almost as music: where it builds, the crisis point, where it drops, the tone. I start to feel the film. Then, what elements can I introduce into this emotional structure? When I'm dealing with an artist, I've got the paintings, the work, which forms the spine, and then I ask, what other elements will bring more life? Is it the work or the person's life? There's lots of debate about that. Ultimately I decided that the work was

the important part and the only thing that I could judge. It was created for me to look at, to respond to, react to. His life isn't there for me to judge, but it is a life nonetheless, and it has something to do with the work, and that's what I'm interested in. I ask, "What can help me understand the work from the life?" So that's the premise.

The sequences of Spain in Tracks and Gestures *interested me because you're hoping to reveal the country life Chambers might have experienced, yet the narration talks of "dark and brooding emotions" in an "impenetrable landscape."*
John. What you quote is from the Chambers diaries in Spain. The Spanish sequences are a little mini-film in themselves: he arrives at the Academy, after four years he feels Spanish and becomes Catholic, but in the end he says, "It was a landscape I couldn't penetrate." After, there was a romantic return to Canada and a whole shift into romanticism. I like working with tension – tension between a person's work and life. In Strand's case I saw an incredible tension.

Was Chambers's style of "perceptual realism" of interest to you as a photographer?
John. Absolutely. Chambers was one of the most interesting painters in Canada. I never met him, but I was really struck by his use of photography in his last exhibition. I'm not an admirer of photo-realism, or hyperrealism. I'm suspicious of that relationship. Chambers went way beyond the photograph. He used the camera and the photo as a reference. The hyper-realists simply paint photographs, often not very interesting ones, often lifeless. To me it's like socialist realism – devoid of any human contact. There seems to be a perverse attraction in proving photography doesn't have any heart or soul, purely a surface, mechanical thing. Chambers is unlike that. His paintings have emotion and all kinds of human elements – that, combined with his training as a classical painter. His work is painterly. It has a texture, a weight, a depth. He knew how to draw a hand, and that I admire. He had that training. I feel very sad that he died so young.

You've worked as a cinematographer on dozens of documentaries. One cliché is that directors don't know how to use the talents of their photographers. Has that been your experience?
John. A cinematographer can only be as good as the director they're working with. It's like a chess game. If you're playing with someone

more experienced than you, you learn from it, expand. I've had both experiences. In the beginning I worked with more experienced directors, but I've ended working with younger people who don't impose on me. I choose carefully. A good director in documentary is another eye. I keep my left eye open, but I'm only seeing a quarter of the world. The director should be the right eye, and also there to protect you: you may be run over. Good directors don't say, "Pan to the left," but they say something like, "There's a person coming in from the left, he's part of our film, watch out for this," thus allowing you to make your own decision. They gently give you a sense of your environment. In documentary you can't really direct. There's much more freedom for the cinematographer. That's why I stayed in documentaries. All your choices are instinctive, emotional responses. A good documentary director gets you into the context and lets you fly.

How conscious were you to try something different for your film on Strand?
John. I moved slowly towards the final form of the film. I was forced by the nature of the material to avoid something traditional. I was driving for a theatrical film that would work on the big screen, a theatrical experience, not a TV film. That was the major decision, though it didn't come right at the beginning. I thought that Strand's photos, with their incredible detail, shot in 35mm, and put on the screen, would be something people hadn't seen before. With most photos that you see on the screen, shot on 35mm, when you make a move or cut into a detail, you're cutting into the grain structure, and the image becomes grainier. With Strand's photos you see *more* detail. That's rare with photos on film, and can only be appreciated on a big screen.

It was a challenge to do a feature-length documentary using only stills. The film is driven, the way all my work is driven, by a sense of myself becoming the viewer. As a cinematographer I like to feel when I'm shooting that I've got the whole audience in my head, or sitting behind me. I want the audience to look through the viewfinder and to feel. For the Strand film I wanted a feeling on the screen that you were sitting quietly in a room, and the content of how you look at photographs was built into the filming. Some photos only require a full-frame shot. Others you follow the way the eye goes, into further detail.

Some of Strand's photos of people have been criticized for aestheticizing his subjects' faces, for treating the lines on a face in the same way he does the grain in wood or rocks. Were Strand's political ideas and his formal concerns ever at odds?

John. The way I view it is that Strand's rocks look like people. All the details of life come forward in a painterly tradition. His landscapes aren't particularly innovative, but what they share is the sense of landscape touched by human labour. In France, Italy, the Hebrides, he's showing landscapes and fields as labour, and architecture as created by the human hand. His books are very informative since they are real books, or films on paper. You see a portrait of a woman's face, then on the next page a rock. The storms, fog, wind, and rain that have weathered the rocks are the same weather that has beaten that woman's face. I don't see that as a criticism.

Criticism of Strand's later work often misunderstood his books. He wasn't going out shooting single images to make commodities. His books deal with juxtaposition. Like in the cinema, not every shot is a masterpiece, there's linking shots – little commas and apostrophes.

I do have some criticism of his work, which I didn't touch on in the film, though I tried. I'm not a critic and it would have shifted the whole tone of the film. He had been criticized for always photographing farmers and peasants, not the working class. He continually drifted to the old faces. In the *Living Egypt* book, for instance, he had to shoot the industrial worker, and the result borders on socialist realism – staged, composed, no life. He photographed material needed by the book, even though it wasn't central to his desires. He wanted to do modern Egypt, but he drifted to the older faces. You see some of that in his earlier work. It's forced, more of an idea. Strand was really good at showing people expressing their insides on the outside, reflecting quiet moments. Workers on a job site didn't suit him.

The Globe and Mail *critic Jay Scott says he was an emotional hermit. What do you think?*

John. I don't know what that means. It negates other elements. There's a movement to the film, tracing his emotional life. You feel sensuality. His portraits of Rebecca, his first wife, are deeply psychological. When she left he was totally shocked. His second wife Virginia, an actress twenty years younger, told me that his mother was not particularly warm with him. He feared the emotional world and distrusted women.

Photography is something you do alone. It encourages aloneness –
in the landscape, under the cloth. You get to like that. Those characters
like photography, and photography helps develop those characters. I
have felt that in my own life. My whole teenage life was spent in the
darkroom and it certainly affected my relationships. There's a lot of
autobiography in the film. During his film period in the thirties and forties he was pushing his world out by working on the bigger themes and
the ideas of socialism. Finally, his third marriage was much better. He
learned to touch and open up. He changed.

*Do you feel better equipped than Strand to go on making films, rather
than returning to the more individual art of photography?*
John. Filmmaking is a killer. But I don't see myself giving up for quite a
while. I'm keen on it. I'm at a good point where a lot of things are happening. If you look back on what you go through you think, "This is
nuts." You need patience. You need to plant seeds way in advance and
not expect immediate results. You go to the funders and broadcasters
and say I've got a proposal and if you can't look at it for this year put it on
your list for next year or the year after, but put it on the list. I'm not going
to go away until you do. The first projects are the toughest. *Strand* took a
long time partly to raise the money, but partly I wasn't enthused about
finishing, since it kept me sane.

*I found the music in the film quite extraordinary. Did you have a way of
describing what you wanted to the musicians?*
John. The one criticism I've heard at festivals concerns the music. I
showed the composer the film about six months before finishing,
describing it sequence by sequence, describing Strand, and his emotional tensions. When you put music over still photos, everything is
absolutely bare. With no movement to track and no sound effects, any
little squeak or squawk is huge. Any influence I would draw on would be
Beckett plays or Bresson, the creaking of lights which heightens. I didn't
want easy-listening background music. And I didn't want the tradition-
soothing emotive support. It's the opposite. It's meant to be intellectual
and perhaps obtrusive. The original idea was to have Glen Gould, and I
actually talked to him three weeks before he died and he was keen. That
would have been interesting. Gould's whole perfectionism, his intense,
hermit-like, Strand-like personality. Then I dropped classical music
altogether. I wanted something original and challenging. There are similarities to directing actors. You ask for twenty per cent and they give you

eighty – way too much. That happened in places with this film. There's ego involved, you don't want to insult the composer. All you can do is eliminate. You can't rewrite, they'd be so upset. At first I was scared to death about the music, but I liked its sense of fore, middle, and background, which allowed us to play with depth.

Was the composer present during the final mix?
John. Yes. We had a lot of discussion about the music. We didn't want stereo, surrounding you. It was unnecessary because the photos are very centred. We wanted the music to come from the centre of the screen. In fact we wanted to build depth – back – like a tunnel. At times there are sounds way off in the background and then "boop," there's sound to bring you back to the front and centre. It's new music. It's challenging. I wanted people to sit up and take notice.

I think that the best film composers have small egos, because music is only one element in a film. Each element of film has to be subverted at one time or another. At times picture dominates, then sound, music, dialogue. Theatre can take a lot more music in ways that don't interrupt. In film, music can easily dominate. Composers have to learn that. It's the most difficult for a younger composer.

Jay Scott in The Globe and Mail *related the music to your personal voice in the film. He called your personal voice "unnecessary."*
John. Filmmakers should ignore what critics say about their work. Scott's comments surprised me, since the response I was getting in Europe showed that people liked my personal voice. That was the film's strength. I like films where the author/filmmaker takes a clear position, and it's their comment. In the Strand film I wanted it clear that this is my voice. It's not an objective biography. It's true that in the Hebrides sequence I come out as a Scot – out from under the cloth. I'm a stand-in for Strand, but the narrator also stands in for me. That was the toughest sequence in the film. I wondered how far I should go in terms of my personal response. But I'm glad I did what I did there.

In fact I tried to set up the personal voice in the opening sequence. In the darkroom, that's me working there making it clear that I am telling the story. However, I didn't want my personality to be obtrusive.

How did the Hand Of Stalin *films come together?*
John. I'm quite proud of those two films. I got six months' free reading to immerse myself and prepare before starting. I read poetry and some

wonderful books, like *Hope Against Hope*, by Mandelstam. Lena
Pomerantz did the interviewing and her husband, Igor, is a Russian poet.
So we had some wonderful conversations, preparing for the shoot. He
said, "Don't have sympathy for anyone, don't try to explain. With the
poet's point of view you can't explain life, you can only experience and
share it. Spit it out." So I was fired up by their passion. I started with the
peasants in the south and their landscape, which I love. My family were
farmers in Scotland, so I'm comfortable with that life.

*Leningradskaya is incredibly beautiful, partly due to the late-afternoon
autumn light that you capture. When did you decide to use the harvest
as a metaphor?*
John. I was reading *And Quiet Flows the Dawn* by Mikhail Sholokhov,
which is about the Cossacks just before the war and revolution. I was
influenced by that. Yet I also felt I was extending the Strand film because
of the landscape. I refused to use the term "interview" and told the crew
we were making portraits. The characters I chose were similar to
Strand's – people who would express. It sounds crude and hard, but we
were casting. That's what documentaries do, but you don't often hear
about it. The film was like a river, flowing. Stories would be told, not
prepackaged. I wanted to show the abundance of the place.

*It wasn't clear to me who the interviewer was in the film. Was she
speaking Russian or English?*
John. The woman on camera works with a group of dissidents called
Moscow Memorial, who have been investigating and researching this
southern rural area. I wanted to show that. Now the group is trendy and
people are rushing to join it, but they started much earlier when it was
dangerous. I didn't want the feeling that this was the West and the BBC
coming in.

Is it possible to make sophisticated films like these in Canada?
John. These films would have had a hell of a time here – without commentary, the general approach. The British system treats documentaries as part of its regular diet. Here you have to fight to get them made
and seen. I got ten serious reviews in major British papers. In the U.S. the
PBS *Civil War* series was a great success – it would have been a tough sell
in Canada.

TVOntario and the other educational networks have shown the Stalin films. With its limited resources TVOntario is functioning nowa-

days as Canada's only truly public-sector broadcaster – like BBC-2. It's ironic that Canadians are making work that's more European at the same time as our broadcasting is becoming more commercialized and American.

Some critics and filmmakers are saying that the documentary as an art form is nearly dead and that audiences are bored. On the other hand, your group, the Film Caucus, is saying that the problems lie with Canadian broadcasting, which ignores documentaries. Are there fundamental problems with the conventional documentary? Or is it a question of different approaches for different audiences?

John. The essay form has been adopted entirely by *The Journal*, and my film *Distress Signals* is a current affairs essay unlike my other work. I made that choice as a challenge, to play with that form. Now I would like to do a purely verité film with no interviews at all, which will be tough because Telefilm now wants to see a script for documentaries. For *Distress Signals* we needed a twenty-three-page treatment! We'd even done the first shoot and quoted from it in the treatment and they said they needed a script. This is totally nuts. At the BBC, on the other hand, we wrote a general initial proposal, we shot, and I did a two-page treatment, with a list of characters and some historical context. When we discussed it, they were very supportive – critical but supportive: not *defend* your point of view and *tell us* why you're doing this. It was totally refreshing. Jane Drabble, the executive producer, organized a party for us. That doesn't happen here.

Somebody said the reason Canadians do well when they leave here is that this country is such a discouraging place to work. I don't know why that's so. We have lots of funding. It's that the support is so fragmented. As if when you do something good you should be quiet and humble about it because somebody might try and get you. I can't describe it. It's a very strange country. We do funny things to each other. We're not gung-ho supporters.

You've talked about the long process in getting Strand *completed. But at the same time you are now fairly well known in Canada for your work. How necessary is it to construct a profile for yourself and be ambitious to get your projects off the ground?*

John. I certainly don't operate with that premise. I'm just totally dedicated to films – pushing the films. Everything's for the film. I don't network in the industry, though everyone else seems to. I shy away from it.

On the other hand I'm president of the Canadian Independent Film Caucus. Your films should speak for you. There's a lot of people out there pushing with glossy packages – all show and no content.

In addition to having something to say, the people I've interviewed for this book have all achieved a measure of success and recognition. This is partly due to perseverance and a certain administrative ability.
John. Perseverance is certainly a key word. With the Strand film I was ambitious – it was a 35mm, feature-length art film, on a relatively unknown person. Hardly a sexy project for broadcasters. If you're asking what's the road to being successful as a documentary filmmaker, success is getting a film completed. You have to choose subjects that you're so committed to that you'll never give up. If I had merely liked Strand but felt no personal influence, the film would have died many years ago from the obstacles. Hundreds of films die. I have ideas every week that die. The strongest one is the one that gets made. You're judged on your films, not how flashy you are. On the other hand, there's great frustration. I've sold *Strand* all over in Europe, with great reviews. It won the Genie award here, but when we showed it to CBC Adrienne Clarkson wrote back saying, sorry, they only have a forty-minute slot. Then I see the fall season opens with an eighty-minute film on Prince Charles. I don't blame Clarkson, it's the system in general.

It's such a shame that documentary is not respected in Canada. The level of non-fiction could be raised by thinking filmmakers, broadcasters, and a critical press, yet it's continually marginalized by all the forces at play. You can measure the size of a film's budget by the size of the newspaper articles. Making documentaries is like trying to survive as a poet. What kills is neglect, lack of enthusiasm. It's our attitude about life, the lack of engagement with life. I know it's a cliché but the dominant popular culture is really having an effect.

I felt my mind had been asleep when I left Canada. British TV will have a gardening show in prime time, then in the next hour a terrific drama about lesbian teenagers, exploring sensuality. They take risks. TV can provide all kinds of forms. The key is diversity. Documentaries are cost-effective. They can play a really interesting role in society.

As long as you have confidence in the audience.
John. Exactly. I find that too often the media want to explore black and white, not the grey. For instance, all the news about priests and sex, well, how about interviewing somebody who's had a good sexual rela-

tionship with a priest? That's also possible. I'm interested in grey areas. There's an independent knee-jerk reaction to the system as well, producing work that feels like propaganda – films I've seen on Nicaragua, for example. They lose credibility. Give me some life and contradictions to chew on.

There's a lot of debate about balance and fairness, and many independents stress the need for point of view and bias. That's sometimes appropriate, but with other current affairs subjects it's often not in your favour to only go with your own point of view. I try to explain this to other filmmakers. I say look, you're doing something on acid rain and you have a particular view, but go out and interview the guys who are producing acid rain, they'll hang themselves and it will only strengthen your story. If you can't get to them, say that you tried and they wouldn't comment, like they do on radio documentaries. That's balance and fairness. What's the problem? *Distress Signals* works that way as point-counterpoint, since we talked to the presidents of Twentieth Century-Fox, M.C.A., etc., and present their point of view against their opposition.

Even if an audience ends up agreeing with the big guys, fine, that's the view of the audience. It's how you interpret that. There's no such thing as objectivity. When you're telling a story presenting two points of view, hot and cold, that sets up a dialectic and creates new meanings, and that's what's interesting to explore.

Distress Signals *includes no outside experts – no TV critic, for example. It's stronger because of that, I think.*
John. We wanted a behind-the-scenes look at the industry. Walking in for that first shot at the MIP TV market in Cannes you immediately see the classic global marketplace, with producers from around the world. You see the enormous economic and cultural pressures facing producers. It's amazing seeing all the TV series, all the cop shows, etc., that never get broadcast in the United States, but are flogged elsewhere. I was looking for Africans, a voice of the Third World, yet I didn't find any the first trip.

It's very depressing seeing what the two men from Zimbabwe TV end up buying.
John. I showed Zimbabwe as a national model. Here you have this struggling filmmaker, Ramius, who wants to tell his own stories, and you have Zimbabwe's only broadcaster, a public one, subverting him – not

giving him the support he needs, telling him he's spending too much money. Yet at the same time they go off and buy all this American material. They don't have to do that. The broadcasters always argue that "We have to fill the airwaves." But not all countries broadcast eighteen hours a day. Why not ten hours? So it's not just a case of the big bad Americans.

Did you consider including material on the CBC?
John. Yes. It was conceived as a three-part series. It began with my interest in Harold Innis, specifically his book *The Bias of Communications*. But I hadn't come up with a way to film that. For the series I wanted to do an international overview, then a developing country program, and finally a strong Canadian program. *Distress Signals* was to be the overview. The CBC felt that a Canadian film would be seen as too self-serving, so they committed themselves to the global overview only. There was too much resistance to the Canadian show.

How did you meet Ramius, the Zimbabwean director?
John. Tom Perlmutter, my co-producer, met him while doing preliminary research. We were searching for countries that would provide a broadcasting model. Ramius was very shy at first. Then he started coming out, gaining confidence.

So he hadn't been interviewed about his situation before, or talked to Western filmmakers about these general TV issues?
John. No. He said he learned a lot. I was able to say to him, "Look, you need support." With a reflector and other simple things he could improve his production quality. They have Betacam in Zimbabwe, all the best cameras. And they have an audience. That was the good news of the film. Anywhere in the world you will have an audience for your work if it's rooted in who you are, culturally, and if you are connected to your community.

It contradicts the old argument that Canadians will only watch American shows. Well, people will watch what's put on the air. It's free. A cop show – you watch it. Unfortunately, much of the Canadian drama being done is very close to the American stuff. And that's because of our tastes. You develop a taste.

I think all people have a range of tastes. I know I do, and I assume everybody else does. I like watching cop shows as well as very personal documentaries. So why should I assume that, for example, people in the

North shouldn't also want that range – from WWF wrestling to Inuit documentary?
John. Exactly. It's an issue of diversity. That's what I discovered in Britain as regular TV fare. Films on gays and lesbians. Sure, you've got an audience. British drama is so different. In *Truly, Madly, Deeply*, when the lead actress cries you see the snot mixed with her tears. It's real people, not beautiful people.

Do you feel any influence from art video or experimental film? Is that source of innovation a way of questioning standard documentary?
John. I'm open to it and feel stimulated, playing with sound etc., but I'm most interested when those films hit me emotionally. I'm quite keen to look more into the experimental side of film. I don't find inspiration from rock video. You just flick through and see some new technology. I can't stand the technical side of film, and with my cinematography I've struggled to make the camera an extension of me. It's that presence of the maker that I was trying for in *Strand*. So personally I want to get away from the technology. I don't want it imposing. I'm interested in relations between people, or between people and the world.

I like to have the camera move as my head moves, not as a detached observer. The camera moves and feels by what interests me. This new technology frightens me when it tries to separate us from the human material. I'm not a manipulator. When I hear that in video editing it's a nightmare to remove three frames, I say to hell with it, I'll stick to film.

Since you've been directing more, have you changed how you work as a cinematographer? Is it more complicated now? Are you ever second-guessing?
John. I made the biggest shift in my cinematography many years ago. It shifted from a visually based practice – a photography background, which was second nature since I'd been taking pictures since I was eight – to one based on listening. Not all cinematographers pay that much attention to listening. Now when I shoot or direct I want to hear what's happening. I wear a headset to hear the microphone, since sometimes in a medium or long shot you can't hear. I shoot with the audio in mind. I've come to realize that bad sound can ruin a good picture. Some of this consciousness of sound comes from editing. With documentary you can't go back or patch up bad sound in the studio. You just can't use it.

Perhaps I take my work too seriously. I find it pretentious to talk of documentary as an art. I feel that art is above me: like trying to attain

something that's impossible. Maybe it's an attitude, and you aspire to it
and push the medium. But it's not something you want to talk about.
When someone says, "I'm doing art," I immediately think, oh fuck off.
What I'm doing is dealing with life. What interests me is that documentary in its purest form is poetry, organizing life in a way that's not
mechanical. I read descriptions of how Mandelstam wrote his poetry
and how he would almost get physically ill with a massive headache and
shake like something was coming. This creative force was moving into
his body and he was preparing. I'm like that when I'm about to do a film.
I get tense and I can't breathe, I'm washing the floor and doing everything else but the film. It's a fear that you're not going to be connected.
So I am conscious that creative process is a state of mind and that I cannot create at the drop of a hat. That terrifies me in trying to do film for
TV deadlines.

7

Anatomy of the New Documentary: A Canadian Avant-Garde

In their work over the past decade or so, the producers of the new documentary have renewed and reworked documentary as a form of media practice. They have tended to take on unlikely subject matter, and in doing this they have followed both personal and political agendas. They have worked at freely mixing conventions, at building radically new forms, and at establishing responsible and creative relationships with their "subjects."

As an aid in analysing the role and work of the producers of the new documentary – and especially to help explore the gap between the major contextual forces (the general histories, the political forces, and major institutions) and the individual producers and their work – we might consider the concept of "intellectual formation" as developed by the Welsh cultural analyst Raymond Williams. [1]

According to Williams, a formation is a group of people who, at minimum, share a cultural perspective in order to establish a distinct role in the larger society. Formations can be *specialist* groups (such as guilds, clubs, professional organizations), *alternative* groups who aim to establish a new cultural viewpoint, but do not wish to alter the general relations of the society (such as the French Impressionists, the Group of Seven, or the New American Cinema), and *oppositional* groups who, as Raymond Williams stated, actively oppose "the established institutions, or more generally . . . the conditions within which these exist" (such as documentary movements within South America during the 1960s and Quebec's Common Front of the 1970s). [2] As Williams points out, grey areas exist between specialist, alternative, and oppositional practices, and one group can at various times adopt different stances.

Formations can be as strictly defined as large institutions with manifes-
tos, fixed memberships, and firm principles, or they can be loose associations, or even tendencies, wherein the members do not even define
themselves as part of the group.

As a tool of analysis the concept of formation allows us to group
people by their similar responses to the more general contexts and conventions pertinent to their art. For example, in considering the introduction of new video equipment, rather than jumping from the invention of
new technology to its use in specific tapes it seems essential to consider
first how specific cultural attitudes within a formation might *shape* the
use of the new equipment. Similarly, outlining the social-class position
of artists does not in itself "explain" why they make certain types of art.
Rather, an hypothesis that groups them within a cultural formation
(which includes information on their class situation, education, and
affiliations) provides a much sharper analytical tool.

All the people discussed in this book occupy positions within the
middle class. This has little to do with birth or income and everything to
do with specific patterns of education and relative comfort. That, in
turn, allows them to develop projects and create with confidence. Along
with confidence comes a degree of power to get things done. Most of
these producers could work in the mainstream, but they choose not to.

Whether the practitioners are defined as artists or cultural workers,
this type of middle-class practice brings with it specific experiences and
attitudes. Some producers can support themselves solely through their
own productions, others take freelance commercial jobs or unrelated
work, but all define themselves primarily as working filmmakers or
videomakers. This is their life work. Even when working inside the
"communities" to which they belong, their situation as art producers
makes them different. They are not merely activists who occasionally
take up a camera – their occupation is filmmaker or videomaker.

Yet their power remains severely limited. Unlike mainstream and
formalist documentary-makers whose work can carry a wide influence,
if only to prop up the social and artistic status-quo, those who choose
oppositional politics generally work at the margins of Canadian society.
Their films and tapes have difficulty finding mass media distribution
and exhibition. A major television broadcast is rare. Of all the films and
tapes discussed in the interviews, only Alanis Obomsawin's *Richard
Cardinal* and John Walker's *Chambers* and *Distress Signals* have been
shown on the CBC. And as far as the critics are concerned, "We're not
even on the map," filmmaker Judith Doyle says.

They demonstrate a racial mix of First Nations, African Canadian, Asian Canadian, Central and South American backgrounds, white English-speakers, and Québécois; also a roughly equal number of women and men. These differences cannot be easily overlooked, nor should they be. Certainly, the existence of a cultural formation composed of such a diverse group could easily break apart in the years just ahead. There are also growing connections among international cinema movements, many powered by non-white producers. And these oppositional ties could establish racial difference among Canadian producers as the key to new developments in the future. Yet to some extent the differences represent an attempt by the producers and by many of the communities documented to build an inclusive multiracial politics in sharp contrast to a mainstream stuck in the mire of ignorance, fear, or outright racism towards others.

The people interviewed for this book comprise an intellectual formation that continues the tradition of committed media. They represent a middle-class fraction that aligns itself with forces trying to disrupt existing society – in Williams's terms, an oppositional practice. The cultural ideas and general world view that they share provide the best way to group them together. These shared views include:

- a belief in the power and influence of the mainstream media in Canada – the media have specific imposing effects and influence over individual viewers and in society.
- a scepticism about received documentary forms and conventions.
- a belief that the old oppositional art strategies based solely on presenting new content will no longer suffice.
- a scepticism about existing "alternative arts movements" such as the "experimental film" and art-video practices.
- a belief that documentary needs to be practised in close collaboration with documentary subjects, that is, with non-artists.
- a discomfort with received notions of the artist – both the romantic and commercial varieties.
- a desire to reach new audiences, that is, to move beyond community groups and galleries.
- a world view based on the major concerns of post-1960s North American radicalism – critiques of capitalism and imperialism, and the politics of race, class, and gender.

Although these shared views fall short of the consistency to be found in a cultural manifesto or political party, they do place this set of people apart from their peers.

A Canadian Avant-Garde

The specific attempts by this group to create alternative and oppositional cultural practices, linked with their concern for innovative formal strategies, also makes them a Canadian avant-garde. I use the term avant-garde warily, since it carries with it a complex European history – often associated exclusively with formalist and aesthetic criteria, as in some currents of mid-century modernism, epitomized in painting by abstract expressionism, and in late-century postmodernism, embodied architecturally in Ottawa's National Gallery and Vancouver's new Public Library. Also, film historians have often linked the terms experimental and avant-garde, in very specific discussions, usually with little bearing on documentary. Indeed, for some critics, the act of placing documentary and avant-garde in the same sentence amounts to a contradiction in terms.

The new documentary producers form an avant-garde for two fairly straightforward reasons. First, the group is concerned with the formal strategies of documentary as a cultural practice. They not only qualify as an artistic formation, they have produced innovations. Second, they deal with key Canadian issues untouched by the mainstream but of great concern and significance nonetheless; they consistently anticipate these issues in advance of their peers. They could play a leading role in setting Canadian cultural agendas into the next century.

Some specific characteristics of the new documentary also make this group an avant-garde formation: the discomfort with received notions of artists and their subjects (those people used as witnesses, or interviewed on camera or off camera); the attempts to challenge both documentary *and* experimental forms; and the desire to reach new audiences. Whether this particular avant-garde will force changes in the dominant media or become co-opted does not undercut their avant-garde status today. The best avant-garde remains an effective one, but many crushed or shunned movements have had their effect nonetheless.

My use of the term avant-garde relates to my earlier discussion of committed media, but also works as a more specific concept. The idea of committed media emphasizes the producer's general outlook and intentions. The term avant-garde, by historical usage, if not consensus, suggests the importance of formal strategies. But in no sense do I wish to link avant-garde with elite or minority tastes or an anti-popular aesthetic. Although these formalist sentiments have been common in past avant-gardes, they need not be here.

The development of First Nations film and video, exemplified by Zach Kunuk, provides one clear example of committed media coupled with formal innovation. Nascent groups such as the First Nations Media Coalition in Ontario and the Chief Dan George Society in British Columbia, with members working in documentary and fiction and as critics, provide support and encouragement. This new awareness has been reflected in the thinking of the white producers interviewed here. There is an awareness that the old ways of visual anthropology, no matter how well intentioned, will no longer suffice; neither neutral observation nor participant observation will continue unchallenged. Ethnographic media-making is on the defensive, and new visual languages for representing First Nations' people will soon dominate this documentary avant-garde formation. Whether the new approach will register on the mainstream media remains to be seen.

Throughout this century many avant-gardes have developed a strict formula that links artistic form and political effect. And mid-twentieth-century attempts by committed film and video groups to codify a political aesthetic have not been fruitless. In the 1970s, efforts by the women's movement to define a woman's or feminist aesthetic fuelled the critique of patriarchy and led as well to new forms within documentary and narrative fiction, such as Michelle Citron's *Daughter Rite*, Anne Claire Poirier's *Mourir à tue-tête* (1979), and Joyce Wieland's *The Far Shore* (1975). Among unconstrained video artists, from Nam June Paik to Lisa Steele, the attempts to carve out an anti-television aesthetic led to a rapid expansion of possibilities for all documentary work. Also in the 1970s, theorists of "counter-cinema" advocated variations on Brecht's formal strategies of distanciation – a cinema of the head in opposition to Hollywood. This Hollywood/anti-Hollywood polarity has waned among committed producers and theorists, partly under the influence of new international practices based instead on concepts such as Third Cinema, diasporic cinema, and the very diverse forms of Third World Cinema. [3] All three of these practices are extraordinarily pluralistic and more open to incorporating popular genres. It is only when a political aesthetic comes to assume that all viewers will respond to it similarly that the various sorts of prescriptive conventions become dead ends.

In terms of formal strategies, this Canadian avant-garde is less prescriptive than many of its predecessors and its formalist peers. The group I've interviewed exhibits nearly unanimous dislike for voice-of-God narration, but many still use it (albeit in more subdued terms, as commentary) and none of them seem inclined to label it the Trojan horse of patriarchal or fascist aesthetics, as some of their predecessors might have. In most of the interviews I asked the question, "Are there particular conventions in mainstream documentary that really bother you?" John Greyson answered, "Voice-of-God narration is pretty high up on my bad list. At the same time I can think of good reasons to use it, as a way to shape content and capture information, etc." Richard Fung said, "You mean that male voice-of-God narration, I suppose? *Orientations* has no narration . . . but I didn't really cut it out for theoretical reasons. It's the rhetoric of truth in documentary that bothers me."

Despite the problems surrounding the concept of avant-garde, the loose ties holding this group together as a formation, and the non-prescriptive aesthetics behind their work, these producers do represent a coherent and distinct force within Canadian documentary. Their shared outlook about innovation and their relations with larger communities have allowed them to achieve a body of distinguished work. Their films and tapes reveal enough similarities to accord them the status of an avant-garde rather than the simple recognition bestowed on individual creative artists.

I believe that without formal experimentation documentary may well die, to be replaced by fiction and personality journalism. In addition, this new reworking of the ethical and political relations between media producers and the people they film, tape, and record epitomizes the only way that documentary can remain viable politically. Producers must rethink their working methods. If they do not their subjects will become ever more wary of co-operating, and audiences will reject any claims of truth or significance that documentary can offer. The future of documentary in Canada is at stake.

Notes

1. The Look, Sound, and Feel of the New Documentary

1. Satellite Video Exchange Society, *Catalogue* (Vancouver, 1977), p.29.
2. I use the term *postmodern* in the most general sense, as it has been applied in the arts since 1980. In contrast to modernism, which for the most part tries to pare down and isolate those elements considered to be unique within an art or within a genre, works of the postmodern revel in the mixed. In architecture the Toronto Dominion Bank building, with its "form follows function" minimal appearance, is decidedly "modern," and the National Gallery in Ottawa, with its mix of gothic elements and basic modernist steel and glass, is frankly "postmodern." In film, a work such as Michael Snow's *Wavelength* (1967), with its forty-five-minute forward zoom, exemplifies modernism; John Greyson's *Urinal*, with its documentary interviews, fictional scenes with actors playing historical characters, high-art references, and low-camp party scenes, is flamboyantly postmodern.

Postmodernism has also acquired meanings that suggest that as an art phenomenon it parallels (or reflects) life in the 1980s and 1990s. But modernist art still claims its adherents, so there is no neat transition like that of French Impressionism followed by Cubism.

I use the term *hybrid* to discuss those documentary films and tapes that mix conventions normally found in another mode or genre. This type of mixing goes beyond the ordinary use of narrative in documentary. Most critical attention has been directed towards those hybrids mixing documentary and fictional drama: in mainstream television, the docu-drama and drama-doc; within the art world, those mixing documentary and theatrical performance. This book concentrates on films and tapes that mix conventions *from within* the expository mode, using conventional documentary as the baseline. Among new documentary practitioners, John Greyson has probed furthest along these lines, and *Uri-*

nal crosses over towards docu-drama in its explicit use not only of narrative and exposition but also of fiction.

3. I am indebted to Bill Nichols for this particular phrase, which helps describe what I am attempting in this book.

4. This is not the first time the word "new" has been applied to a particular type of documentary, and I'm sure it won't be the last. Alan Rosenthal used the term twenty years ago to cover everything from *A Married Couple* to the most conventional TV news specials. See his *The New Documentary in Action* (Berkeley: University of California Press, 1971).

5. Bill Nichols, *Representing Reality: Issues and Concepts in Documentary* (Bloomington: Indiana University Press, 1991), p.ix. The books he mentions are listed here in the Bibliography.

6. Gary Evans, *In the National Interest* (Toronto: University of Toronto Press, 1991).

7. The dictionary defines *rhetoric* as a logical or persuasive argument, and in the visual media critics usually associate the term with direct-address documentary. But other types of media also employ it. There is a rhetoric to much fiction and observational documentary as well. This conforms to a more general, and modern, use of the word to describe any fairly elaborate system of communicating (the rhetoric of journalism, or the rhetoric of fashion, for instance). In this book I define rhetoric as a set of conventions that together form a conventional practice, both social and ideological.

8. Gary Evans provides a fascinating overview of the Billy Bishop affair in *In the National Interest*, pp.295-298. For a vigorous attack on the film, see H. Clifford Chadderton, ed., *Hanging a Legend: The NFB's Shameful Attempt to Discredit Billy Bishop VC* (Ottawa: War Amputations of Canada, 1986).

9. "Donald Brittain: Filmmaker Needed an Outsider's Touch, Robert Fulford Explains," *The Globe and Mail*, December 9, 1992, p.C-1.

10. I take this definition of formalism from Chuck Kleinhans, "Forms, Politics, Makers and Contexts: Basic Issues for a Theory of Radical Political Documentary," in Tom Waugh, ed., *Show Us Life* (Metuchen, N.J.: Scarecrow Press, 1984), pp.318-344.

11. I should point out that the works of Vera Frenkel, Gary Kibbins, Robert Morin and Lorraine Dufour, and Norman Cohn that I have seen deal for the most part with issues of concern to left and feminist politics: women's representation in the media, the colonial history of Canada, marginalized racial groups, and working people. Some of their work fits my definition of the new documentary, but the tapes I cite here do not. These, in contrast to the new documentary, seem produced in a vacuum and unlikely to connect with audiences to produce social change.

12. The quoted phrase is from Kleinhans, "Forms, Politics, Makers and Context," p.322.

13. Réal La Rochelle, "Committed Documentary in Quebec: A Still-Birth?" in Waugh, *Show Us Life*, pp.280-301.

14. Julia Lesage, "Feminist Documentary: Aesthetics and Politics," in Waugh, *Show Us Life*, p.226. Here I should point out that Lesage's influential article does not dismiss out of hand those feminist documentaries that focus on "problems of identity in the private sphere," since they often carried a deep structure that paralleled the consciousness-raising groups of the 1970s.

15. Throughout the book I use the term *producer* as a convenient shorthand to refer to the person most central in the creation of a film, video, or television program. In the film world the person at the creative centre of production work is usually called the "director," while the money person and general organizer is the "producer"; in video art and television the person equivalent to the director in film is referred to as a producer.

16. Use and gratifications studies usually attempt to show the variety of functions that the mass media normally serve in fulfilling needs within the so-called mass audience. These include the needs to acquire information, to experience emotion and aesthetic experience, to develop self-confidence, to strengthen contacts with others, and to escape and find diversion. This sort of framework creates a strong bias towards a philosophy of individualism and seeing the media as simply a matter of communication. Other types of audience theory attempt to show the media and their audiences more in terms of power relations and group dynamics. For a good summary of the use and gratifications tradition, see J. Fiske and J. Hartley, *Reading Television* (London: Methuen, 1978), pp.68-84.

17. Quoted from La Rochelle, "Committed Documentary," pp.280-301.

2. The Changing Face of Documentary 1960–80

1. Louis Marcorelles, *Living Cinema: New Directions in Contemporary Film-Making* (New York: Praeger, 1973), p.30.

2. Michel Brault, interviewed by Pierre Jutras and translated by Will Straw, *Cinétracts* 10, Vol.3, No.2 (Spring 1980), pp.37-48.

3. Bruce Elder, *Image and Identity* (Waterloo, Ont.: Wilfrid Laurier University Press, 1989), pp.103-118.

4. For Rouch's views on Quebec cinéma direct, which he largely praised, see Eric Rohmer and Louis Marcorelles, "Entretien avec Jean Rouch," *Cahiers du Cinéma*, Vol.144 (June 1963), pp.1-22.

5. Quoted in "Television's School of Storm and Stress: Robert Drew's Documentaries Aim at Photographic Realism," *Broadcasting*, March 6, 1961, p.82.

6. James Blue, "Thoughts on Cinéma Vérité and a Discussion with the Maysles,"

Film Comment, Vol.2, No.4 (Summer 1965), p.22. For a provocative, thoroughly researched essay on the rhetoric of U.S. direct cinema, see Jeanne Hall, "Realism as a Style in Cinéma Vérité: A Critical Analysis of *Primary*," *Cinema Journal*, Vol.30, No.4 (Summer 1991), pp.24-50.

7. For more information on these films and an analysis of narration in Latin American documentaries, see Julianne Burton's wide-ranging article, "Democratizing Documentary: Modes of Address in the Latin American Cinema, 1958–72," in Waugh, *Show Us Life*, pp.344-383.

8. Interviews can take many different forms, from the quick snatches of vox populi favoured by TV news programs to long, wide-ranging conversations. Interviews and interview segments can take different forms on screen as well. Interviewer and interviewee can both be seen on camera facing each other; the interviewee can face the camera/interviewer/audience directly; or the interviewee can be alone, facing slightly off centre. This last strategy usually takes the "masked interview" form, whereby an interviewer is implied but not seen or heard. It is by far the most popular interview set-up in conventional documentary.

9. *Ballad Of Hard Times*, Richard Boutet, Pascal Gelinas, Lucille Veilleux, Quebec; *A Wives' Tale*, Sophie Bissonnette, Martin Duckworth, and Joyce Rock, Quebec; *Harlan County U.S.A.*, Barbara Kopple, U.S.; *The Wobblies*, Stewart Bird, Deborah Schaffer, U.S.; *The Battle Of Chile*, Patricio Guzman, Chile/Cuba; *El Salvador: The People Will Win*, Diego de la Texera, Revolutionary Film Institute of El Salvador, El Salvador.

10. Gary Evans describes the historical relations between the NFB and the CBC in *In the National Interest*.

11. Brian Winston, "Documentary: I Think We Are in Trouble," *Sight and Sound*, Vol.48, No.1; reprinted in Alan Rosenthal, ed., *New Challenges For Documentary* (Berkeley: University of California Press, 1988), pp.21-34.

12. See in particular, Bill Nichols, "The Voice of Documentary," in Bill Nichols, ed. *Movies and Methods*, Vol.2 (Berkeley: University of California Press, 1985), pp.259-273.

13. Peter Wollen, *Signs and Meaning in the Cinema* (London: Secker & Warburg, 1969).

14. David MacDougall provides a good summary of his position in "Beyond Observational Cinema," in Nichols, *Movies and Methods*, Vol.2, pp.274-287.

15. See UNESCO, *Many Voices, One World*, final report of the International Commission for the Study of Communication Problems, or McBride Commission (Paris: UNESCO, 1980). For a broader discussion of the New World Information and Communications Order, see Armand Mattelart, Xavier Delcourt, and Michelle Mattelart, *International Image Markets: In Search of an Alternative Perspective* (London: Comedia, 1984).

16. The extremely useful theoretical framework of invention, innovation, and diffusion is taken from Robert Allen and Douglas Gomery, *Film History: Theory and Practice* (New York: Random House, 1985), pp.114-115.

17. Brian Winston, *Misunderstanding Media* (London: Routledge, 1986). Winston uses slightly different terminology than Allen and Gomery and provides a more sophisticated (and entertaining) account of the relations among science, industrial technology, and social necessity. My description of video technology and its adaptation by the broadcast industry relies on Winston's account.

18. The information in figures 2 and 3 comes from John Bishop, *Making It in Video* (New York: McGraw Hill, 1989); Winston, *Misunderstanding Media*; Eric Barnouw, *The Image Empire* (New York: Oxford, 1970); and Kim Tomczak, co-director of V-Tape, Toronto, interview with the author, January 1992.

Figure 2 lists only the "inventions" of video technology (the machines produced by the industry), not the prototypes or scientific experiments stretching well back into the nineteenth century that made video possible. Figure 2 also concentrates on video production, rather than consumption, and lists the date that new machines entered the market. In the case of artist-run centres and community TV enterprises, the editing machines especially were not purchased immediately because of cost. The diffusion was certainly uneven.

Figure 3 suggests some of the basic "properties" of video that producers have had to reckon with. These "properties" are not inherent. They represent the mixing of invention, innovation, and diffusion by the video industry, largely determined by the huge video corporations and the needs of broadcast television.

19. This comparison of, first, North American television's 525 lines with 16mm and, second, HDTV with the resolution of 35mm film is discussed in Winston, *Misunderstanding Media*, p.58.

20. Allen and Gomery, *Film History*, p.115.

21. For a brief discussion of the switch from kinescope to videotape at the U.S. networks, see Barnouw, *The Image Empire*, p.79.

22. Martha Rosler, "Shedding The Utopian Moment," and Renee Baert, "Video in Canada: In Search of Authority," both in *Video* (Montreal: Artexte, 1986).

23. Marty Dunn, "Introduction," *Videoscape* (Toronto: Art Gallery of Ontario, 1973).

24. Peggy Gale, "Video Art Has Captured Our Imagination," *Parachute*, Summer 1977; reprinted as the "Introduction" to the exhibition catalogue *In Video* (Halifax: Dalhousie Art Gallery, 1977).

25. Clive Robertson, review of the Video/Vidéo exhibition held at Toronto's 1981 Festival of Festivals Trade Forum, in *Fuse* November/December 1981) pp.266-270.

26. Herschel Hardin's angry book *Closed Circuits* (Vancouver: Douglas and McIntyre, 1985) describes some of the history of cable TV in Canada, including the unusual experience of Saskatchewan where the government-owned Sask-Tel provided the cable infrastructure so that real community programming became a possibility: unfortunately short-lived. In the other provinces private cable companies owned the distribution system and thus were able to control programming and set rates.

27. Lisa Steele et al., "Introduction," *Women and Film Catalogue* (Toronto: Women and Film International Festival, 1973), p.6.

28. See Evans, *In the National Interest*, p.161.

29. Ibid., p.168.

30. For a brief history of this split, see Judith Doyle, "Negotiating Representation: Notes on Community-Based Film and Video in Canada," *Independent Eye*, Spring 1991.

31. Clive Robertson, "The Second Independent Video Open," in *Fuse* January 1980.

32. Kim Tomczak of V-Tape disputes this statement and says Canada has produced little that can be termed avant-garde, high-art video. Canada's tradition, Tomczak argues, actually shows much more interest in documentary when compared to the situation in Europe. Still, it seems to me that if we compare levels of funding and levels of critical recognition, art video dominated the Canadian scene until the mid-1980s.

33. Gale, "Video Art."

34. Baert, "Video in Canada."

35. See Waugh, *Show Us Life*.

36. Blakeston's article, "Two Vertov Films," appeared in *Close Up* magazine, August 1929; reprinted in Lewis Jacobs, ed. *The Documentary Tradition*, 2nd ed. (New York: Norton, 1979), pp.49-53.

37. Esther Shub (1894–1959), a major force in Soviet cinema in the 1920s and one of the first women directors, is best known for her compilation films, *The Fall of the Romanov Dynasty* (1927) and *The Russia of Nicholas II and Leo Tolstoy* (1928). These were powerful reworkings of footage originally shot for pre-revolutionary newsreels.

3. The Canadian Context

1. Refugee figures are from Immigration Canada, "Report to Parliament," Ottawa, 1989. See also *Managing Immigration: A Framework for the 1990s* (Ottawa: Immigration Canada, 1992).

2. Peter Harcourt, "The Innocent Eye," in Seth Feldman and Joyce Nelson, eds., *Canadian Film Reader*, (Toronto: Peter Martin, 1977), p.72.

3. D.B. Jones, *Movies and Memoranda* (Ottawa: Canadian Film Institute, 1981), p.74.

4. Elder, *Image and Identity*, p.135.

5. Susie Mah as quoted in Arlene Moscovitch, *Media and Society* (Montreal: NFB, 1989), p.52.

6. Winston, "Documentary: I Think We Are in Trouble."

7. The CBC is a Crown corporation, whereas the NFB maintains only an "arms-length" status, accountable to cabinet.

8. Ian Taylor, "*The Journal*," *Borderlines*, Summer 1986, pp.14-18.

9. Telephone conversation with the author. Confidence in the audience demand for non-narrative fuels the provincial broadcasters to a greater degree. TVOntario, the largest, shows hundreds of documentaries, programmed to stand alone and as series. Unfortunately, few Canadian works other than NFB products make the cut. Radio-Québec provides its viewers with a greater range of Canadian independent and internationally produced works.

10. Joyce Nelson, *The Colonized Eye: Rethinking the Grierson Legend* (Toronto: Between the Lines, 1988); Peter Morris, "Praxis into Process: John Grierson and the N.F.B.," *Historical Journal of Film, Radio, T.V.*, Vol.9, No.3 (1978).

11. This phrase was used in the Film Act of 1950. The original wording by Grierson in 1939 was "to help Canadians in all parts of Canada . . . understand the ways of living and the problems of Canadians in other parts." For more detail, see Evans, *In the National Interest*, p.17.

12. Peter Morris, "Backwards to the Future: John Grierson's Film Policy for Canada," in Gene Walz, ed., *Flashback* (Montreal: Mediatext, 1986), p.27.

13. Nelson, *Colonized Eye*, pp.127-129.

14. Marc Raboy, *Missed Opportunities: The Story of Canada's Broadcasting Policy* (Montreal: McGill-Queen's University Press, 1990).

15. See Canada Council, *Report on Access*, Ottawa, January 1992, for some evidence of movement in this area. See also "No Council Guidelines on Cultural Appropriation," in *Bulletin*, No.37 (Spring 1992), for the Council's official response to questions of cultural appropriation.

16. Richard Fung, "Colouring the Screen: Four Strategies in Anti-Racist Film and Video," *Parallelogramme*, Vol.18, No.3 (1993), pp.38-54.

17. Winston, "Documentary, I Think We Are in Trouble."

18. For a strong statement by a filmmaker on the appropriation of Native stories and imagery, see Loretta Todd, "Notes on Appropriation," *Parallelogramme*, Vol.16, No.1 (Summer 1990), pp.24-33.

19. Trinh T. Minh-ha, "Documentary Is/Not a Name," *October*, Summer 1990, p.94.

4. The Elements of Documentary Distribution

1. When a large distributor forces an exhibitor to screen "B" pictures or those with weak box-office potential as part of a deal to secure exhibition rights for an "A"

film, the practice is known as block booking. Although it now occurs less often than in the heyday of Hollywood, the practice still does take place.

2. This section on distribution is based on my experience at DEC and Full Frame. Other distributors, at Video Femmes, IDERA, and V-Tape, for example, will undoubtedly have collected slightly different experiences.

3. *Our Marilyn* is discussed in the interview with Brenda Longfellow; *Sima's Story* is an impressionistic testimony of life in Alberta for new refugees from Iran, the family of the filmmaker; *The Forgotten War* is a fiction based on the true story of German soldiers who escaped from a prison in Quebec during World War I.

4. Quoted in Ferne Cristall and Barbara Emanuel, *Images In Action: A Guide to Using Women's Film and Video* (Toronto: Between the Lines, 1986), p.34.

5. I am using the term *representation* in the conventional, fairly broad, sense of how people are treated on the screen, rather than in the full theoretical, and narrower, sense, which has replaced notions of truth or realism in modern media theory.

6. See in particular Alan Rosenthal, *The Documentary Conscience* (Berkeley: University of California Press, 1982); Calvin Pryluck, "Ultimately We Are All Outsiders: The Ethics of Documentary Filmmaking," in Rosenthal, *New Challenges For Documentary*, pp.255-269; and John Katz et al., eds., *Image Ethics* (New York: Oxford University Press, 1988).

7. Statistics taken from the report of the Task Force on the Canadian Non-Theatrical Film Industry, *The Other Film Industry* (Ottawa: Department of Communications, 1986).

5. Audiences: The Ideal and the Real

1. Claire McCaughey, a researcher for the Canada Council, compiled a study showing that cultural programs on television were watched in disproportionate numbers by older, university-trained women. The study did not deal with social-issue documentary, so its bearing on the new documentary is unclear. See Claire McCaughey, *A Survey of Arts Audience Studies: A Canadian Perspective, 1976–1984* (Ottawa: Canada Council, 1984).

   The Department of Communications, the Canada Council, and Statistics Canada occasionally publish relevant statistics on audiences. Gary Evans touches on the work of the NFB's Audience Needs and Reactions Unit in his *In the National Interest*, for example on p.193.

2. Solid evidence of Chomsky's views on television and popular culture can be found in the Canadian film *Manufacturing Consent* (1992), directed by Mark Achbar and Peter Wintonick for the NFB. Nelson develops her views on the power of TV, which she links to the development of the atomic bomb, in *The Perfect Machine: TV in the Nuclear Age* (Toronto: Between the Lines, 1987).

3. See Ien Ang, *Desperately Seeking the Audience* (London: Routledge, 1991), p.ix.

4. In addition to Ang's *Desperately Seeking the Audience*, the most sophisticated and useful book-length studies of audiences include: Ien Ang, *Watching Dallas: Soap Opera and the Melodramatic Imagination* (New York: Routledge, 1985); James Lull, *Inside Family Viewing* (New York: Routledge, 1990); David Morley, *Family Television: Cultural Power and Domestic Leisure* (London: Comedia, 1988); David Morley, *The Nationwide Audience* (London: British Film Institute, 1980); and Ellen Seiter et al., eds., *Remote Control: Television, Audiences, and Cultural Power* (New York: Routledge, 1991).

5. On the level of the viewer and the film or tape, we need to know how specific viewers engage with documentary as opposed to narrative fiction: whether, for example, the frameworks of learning take precedence over those of entertainment, whether viewers are more apt to see themselves as part of a social group than when viewing fiction. I develop some of these ideas later in the chapter.

   In terms of the documentary in society, demographic studies by race, class, age, and gender can help to postulate a theory of documentary in the social fabric. Conventional market research and the sophisticated studies of British current affairs programs and U.S. soap operas might serve as starting points, but we need to develop empirical, analytical studies of conventional as well as unorthodox documentary.

6. See Tania Modleski, *Loving With A Vengeance: Mass-Produced Fantasies for Women* (Hamden, Conn.: Archon Books, 1982).

7. See in particular Bill Nichols, *Ideology and the Image: Social Representation in the Cinema and Other Media* (Bloomington: Indiana University Press, 1981).

8. Media theorists have noted the problems in trying to set strict limits to the terms "text" and "audience." Some even argue that the terms should be dropped altogether since they reify what are in fact relationships. But dropping the terms altogether seems a theoretical extreme, because audiences are certainly capable of using a term like "text" as a convenient shorthand, while knowing that it is made up of a set of relationships with no fixed boundaries.

9. Film, television, and literary theory often refer to the text as a site of competing discourses. A *discourse* is a set of ideas, values, or feelings shared by a social group, just as often unconscious as conscious.

10. The term "supertext" is taken from Nick Browne, "The Political Economy of the TV (Super)Text," *Quarterly Review of Film Studies*, Vol.9, No.3.

11. Analysis of the mainstream TV audience has become more complex with the advent of late 1980s feminist theory. Charlotte Brunsdon argues: "The use of autobiographical data, and the validation of the pronoun "I" makes an important contribution to theory." Women and other groups "have worked to construct autobiographical data as "proper" data." See Charlotte Brunsdon, "Text and Audience," in Seiter et al., *Remote Control*, pp.116-129.

   In ethnography, a field much closer to documentary than commercial TV fiction, the role of scientist observer has been under scrutiny for years, forcing the field worker as well as the theorist to analyse their links to "their subjects." To keep up with these developments the analyst of the audience must write her/himself into the equation in a way that traditional communications theory did not require. In the study of popular culture, writing oneself in can sustain political motives as well – working as a statement of solidarity (or duplicity) with the audience. This can be tricky if the result only validates in populist fashion any media product enjoyed by both audience and theorist: "I like *Dallas* and I'm a sophisticated viewer, so maybe the general audience isn't so naive after all."

12. The terms "dominant," "negotiated," and "oppositional" reading originate in the work of the British sociologist Frank Parkin and were adapted by Stuart Hall in his influential article, "Encoding/Decoding," in Stuart Hall, Dorothy Hobson, Andrew Lowe and Paul Willis, eds., *Culture, Media, Language* (London: Hutchinson), pp.128-138. Hall argues that these terms represent the three potential types of decoding that viewers can engage in.

13. Tamar Liebes and Elihu Katz have developed a series of categories for analysing the critical abilities of viewers. They showed episodes from *Dallas* to small groups in different countries, then during interviews coded all the verbal responses as referential or various types of critical. See "On the Critical Abilities of Television Viewers," in Seiter et al., *Remote Control*, pp.205-221.

14. Morley also draws on the work of Dorothy Hobson, Ien Ang, Charlotte Brunsdon, Stuart Hall, and others. An overview of all this work is contained in Morley, "Changing Paradigms in Audience Studies," in Seiter et al., *Remote Control*, pp.16-44.

15. For an excellent analysis on how particular audience groups understand and use film stars, see Richard Dyer, *Heavenly Bodies: Film Stars and Society* (New York: St. Martin's Press, 1986). Dyer examines how Marilyn Monroe, Paul Robeson, and Judy Garland were "read" by women, Black, and gay audiences respectively.

16. See Marshall McLuhan, *Understanding Media: The Extensions of Man* (New York: McGraw-Hill, 1964).

17. See Horace Newcombe and Paul Hirsch, eds., *Television: The Critical View* (New York: Oxford University Press, 1987).

18. Theoretical models help frame some of the questions, but without empirical studies it remains extremely difficult to predict whether a film or tape will be more thoroughly appreciated or effective in one medium or another. Empirical studies comparing the response to, and effect of, a medium and setting for a given film or tape will need to consider other contextual factors, such as public awareness of the issues in the work and awareness of the director and genre. Given an adequate theory combined with empirical investigation, it is possible

to conclude that a work will be better received in one setting over another – via one medium over another.

19. A rhapsodic 1992 article in *This Magazine* delights in the fact that feature documentaries have been reborn, largely because they have made money on the arthouse circuit. See Ian Pearson, "Ext./Int.: Documenting the Remarkable Comeback of Canadian Documentaries," *This Magazine*, May 1992, pp.27-31.

20. For a concise history of the film club movement in Canada, launched in 1935, see Yvette Hackett "The National Film Society of Canada, 1935–1951: Its Origins and Development," in Walz, *Flashback*.

21. These observations are based on my experience as a distributor of new documentary and my conversations with other distributors and producers. One exception is the annual Mayworks Festival of Labour and the Arts held in Toronto and Vancouver.

22. This is a slight exaggeration, because Laura Sky and Sara Diamond have worked closely with unions, and their films and tapes have achieved success in finding union audiences.

6. Interviews with Film and Video Producers

1. Readers wishing to pursue this key period of film and politics in Quebec will find solid analysis in Evans, *In the National Interest*; La Rochelle, "Committed Documentary"; and Marc Raboy, *Movements and Messages: Media and Radical Politics in Quebec* (Toronto: Between the Lines, 1984).

2. Ron Geyshick, *Te Bwe Win* (Toronto: Summerhill Press, 1988).

3. Midi Onodera's *Displaced View* is an innovative documentary on three generations of Japanese-Canadian women.

4. *The Body Politic* was an influential gay newspaper published in Toronto from 1972 to 1986.

5. See, for example, "The Search for Voice: *La Femme de l'hotel*," included in *Dialogue: Canadian and Quebec Cinema* (Montreal: Mediatext, 1986), and "Postmodernism and the Body," *Canadian Journal of Political and Social Theory*, Vol.XIV, Nos.1-2-3 (1990).

6. *Scandal* (U.K., 1989) tells the story of Christine Keeler and her entanglements with the British war minister John Profumo and a Soviet military attaché in the early 1960s.

7. Chris Marker is a noted French documentary filmmaker, born in 1921. His *Sans Soleil* was produced in 1980.

8. See, for example, Fred Landon, "Social Conditions Among the Negroes in Upper Canada Before 1865," *Ontario Historical Society*, Vol.XXII (1925); and Robin Winks, *The Blacks in Canada: A History* (Montreal: McGill-Queen's University Press, 1971).

9. *Cinema Canada*, December 1988.
10. Fred Wiseman's *Titicut Follies* was produced in the United States in 1967.

7. Anatomy of the New Documentary: A Canadian Avant-Garde

1. Raymond Williams described the concept of formation most succinctly in his *Culture* (Glasgow: Fontana, 1981) and *Problems of Materialism and Culture* (London: Verso, 1980), analysing the Bloomsbury Group (Virginia and Leonard Woolf et al.) as an intellectual formation. My thinking on the new documentary producers as a group is based largely on these works.

2. Williams, *Culture*, p.70. The term New American Cinema was first coined by a diverse group of New York filmmakers and critic Jonas Mekas to describe the diverse experimental cinema flourishing in the United States in the early 1960s – the films of Robert Frank, Shirley Clarke, Stan Brakhage, John Cassevetes, and others. The Common Front was launched in 1972 by the three largest union centrals in Quebec, the CSN (Centrale des syndicats democratiques), the FTQ (Federation des travailleurs du Québec), and the CEQ (Central de l'enseignement du Québec). A wide range of radical social and media groups linked up with the unions to become what political analyst Marc Raboy described as the "largest protest movement ever in modern Quebec (some would say, in North America), a movement involving more than three hundred thousand workers." See Raboy, *Movements and Messages*.

3. The concept of Third Cinema derives partly from the famous 1969 manifesto by Fernando Solanis and Octavio Getino entitled "Towards a Third Cinema," reprinted in Nichols, ed., *Movies and Methods*, pp.44-64. The authors call for a third type of cinematic practice in opposition to Hollywood and to the art cinema – a practice "outside and against the System."

   Contemporary adaptation of the term Third Cinema, the source of heated debate in Britain, embraces work produced in the Third World and the capitalist West, but there is considerable disagreement over the scope and applicability of the concept. For discussions of Third Cinema see Jim Pines and Paul Willemen, eds., *Questions of Third Cinema* (London: British Film Institute, 1989), especially Willemen's "Introduction" and the essay by Reece Auguiste, "Black Independents and Third Cinema: The British Context," pp.212-217. Auguiste states that the conceptual framework called Third Cinema "does not allow adequate space for a critical evaluation of the distinctiveness of films emerging from Britain and other western metropolitan centres," especially African and Asian peoples of the diaspora – a diasporic cinema (p.215). See also Teshome H. Gabriel, *Third Cinema in the Third World* (Ann Arbor, Michigan: UMI Press, 1982). Also, John Downing has edited a superb anthology of Third World cinema writings in *Film and Politics in the Third World* (New York: Autonomedia, 1987).

A major source of inspiration for all these practices has been "For An Imperfect Cinema," by the Cuban filmmaker Julio Garcia Espinosa, reprinted in Michael Channon, ed., *Twenty-five Years of the New Latin American Cinema* (London: British Film Institute, 1983), pp.28-33.

The Producers' Films and Tapes

Maurice Bulbulian
(all works on film)

1968. *La P'tite Bourgogne* (Little Burgundy). 43 min. Portrait of a poor neighbourhood in Montreal.

1970. *Un lendemain comme hier.* 41 min. The fictional story of a Québécois working-class family's generational conflicts.

1971. *En ce jour mémorable.* 14 min. A detailed documentary portrait of the same family as in *Un lendemain comme hier.*

1971. *Dans nos forêts.* 89 min. A cinéma direct investigation into Quebec's forest industry, using interviews, montage sequences, and observational sequences with long takes.

1973. *Richesse des autres.* 94 min. Miners and the mining industry in Quebec, and a miner's delegation to Chile during the time of the Salvador Allende government. A major work of Quebec documentary in the 1970s.

1974. *Salvador Allende Gossens.* 18 min. A portrait of Chile's mining industry based on a speech by Allende to a delegation of Quebec miners in 1972. The film was denied international distribution by the NFB (for details, see Evans, *In the National Interest*, p.191).

1974. *La revanche.* 22 min. Bulbulian returns to investigate Quebec's forest industry, this time putting more emphasis on foreign control. A faster-paced, less observational film than *Dans nos forêts.*

1976. *La lutte des travailleurs d'hopitaux* (with Denys Arcand).

1976. *Y'a rien là.*

1977. *Les gars du tabac* (On the Tobacco Road). 26 min. Young Québécois workers in their annual migration to the tobacco fields of southwestern Ontario, their conflicts with "English" gangs and Mexican migrant workers. Fast-paced and rapidly edited to a rock and blues sound track.

1978. *Tierra y Libertad*. 93 min. A gruesome portrait of the Tierra y Libertad slum on the outskirts of Monterrey, Mexico. Featuring very long takes – with people standing facing the camera and testifying about their lives – no music, and minimal montage, but with a voice-of-God narration.

1978. *Les délaissés*. 26 min. Life for some of South America's most impoverished peoples, living in communities in the heart of cities.

1978. *Ameshkuatan – les sorties du castor*. 24 min. A mix of ethnographic observation and social documentary on life among the Montagnais in Eastern Quebec, focusing especially on the traditions of beaver hunting.

1983. *Cissin . . . 5 ans plus tard*. 37 min. A report on the African country of Upper Volta (now Burkina Faso) and its attempts to provide housing in rural areas. (co-produced with the United Nations.)

1983. *Debut sur leur terre* (Our Land, Our Truth). 54 min. Shot in the Inuit communities of Ivujivik, Povungnituk, and Sugluk of Northern Quebec, a matter-of-fact, non-romantic documentary on economics, language, family life, and the law.

1985. *Surs nos propres forces*. 43 min. Bulbulian returns to Burkina Faso after independence and documents new housing and transportation systems plus the conflicts between traditional chiefs and young revolutionaries.

1987. *Dancing Around the Table*. Part One. 57 min. The first three constitutional conferences to discuss aboriginal rights, featuring Pierre Trudeau at his most belligerent and four major First Nations representatives. Bulbulian accompanies the Native leaders back to their communities to show the reality of their positions in the talks.

1989. *Dancing Around the Table*. Part Two. 50 min. Mulroney, the provincial premiers (excluding Bourassa of Quebec) and Canada's First Nations' leaders make one final effort to negotiate at the fourth and final Aboriginal Constitutional Conference. Featuring the analysis of Ethel Pearson, a Kwakiutl elder from British Columbia.

1992. *Salt Water People*. 121 min. A study of the fishing ecosystem of British Columbia as seen through the eyes of the Kwakiutl Nation.

Sara Diamond
(all works in video)

1980-82. *Concerned Aboriginal Women.* 58 min. A cinéma vérité documentary of an occupation by B.C. Native women at the Department of Indian Affairs offices. *This Line Is Not in Service.* 30 min. A document of the strike among women operators at B.C. Telephone. (both as co-producer, as a member of Amelia Productions)

1982. *Influences of My Mother.* 24 min. Biographical and autobiographical sketches with staged vignettes about Diamond and her mother.

1984. *Heroics.* 38 min. *Heroics: A Quest.* 3 ½ hour installation. Heroes in "the feminine," with the presentation of women speaking directly to the audience about the notion of the hero and heroic moments in their lives.

1988. *Keeping the Home Fires Burning: Women, War Work, and Unions in British Columbia.* 49 min. A rich blend of social-issue documentary with performance and staged scenes of popular theatre as it might have looked in the union halls of the 1930s and 1940s.

1989. *Ten Dollars or Nothing!* 11 min. The reminiscences of Josephine Charlie, a Native woman from Lake Cowichan, Vancouver Island, are mixed with dense, rapid-fire images culled from historical footage of B.C.'s First Nations. The images are reworked, slowed down, coloured, and reversed through optical printing.

1990. *The Lull Before the Storm.* 2 parts. *The Forties.* 48 min. *The Fifties.* 50 min. A drama that also integrates historical footage, which tells a story of women's work in the paid labour force and at home.

1991. *The Lull Before the Storm.* 2 parts. *Women Of Wood. Community Acts.* Each 48 min. Interviews with women whose lives revolved around British Columbia's largest industry from the 1930s to the 1950s: wood, especially logging and millworking, with a focus on South Asian and white women.

1991. *Patternity.* Video installation – première, Vancouver Art Gallery. "Relationships between parent and child, and the experience of memory as it is transferred from one generation to the next. Three video tapes projected simultaneously on eight monitors. Screenprint, multiple media, and phototransfer on fabric and furniture." (from the National Gallery of Canada program)

1992. *On to Ottawa Trek.* 53 min. A multi-layered work of documentary and performance based on a play by Tom Hawker about the

1935 demonstrations of the unemployed, which were violently broken up by the RCMP in Regina.

1992. "Memories Revisited, History Retold," A Retrospective Exhibition of video works by Sara Diamond. (National Gallery of Canada)

1992-93. *29/92* and *Fit to be Tied*. Two histories of British Columbia domestic workers, in the country and in the city.

Judith Doyle

1982. *Private Property, Public History*. Super 8. 20 min. A work of experimental cinema examining the lives and stories of women in the Creemore, Ontario, area.

1982. *Launch*. Super 8. 12 min. An experimental work dealing with shipyard union organizing in Collingwood, Ontario.

1983. *Eye of the Mask: Theatre In Nicaragua*. 16mm. 58 min. A cross-section of Nicaraguan culture during the early years of the Sandinista revolution, focusing on the popular theatre movement and the work of Alan Bolt's Nixtayalero company.

1988. *Neguaquan – Lac La Croix*. 16mm. 58 min. A portrait of the Ojibwa community of Lac La Croix, Ontario, situated near Quetico Provincial Park just northwest of Lake Superior.

1991. *Whitefish Bay: Self-Government*. Video. 30 min. Produced for the Whitefish Bay First Nation of northwestern Ontario to explain the process of achieving self-government being negotiated with the federal government.

1991. *Seventh Fire*. Video. 17 min. Produced for the Anishinabe Health Centre, Toronto. Portraits of Native healers examining the philosophies of traditional medicine as they apply today.

Richard Fung

(all works in video)

1985. *Orientations*. 56 min. Portraits of gay and lesbian Asians involving testimony, self-validation, and analysis, and concentrating on the relations between gender and race. The tape mixes loose storytelling with a more conventional talking-head approach.

1986. *Chinese Characters*. 20 min. A tightly constructed essay commenting on and deconstructing the conventions of documentary as seen in *Orientations*. A parody of documentary and pornography, aimed primarily at gay Asian audiences.

1988. *The Way to My Father's Village.* 38 min. The first of two family biographies that trace Fung's parents from China to Trinidad to Canada. This tape shifts between the tension of storytelling and a much cooler formal structure that examines how we attempt to gain historical knowledge.

1989. *Safe Place: A Tape for Refugee Rights in Canada.* 35 min. Co-produced with Peter Steven. Interviews with new refugees to Canada, with a focus on their reception on arrival.

1990. *My Mother's Place.* 49 min. The life of Rita Fung in Trinidad and Canada as presented through interviews, home movies, a trip home to Trinidad, and attempts to establish a context for such a life through analysis by feminist intellectuals.

1990. *Fighting Chance.* 30 min. Four Asian men at different stages in their life struggles with HIV.

1991. *Out of the Blue.* 28 min. The story of a young Black man from Scarborough, Ontario, who was falsely arrested for a robbery committed in another town while he was in church.

John Greyson
(all works in video unless indicated)

1980. *The Visitation.* 40 min. A pseudo-documentary with performance sequences on gay life in Toronto, "narrated" by activists at a gay radio station.

1983. *Manzana Por Manzana.* 35 min. A portrait of the Nicaraguan city of Esteli, focusing on farmworkers and grassroots Sandinista militants.

1984. *To Pick is Not to Choose.* 44 min. Produced for the Ontario Farmworkers Union, a tape that outlines the joys and hardships of seasonal farmworkers in southwestern Ontario.

1986. *Moscow Does Not Believe in Queers.* 27 min. A "construction" using documentary sequences, as well as a documentary frame using constructions. Based on a trip to a Soviet youth conference and featuring Rock Hudson submarine movies.

1989. *Urinal.* 16mm. 100 min. A drama-documentary hybrid based on the arrests of gay men in Ontario public washrooms, featuring analysis by Sergei Eisenstein, Langston Hughes, and other gay and lesbian historical figures.

1989. *The World Is Sick (Sic).* 38 min. On the Fifth International Conference on AIDS, 1989, Montreal, featuring analysis by members of

Toronto's AIDS Action Now, a CBC narrator in drag, Pink Panther cartoons, and a dizzy array of cheap video effects.

1989. *The Pink Pimpernel*. 32 min. The lead character as dandy activist, smuggling AIDS treatment drugs into Canada. His escapades jostle with documentary and performance sequences.

1991. *The Making Of Monsters*. 16mm. 35 min. "Originating in an actual case in which a group of teenage boys brutally murdered a gay man in a park ... brilliantly incorporating everything from Marxist aesthetics to hockey machismo, to tire fires – a strong fearless statement of gay pride." (from the Festival of Festivals catalogue)

1993. *Zero Patience*. 16mm. A $1.2-million feature-length musical comedy debating the theory that one man, "Patient Zero," brought AIDS to North America.

Other works, best described as short fictional constructions, include *First Draft* (1980), *Breathing Through Opposite Nostrils* (1982), *The Perils Of Pedagogy* (1984), *The Jungle Boy* (1985), *A Moffie Called Simon* (1985), *Kipling Meets the Cowboys* (1985), *The Ads Epidemic* (1986), and *You Taste American* (1986).

Zach Kunuk
(all works in video)

1983 to present. Directs a weekly program as station manager and senior producer at the Inuit Broadcasting Corporation (IBC) Production Centre in Igloolik, Northwest Territories.

1985. *Walrus Hunter*. VHS. 30 min. One of fifty programs produced through Igloolik IBC.

1985-89. *From Inuk Point of View*. Includes the program *Inuit Life*. 30 min.

1988. *Amittuqmiut*. A weekly television program produced by Kunuk and Simon Quassa.

1989. *Qaggiq* (Gathering Place). 58 min. Inuktituk with English subtitles. Co-produced with Norman Cohn. Documents aspects of the Inuit way of life near Igloolik around the turn of the century. It re-creates the gathering together of several nomadic families, the building of a communal igloo (*qaggiq*), and the celebrations that follow – games, singing, and drum dancing. Although the story-line of the tape was carefully scripted, the dialogue and interaction between characters were improvised throughout.

1989. *Alert Bay*. 58 min. A portrait of a West Coast B.C. First Nation settlement, showing culture, history, the natural surroundings (including whales), and interviews with elders. Shot while Kunuk was an artist in residence at Vancouver's Video In.

1991. *Nunaqpa* (Going Inland – Summer Hunt). 58 min. Co-produced with Norman Cohn. Three families re-create life during the summer for the Inuit of the Igloolik area at the turn of the century. A sequel to *Qaggiq*.

1993. *Saputi* (Fishtrap). The third tape in the series of historical re-creations.

Brenda Longfellow
(all works on film)
1984. *Breaking Out.* 28 min. An experimental documentary that uses a script and dramatized sequences to highlight the problems of Canadian single mothers, many of them victims of spousal abuse.

1989. *Our Marilyn.* 29 min. An analytic yet emotionally moving account of the 1954 Lake Ontario marathon swim by seventeen-year-old Marilyn Bell, as compared to the media image of Marilyn Monroe, a world icon at the time. The film uses archival footage, rephotographed and altered by optical printing, and a fictional narrator named Marilyn.

1992. *Gerda.* 80 min. A docu-drama based loosely on the 1960s sex and security scandals in Canada involving Gerda Munsinger and cabinet ministers in the Diefenbaker government.

Alanis Obomsawin
(all works on film, produced at the NFB)
1971. *Christmas at Moose Factory.* 13 min. Children's crayon drawings tell of life at Moose Factory, an old settlement on James Bay. The first filmed result of Obomsawin's work with Native children.

1977. *Amisk.* 40 min. A recording of Inuit and Indian performances in Montreal to raise funds for the Cree to fight the James Bay hydro project. The film also glimpses the organizing efforts of the Cree of Mistassini, Quebec.

1977. *Mother of Many Children.* 57 min. A portrait of several First Nations' women from different cultures.

1984. *Incident at Restigouche.* 46 min. The first film to bring Obomsawin wide recognition. It retells the story of the violent 1981 Quebec Provincial Police raids on the Mik'maq reserve of Restigouche, New Brunswick – an attempt to restrict Mik'maq salmon fishing. The film sets up a dramatic "crisis structure," using still photos taken during the raids by participants, TV news footage, interviews, and re-enactments. It also includes a famous heated interview between Obomsawin (seen on camera) and the Quebec fisheries minister.

1986. *Richard Cardinal: Cry From a Diary of a Métis Child.* 29 min. The tragic story of a seventeen-year-old Métis boy who committed suicide after living in twenty-eight foster homes, shelters, and lock-ups in Alberta. The film mixes interviews, reminiscences, and lyrical re-creations of Richard's life as a young boy.

1987. *Poundmaker's Lodge.* 29 min. A portrait of an innovative Native-run institution in Alberta that helps Native and Métis people with alcohol and family problems. The film uses Obomsawin's characteristic personal voice-over, using phrases such as "our people," and features clips from workshops and discussion sessions. There are many victims, with stories of horrible family lives, but all of them are placed within the framework of a positive institution.

1989. *No Address.* 58 min. A film about homeless Native youth in Montreal in the style of investigative journalism, but told from the vantage point of a concerned insider. As in *Poundmaker's Lodge,* Obomsawin balances the tragic stories of young Native people with portraits of healthy Native institutions, in this case the Montreal Native Friendship Centre and the women's radio station in Kahnawake. The story centres on two young people who sleep on the street but get help through the Friendship Centre.

1993. *Kanehsatake: 270 Years of Resistance.* 120 min.

Yvan Patry and Danièle Lacourse
(all works on film unless indicated)

1982. *Guerrilla Priest.* 28 min. The story of a priest in the combat zones of El Salvador.

1982. *Les refugies salvadoriens.* 23 min. The drama of Salvadorian refugees within El Salvador itself and in Honduras.

1983. *Central America, A Time of War.* 8 parts. *La strategie Americaine, Ballots and Bullets, El Salvador: The Powderkeg, Priests in Arms, Flight From Terror, Women in Nicaragua: The Second Revolution, Miskito Native People: Challenge for Nicaragua, Honduras, America's New Policeman.* Each 23 min.

1983. *Le Honduras.* 22 min. A portrait of the situation in Honduras and of that country's role in Central America.

1983. *Les contras.* 22 min. Exclusive footage of the pro-Somoza military camps in Honduras, training-grounds for the armed opposition to Nicaragua's Sandinista government.

1984. *Nicaragua/Honduras: entre deux guerres.* 85 min. The reforms and the difficulties of Nicaragua's government and its relations with neighbouring Honduras.

1984. *The Vote and the Gun.* 26 min. Nicaragua on the eve of the 1984 elections.

1984. *Prime Target.* 13 min. The life of a woman doctor from Quebec in Nicaragua's war zone.

1985. *Nicaragua, la guerre sale.* 67 min. The consequences of the ongoing war on daily life in Nicaragua.

1986. *La longue marche des enfants de la faim.* 14 min. Ethiopia's controversial resettlement program following the 1984 famine.

1986. *Getting Through.* 16 min. Canadian aid to the victims of the Ethiopian famine.

1986. *Ethiopia's Death Camps.* 5 min. Ethiopia's resettlement program. (for CBS.)

1986. *Erythree, la guerre la plus longue.* 12 min. Eritrea's liberated zones and the issues at stake in its struggle for independence.

1987. *Eritrea Series.* 3 parts. *The Forgotten War.* The origin and the issues at stake in Eritrea's struggle for independence. *A Time to Heal.* A young woman barefoot doctor helps us examine the issue of health in Eritrea's liberated zone. *Songs of the Next Harvest.* Agricultural development under the prevailing drought and war conditions in Eritrea. Each 28 min. (NFB)

1987. *Fighting for Survival.* 18 min. Portrait of Mozambique.

1987. *Bridging the Gap.* 12 min. Two Canadian development workers in Mozambique.

1987. *Fighting for a Living Wage.* 15 min. The miners' strike in South Africa.

1987. *The Man in the Middle.* 16 min. Portrait of Van Zyl Slabbert, a white South African politician opposed to the apartheid regime.

1988. *Retornados.* 15 min. Chilean exiles returning home.

1988. *Médecin sequestre.* Testimony of a Chilean doctor who has been kidnapped by an armed commando in Chile.

1988. *Carmen Gloria.* 20 min. Documentary on Carmen Gloria Quintana and Rodrigo Rojas, the two Chileans who were burned in July 1986.

1988. *Harvest of War.* 19 min. The continuing war and famine in Eritrea.

1989. *Guatemala: The Official Story.* 20 min. Daily life in Guatemala and the story of the village of Aguacate, site of a 1988 army massacre.

1989. *Nicaragua: après l'ouragan.* 12 min. The devastation caused by Hurricane Joan in late 1988.

1989. *Food Under Siege.* 23 min. Report of the war and famine in Eritrea.

1989. *Mozambique: Riding out the Storm.* 30 min. Report on the war in the Nampula region in Mozambique.

1989. *I Don't Feel Your Touch.* Videoclip featuring Bruce Cockburn in Mozambique.

1989. *The Forbidden Land.* 55 min. Eritrea and northern Ethiopia five years after the famine.

1989. *Salvador, o secours.* 8 min. The necessity of peace in El Salvador. (with Raoul Duguay.)

1989. *Crowbars.* 16 min. The special counter-insurrectional unit created by the South Africans in Northern Namibia.

1989. *Namibie: à l'aube de l'indépendance.* 21 min. The challenges of Namibia's independence for the country and the region.

1990. *Guatemala: Aguacate Update.* 12 min. The story of the massacre in Aguacate goes before the Organization of American States and is investigated in Washington, Guatemala City, and Aguacate itself.

1990. *Abuse of Power.* 16 min. Report on the Willowgate scandal in Zimbabwe, involving high government officials. The report focuses on the role of the press in exposing that scandal.

1990. *Toivo, Child of Hope.* 28 min. Portrait of Andimba Toivo Ya Toivo, secretary general of SWAPO: his years in prison, his return from exile, his role in the new independent Namibia.

1991. *Night and Silence.* 47 min. The last campaigns in the savage war to liberate Eritrea from Ethiopia. Featuring the testimony and analysis of Dr. Assefaw Tekeste. Winner of the Canadian Association of Journalists' Award for Best TV Program on a National Network, 1991.

1991. *Out of the Ashes.* 45 min. Produced by Patry, directed by Magnus Issacson. The overthrow of the Mengistu regime in Ethiopia and the hopes for rebuilding the country.

1991. *Winning the Peace.* 28 min. The May 1991 national liberation of Eritrea and prospects for the future.

Claire Prieto and Roger McTair
(all works directed by McTair and produced by Prieto unless noted; all on film)

1976. *Some Black Women.* 22 min. An introduction to the history of Black women in Ontario. A ground-breaking work reaching beyond a positive images approach.

1979. *It's Not an Illness.* The value of regular exercise during pregnancy, featuring the birth of Prieto's and McTair's son. (CBC)

1987. *Home To Buxton.* 28 min. A portrait of Buxton, Ontario, a small town in southwestern Ontario and a key Black settlement during and after the period of the Underground Railroad.

1989. *Challenge to Diversity.* A film to encourage employment equity on the basis of gender and race. (CBC)

1989. *Older, Stronger, Wiser.* 28 min. Directed by Claire Prieto. "The rich record of our foremothers' lives which have been hidden from us." Portraits of key Black community activists in Ontario. (NFB)

1989. *Black Mother, Black Daughter.* 29 min. Directed by Claire Prieto and Sylvia Hamilton. A history of Black settlement in Nova Scotia as told through the lives of women active in various communities. (NFB Atlantic)

1992. *Children Are Not the Problem.* 28 min. The prospects for anti-racist education among elementary school children. A unique film that combines analysis and ideas for practical action. (produced for the Congress of Black Women, Toronto Chapter.)

1992. *Jennifer Hodge: The Glory and the Pain.* 28 min. A portrait of the late African-Canadian filmmaker whose best known work, *Home Feeling*, documented racial tensions in the Jane-Finch area of Toronto.

Laura Sky
(all works on film, unless noted)

1973-78. Series of short videotapes for the NFB's Ontario Region Challenge For Change Programme. *Co-op Housing: Getting It Together.* 1975. *Co-op Housing: The Best Move We Ever Made.* 1975.

1979. *Shut Down.* 30 min. The closing of a U.S.-owned branch plant in Windsor, Ontario, and the trauma that such a decision causes the workers. (NFB)

1981. *Moving Mountains.* 23 min. An examination of women workers at an open-pit mine in Elkford, British Columbia. (produced for the United Steelworkers of America.)

1981. *Houdaille: Days of Courage, Days of Rage.* 20 min. The closing of a U.S.-owned branch plant in Oshawa, Ontario. (produced for the
United Auto Workers.)

1983. *All Our Lives.* 28 min. A series of portraits of older Canadian
women.

1984. *Good Monday Morning.* 30 min. The effects of new computer
technology on women workers in a range of occupations.

1984. *Yes We Can.* 30 min. The process that women go through in
becoming active in unions. (produced for the Canadian Union of Public
Employees [CUPE].)

1986. *To Hurt and to Heal.* Part 1. 45 min. An extended, cinéma
vérité-style interview with the parents of a baby who died in infancy –
the first of Sky's works to break from conventional exposition, and the
first to deal with medical ethics.

1987. *To Hurt and to Heal.* Part 2. 45 min. A series of interviews
with parents, nurses, and doctors about critically sick babies, and the
ethics of treatment.

1987. *Proud Women, Strong Steps.* 30 min. Portraits of two politically active young women, both second-generation immigrants – one
Italian, one South Asian. (produced for Women Working With Immigrant Women, Toronto.)

1990. *Crying for Happiness.* 90 min. An examination of an institution that treats depression among seniors, made in collaboration with
staff and women patients, and raising in more specific terms the themes
of medical and documentary film ethics.

1991. *The Right to Care.* 58 min. The health-care crisis in Canada,
seen through the eyes of five nurses with strong opinions. Unlike the
other medical films, this one was designed as much for a general as a professional audience.

John Walker
(all works on film)

1982. *Chambers – Tracks and Gestures.* A biography of the London,
Ontario, painter and filmmaker Jack Chambers. (Atlantis Films)

1989. *Strand: Under the Dark Cloth.* 35mm. 81 min. A biography-
portrait of the U.S. photographer and filmmaker Paul Strand. Combining many interviews with Strand's colleagues, including Georgia
O'Keeffe, Walker's personal commentary, and hundreds of Strand's

photographs, beautifully shot in 35mm black and white. Walker's major work, seven years in the making.

1990. *The Hand of Stalin: Leningrad*. 60 min. The story of both victims and perpetrators of Stalin's secret police in the 1930s, told through a series of spellbinding, unflinching monologues. (BBC/ TVO)

1990. *The Hand of Stalin: Leningradskaya*. 60 min. The effects of Stalinism in the rural USSR. Beautiful fall light in an evocative rich countryside at harvest – a sombre work with a careful posing of subjects, reminiscent of Strand's aesthetic – captured in superb cinematography as farmers talk of past famines. (BBC/TVO)

1991. *Distress Signals*. 60 min. A current affairs essay on the Americanization and globalization of television around the world. With sequences filmed in Zimbabwe, Newfoundland, Europe, and Atlanta, Georgia. (CBC/NFB)

(John Walker has acted as cinematographer on more than fifty other documentaries and co-directed *A Winter Tan* (1987), a fiction feature starring Jackie Burroughs.)

Finding the Films and Tapes:
Producers & Distributors

Maurice Bulbulian
National Film Board of Canada (NFB) (Head Office, 200 Réne-Lévesque Blvd. W., Montreal, Que. H2Z 1X4)

Sara Diamond
Video Out (1102 Homer St., Vancouver, B.C. V6B 2X6)
V-Tape (183 Bathurst St., Toronto, Ont. M5T 2R7)

Judith Doyle
Full Frame Film and Video (394 Euclid Ave., Toronto, Ont. M6G 2S9)

Richard Fung
Full Frame Film and Video
Video Out
V-Tape

John Greyson
Full Frame Film and Video
Video Out
V-Tape

Brenda Longfellow
Full Frame Film and Video

Zach Kunuk
Igloolik Isuma Productions Inc. (Box 223, Igloolik, NWT. X0A 0L0, 819-934-8809, fax 819-934-8782)
V-Tape

Alanis Obomsawin
NFB

Yvan Patry and Danièle Lacourse
Alter-Ciné (5371 L'esplanade, Montreal, Que. H2T 2Z8)
Full Frame Film and Video
Group MultiMedia (5225 Berrie, Montreal, Que. H2T 2S4)

Claire Prieto and Roger McTair
Full Frame Film and Video
McNabb & Connolly (65 Heward Ave., Toronto, Ont. M4M 2T5)
NFB

Laura Sky
Full Frame Film and Video
Skyworks (566 Palmerston Ave, Toronto, Ont. M6G 2P7)

John Walker
Creative Exposure (2236 Queen St. E., Toronto, Ont. M4E 1G2)
NFB John Walker Productions (490 Adelaide St. W., Toronto, Ont.
M5V 1T3)

Bibliography

Alexander, William. *Film on the Left: American Documentary Film from 1931–1942.* Princeton, N.J.: Princeton University Press, 1981.

Allen, Robert, ed. *Channels of Discourse.* Chapel Hill: University of North Carolina Press, 1987.

Allen, Robert, and Douglas Gomery. *Film History: Theory and Practice.* New York: Knopf, 1985.

Ang, Ien. *Desperately Seeking the Audience.* London: Routledge, 1991.

Aristotle. *The Rhetoric of Aristotle.* Trans. J.E.C. Welldon. London: Macmillan, 1886.

Audley, Paul. *Canada's Cultural Industries: Broadcasting, Publishing, Records and Film.* Toronto: James Lorimer, 1983.

Auguiste, Reece/Black Audio Film Collective. "Black Independents and Third Cinema: The British Context." In *Questions of Third Cinema*, ed. Pines and Willemen.

Baert, Renee. "Video in Canada: In Search of Authority." In *Video*, Montreal: Mediatexte, 1986.

Bailey, Cameron. "A Cinema of Duty: The Films of Jennifer Hodge-De Silva." *Cineaction*, No.23 (Winter 1990–91).

Balcer, René. "A Camera and a Purpose: Maurice Bulbulian." *Cinema Canada*, August 1978.

Barnouw, Eric. *Documentary: A History of the Non-Fiction Film.* London: Oxford University Press, 1974.

———. *The Image Empire: A History of Broadcasting in the United States.* Vol.III, *From 1953.* New York: Oxford University Press, 1970.

273

Berger, John. "Paul Strand." In *About Looking*. New York: Pantheon, 1980.

Berson, Alain. *Pierre Perrault*. Montreal: Conseil québécois pour diffusion du cinéma, 1970.

Bishop, John. *Making It in Video*. New York: McGraw-Hill, 1989.

Bissonnette, Sophie. "Women and Political Documentary in Quebec." An interview by Barbara Evans and Scott Forsyth, *Cineaction*, No.28 (Spring 1992).

Brisebois, Debbie. "Whiteout Warning." Ottawa, Inuit Broadcasting Corporation, October 1990.

Blue, James. "Direct Cinema." *Film Comment*, Fall-Winter 1967.

Brault, Michel. "On the Origins of Cinéma-Vérité and the Documentary Film." *Ciné-Tracts*, Vol.3, No.2 (Spring 1980).

———. "Interview." By Pierre Jutras, *Ciné-Tracts*, Vol.3, No.2 (Spring 1980).

Brecht, Bertolt. *On Theatre*. Ed. John Willett. New York: Hill and Wang, 1957.

Burgess, Marilyn. "Proudly She Marches: Wartime Propaganda and the Lesbian Spectator." *Cineaction*, No.23 (Winter 1990–91).

Burton, Julianne. *Cinema and Social Change in Latin America*. Austin: University of Texas Press, 1986.

———. "Democratizing Documentary: Modes of Address in the Latin American Cinema, 1958–72." In *Show Us Life*, ed. Waugh.

———. *The Social Documentary in Latin America*. Pittsburgh: University of Pittsburgh Press, 1990.

Canada, Department of Communications. *The Other Film Industry: Report of the Non-Theatrical Film Industry Taskforce*. Ottawa, 1986.

Cartier-Bresson, Henri. *The Decisive Moment*. New York: Simon and Schuster, 1952.

Chodos, Robert, and Eric Hamovitch. *Quebec and the American Dream*. Toronto: Between the Lines, 1991.

Clandfield, David. "From the Picturesque to the Familiar: Films of the French Unit at the NFB (1958–1964)." *Ciné-Tracts*, No.4 (Spring-Summer 1978).

Corner, John, ed. *Documentary and Mass Media*. London: Edward Arnold, 1986.

Clifford, James. *The Predicament of Culture: Twentieth Century Ethnography, Literature, and Art*. Cambridge, Mass.: Harvard University Press, 1988.

Cristall, Ferne, and Barbara Emanuel. *Images and Action: A Guide to Using Women's Film and Video.* Toronto: Between the Lines, 1986.

Cunningham, Frank, Sue Findlay, Marlene Kadar, Alan Lennon, and Ed Silva. *Social Movements, Social Change: The Politics and Practice of Organizing.* Toronto: Between the Lines, 1988.

Daudelin, Robert. *Gilles Groulx.* Montreal: Conseil québécois pour diffusion du cinéma, 1969.

Downing, John. *Film and Politics in the Third World.* New York: Autonomedia, 1987.

Doyle, Judith. "Negotiating Representation." *Independent Eye,* Spring 1991.

Dyer, Richard. *Heavenly Bodies.* New York: St. Martin's Press, 1986.

Elder, R. Bruce. *Image and Identity: Reflections in Canadian Film and Culture.* Waterloo, Ont.: Wilfrid Laurier University Press, 1989.

Espinosa, Julio Garcia. "For an Imperfect Cinema." In *Twenty-Five Years of the New Latin American Cinema,* ed. Michael Channon. London: British Film Institute, 1983.

Evans, Gary. *In the National Interest: A Chronicle of the National Film Board of Canada from 1949–1989.* Toronto: University of Toronto Press, 1991.

———. *John Grierson and the National Film Board.* Toronto: University of Toronto Press, 1984.

Feldman, Seth, ed. *Take Two: A Tribute to Film in Canada.* Richmond Hill, Ont.: Irwin, 1984.

Fiske, John, and John Hartley. *Reading Television.* London: Methuen, 1978.

Frye, Northrop. *Anatomy of Criticism.* Princeton, N.J.: Princeton University Press, 1957.

Fung, Richard. "Colouring the Screen." *Parallelogramme,* Vol.18, No.3 (1993).

Gabriel, Teshome H. *Third Cinema in the Third World.* Ann Arbor: University of Michigan Press, 1982.

Gale, Peggy. "Video Art Has Captured Our Imagination." *Parachute,* Summer 1977.

Geyshick, Ron, with Judith Doyle. *Te Bwe Win: Truth: Stories by an Ojibway Healer.* Toronto: Summerhill Press, 1989.

Grierson, John. *Grierson on Documentary.* 2nd ed., ed. Forsyth Hardy. New York: Praeger, 1971.

Gross, Larry, John Katz, and Jay Ruby, eds. *Image Ethics: The Moral Rights of Subjects in Photography, Film, and Television.* New York: Oxford University Press, 1988.

Guynn, William. *A Cinema of Nonfiction*. London and Toronto: Associated University Presses, 1990.

Hackett, Yvette. "The National Film Society of Canada, 1935–1951: Its Origins and Development." In *Flashback*, ed. Walz.

Hall, Jeanne. "Realism as a Style in Cinéma Vérité: A Critical Analysis of *Primary*." *Cinema Journal*, Vol.30, No.4, (Summer 1991).

Hall, Stuart. "Encoding/Decoding." In *Culture, Media and Language*, ed. Stuart Hall et al. London: Hutchinson, 1980.

Handling, Piers, and Pierre Verroneau, eds. *Self-Portrait: Essays on the Canadian and Quebec Cinemas*. Ottawa: Canadian Film Institute, 1980. Harcourt, Peter. "Pierre Perrault and Le Cinéma Vécu." In *Take Two*, ed. Feldman.

———. "The Innocent Eye." In *Canadian Film Reader*, ed. Seth Feldman and Joyce Nelson. Toronto: Peter Martin, 1977.

Hardin, Herschel. *Closed Circuits*. Vancouver: Douglas and McIntyre, 1985.

Hardy, Forsyth. *John Grierson: A Documentary Biography*. London: Faber and Faber, 1979.

Hathaway, James C. *The Law of Refugee Status*. Toronto: Butterworths, 1991.

Hill, Daniel G. *Blacks in Early Canada*. Agincourt, Ont.: The Book Society of Canada, 1981.

Jacobs, Lewis, ed. *The Documentary Tradition*. New York: Norton, 1979.

Jones, D.B. *Movies and Memoranda: An Interpretative History of the National Film Board of Canada*. Ottawa: Deneau, 1981.

Kleinhans, Chuck. "Forms, Politics, Makers and Contexts: Basic Issues for a Theory of Radical Political Documentary." In *Show Us Life*, ed. Waugh.

La Rochelle, Réal. "Committed Documentary in Quebec: A Still-Birth?" In *Show Us Life*, ed. Waugh.

Lesage, Julia. "The Political Aesthetics of the Feminist Documentary Film." *Quarterly Review of Film Studies*, Vol.3, No.4 (Fall 1978), reprinted in *Show Us Life*, ed. Waugh.

Levin, G. Roy. *Documentary Explorations*. Garden City, N.Y.: Doubleday, 1971. See especially the interview with Jean Rouch.

Leyda, Jay. *Films Beget Films: A Study of the Compilation Film*. London: George Allen & Unwin, 1964.

———. *Kino: A History of the Russian and Soviet Film*. London: George Allen & Unwin, 1960.

Lovell, Alan, and Jim Hillier. *Studies in Documentary.* London: British Film Institute, 1972.

Lukács, Georg. *Writer and Critic.* London: Merlin Press, 1970. See especially the essay, "Narrate or Describe."

McCaughey, Claire. *A Survey of Arts Audience Studies: A Canadian Perspective, 1976–1984.* Ottawa: The Canada Council, 1984.

McCaskell, Tim. "The Bath Raids and Gay Politics." In *Social Movements, Social Change,* ed. Cunningham et al.

McLuhan, Marshall. *Understanding Media: The Extensions of Man.* New York: McGraw-Hill, 1964.

McMillan, Alan. *Native Peoples and Cultures of Canada: An Anthropological Overview.* Vancouver: Douglas & McIntyre, 1988.

Marcorelles, Louis. *Living Cinema.* New York: Praeger, 1973.

Marsolais, Gilles. *Le Cinéma Canadien.* Montreal: Editions du Jour, 1968.

———. *Michel Brault.* Montreal: Conseil québécois pour diffusion du cinéma, 1972.

Mattelart, Armand, et al. *International Image Markets.* London: Comedia, 1984.

Minh-ha, Trinh T. "Documentary Is/Is Not a Name." *October,* Summer 1990.

Modleski, Tania. *Loving With a Vengeance: Mass-Produced Fantasies for Women.* Hamden, Conn.: Archon Books, 1982.

Morley, David. *The "Nationwide" Audience: Structure and Decoding.* London: British Film Institute, 1980.

———. *Family Television: Cultural Power and Domestic Leisure.* London: Comedia, 1986.

Morris, Peter. "Backwards To the Future: John Grierson's Film Policy for Canada." In *Flashback,* ed. Walz.

———. *Embattled Shadows.* Montreal: McGill-Queen's University Press, 1978.

———. *The Film Companion.* Toronto: Irwin, 1984.

———. "Praxis Into Process." *Historical Journal of Film, Radio, TV,* Vol.9, No.3 (1978).

Moscovitch, Arlene. *Media and Society.* Montreal: National Film Board of Canada, 1989.

Nelson, Joyce. *The Colonized Eye: Rethinking the Grierson Legend.* Toronto: Between the Lines, 1988.

———. *The Perfect Machine: TV in the Nuclear Age.* Toronto: Between the Lines, 1987.

Newcomb, Horace. *Television: The Critical View*. New York: Oxford University Press, 1987.

Nichols, Bill. "The Voice of Documentary." *Film Quarterly*, Vol.36, No.3 (Spring 1983).

———. *Ideology and the Image*. Bloomington: Indiana University Press, 1981.

———. *Representing Reality: Issues and Concepts in Documentary*. Bloomington: Indiana University Press, 1991.

Penner, Norman. *The Canadian Left*. Toronto: Prentice-Hall, 1977.

Pevere, Geoff. "Aching To Speak: Power and Language in Pierre Perrault's *La Bête Lumineuse*," *Cineaction*, No.8 (March 1987).

Pendakur, Manjunath. *Canadian Dreams and American Control: The Political Economy of the Canadian Film Industry*. Toronto: Garamond Press, 1990.

Pines, Jim, and Paul Willemen, eds. *Questions of Third Cinema*. London: British Film Institute, 1989.

Raboy, Marc. *Movements and Messages: Media and Radical Politics in Quebec*. Toronto: Between the Lines, 1984.

———. *Missed Opportunities: The Story of Canada's Broadcasting Policy*. Montreal: McGill-Queen's University Press, 1990.

Richards, Glen. "Is This the Voice of God Speaking?" *Borderlines*, No.3 (Fall 1985).

Robertson, Clive. "The Second Independent Video Open." *Fuse*, January 1980.

Rosenthal, Alan, ed. *New Challenges for Documentary* (Berkeley: University of California Press, 1988.

———. *The Documentary Conscience: A Casebook in Film Making*. Berkeley: University of California Press, 1980.

———. *The New Documentary in Action*. Berkeley: University of California Press, 1971.

Rosler, Martha. "Shedding the Utopian Moment." In *Video*. Montreal: Mediatexte, 1986.

Rouch, Jean. "Interview." *Cahiers du Cinéma*, June 1963.

Ruby, Jay. "The Image Mirrored: Reflexivity and the Documentary Film." In *New Challenges for Documentary*, ed. Rosenthal.

Seiter, Ellen, Hans Borchers, Gabriele Kreutzner, and Eva-Maria Warth, eds. *Remote Control: Television, Audiences, and Cultural Power*. London: Routledge, 1991.

Steele, Lisa et al. "Introduction." In *Women and Film*. Catalogue of the Toronto Women and Film International Festival, 1973.

Sky, Laura. "Letter to Moira Simpson – Vancouver." *Cinema Canada*, December 1988.

Stott, William. *Documentary Expression and Thirties America*. New York: Oxford University Press, 1973.

Taylor, Ian. "Depoliticizing Current Affairs Television: The Nightly Project of *The Journal*." *Borderlines*, No.5 (Summer 1986).

Todd, Loretta. "Notes on Appropriation." *Parallelogramme*, Vol.16, No.1 (Summer 1990).

UNESCO. *Many Voices, One World*. Paris: UNESCO, 1980.

Walz, Gene, ed. *Flashback: People and Institutions in Canadian Film History*. Montreal: Mediatexte, 1986.

Waugh, Thomas, ed. *Show Us Life: Toward a History and Aesthetics of the Committed Documentary*. Metuchen, N.J.: Scarecrow Press, 1984.

Whitaker, Reg. *The Secret History of Canadian Immigration*. Toronto: Lester & Orpen Dennys, 1987.

Williams, Raymond. *Culture*. London: Fontana, 1981.

———. *Problems in Materialism and Culture*. London: Verso, 1980.

———. *Raymond Williams on Television*. Ed. Alan O'Connor. Toronto: Between the Lines, 1989.

———. *Television: Technology and Cultural Form*. New York: Schocken Books, 1975.

Winks, Robin. *The Blacks in Canada*. Montreal: McGill-Queen's University Press, 1971.

Winston, Brian. "Documentary, I Think We Are In Trouble." In *New Challenges For Documentary*, ed. Rosenthal.

———. "The Tradition of the Victim in Griersonian Documentary." In *Image Ethics*, ed. Gross, Katz, and Ruby.

———. *Misunderstanding Media*. London: Routledge & Kegan Paul, 1986.

Wollen, Peter. *Signs and Meaning in the Cinema*. 2nd ed. London: Thames & Hudson, 1970.

———. "'Ontology' and 'Materialism' in Film." *Screen* Vol.17, No.1 (1976).

Worth, Sol, and John Adair. *Through Navajo Eyes: An Exploration in Film Communication and Anthropology*. Bloomington: University of Indiana Press, 1972.

Index

Index of Film and Video Titles

BESÙ

PRINTED IN CANADA